Aux Trois Saisons

An Inn in Burgundy

❦

MORT SOBEL

No part of this publication may be reproduced
in whole or in part, or stored in a retrieval system,
or transmitted in any form or by any means,
electronic, mechanical, photocopying, recording,
or otherwise, without written permission of the author,
except for the inclusion of brief quotations in a review.
For information regarding permission, please write to:
info@barringerpublishing.com

Copyright © 2012 Mort Sobel
All rights reserved.

Barringer Publishing, Naples, Florida
www.barringerpublishing.com
Cover, graphics, layout design by Lisa Camp
Editing by Carole Greene

ISBN: 978-0-9851184-3-3

Library of Congress Cataloging-in-Publication Data
Aux Trois Saisons / Mort Sobel

Printed in U.S.A.

Table of Contents

Prologue: Two Letters
Part I: Awakenings
Chapter 1: Awakenings 13
Chapter 2: Pas de Problème, Papers, and Partners 23
Chapter 3: Surprises. 30
Chapter 4: Les Voisins 38
Chapter 5: La Fin de La Semaine Prochaine 48
Chapter 6: Le Départ. 57

Part II: Between-Times
Chapter 7: La Rentrée de Mademoiselle 66
Chapter 8: Native Customs. 72
Chapter 9: Le Syndic. 77
Chapter 10: Au Café 85
Chapter 11: Pére Lachaise 92
Chapter 12: Renato 97
Chapter 13: La Baptême 99
Chapter 14: À Pied 105
Chapter 15: Le Retour 116

Part III: L'Auberge Aux Trois Saisons
Chapter 16: La Carte de Vin. 123
Chapter 17: Grand Opening 146
Chapter 18: Guide Rivage 154
Chapter 19: Good Times And Others 158
Chapter 20: "Do you have any chickens?". 171
Chapter 21: Up, Up, and Away 176
Chapter 22: À la campagne, à Paris 179
Chapter 23: Harvest. 186

Part IV: Le 4eme Saison
Chapter 24: All Aboard 190
Chapter 25: À La Table Des Rois 194
Chapter 26: Politically Correct 201
Chapter 27: Les Ambassadeurs 206
Chapter 28: Le Marais 213
Chapter 29: Mademoiselle 216
Chapter 30: Candles and Torches 221
Chapter 31: Beaujolais Nouveau 228
Chapter 32: Marie 235

Part V: No Room At The Inn
Chapter 33: Les Guides 247
Chapter 34: Place de la Corinne 253
Chapter 35: Two Weddings and a Birthday 257
Chapter 36: The Annual 30-Year Flood 264
Chapter 37: Assignations 267
Chapter 38: The Countess, Jus d'Orange, and I 273
Chapter 39: After the Fall 277
Chapter 40: La Fin 282
Chapter 41: Au Revoir 288

Part VI: Menus "Aux Trois Saisons:…and why…
Chapter 42: Menus "Aux Trois Saisons:…and why… 292
Menu One 299
Menu Two 299
Epilogue: The French 300
Acknowledgments 301

Recipes
Poulet Patronale (Chicken with grapes) 47
Gougères 64
Cassoulet 83

Floating Islands (Oeufs sur la neige) 84
Tarte Tatin 90
Stuffed Quail in Calvados. 104
Galette des Rois. 114
Soupe d'Oignon à "Le Fregate" 121
Boeuf Bourguignon 134
Crème Concombre (Chilled cucumber soup) 152
Mozart Soup. 153
Roulade de Veau (Mystery Weekend Veal Rolls) 169
Timbale d'Èpinards (Spinach Timbales) 170
Canard Aigre-Doux (Sweet and sour duck breasts). 183
"Nutty Chicken" 184
Nuage de Citron (Lemon Cloud) 193
Canard aux Huitres (Duck with Oysters). 198
Surprise de Terr (Crêpes)i. 210
Mousse au chocolat 211
Raspberry coulis. 212
Poulet Citron (Lemon Chicken) 226
Marion's Okra Recipe. 227
Baguette 233
Rillette 234
Pesto. 242
Marie's Soupe de Pesto. 243
Tapenade. 244
Délice de Julia 245
Gâteau Maison 251
Babotie. 252
Mousse au Saumon avec Sauce Aneth
(Salmon Mousse with Dill Sauce) 262
Potage Michelle. 272

Prologue
Two Letters

We sat at our dining table in Paris and wrote the letter that would formally end the dream that started as "L'Auberge *Aux Trois Saisons*" and ended as an all-consuming, albeit fascinating reality. We wrote it with a mixture of sadness, relief, and nostalgia…sadness because we would never again see some of the people who had entered our lives over the past seven years and become friends, relief because the eighteen-hour workdays were over, and nostalgia for the good times which, in our memory, outnumbered the others. We addressed the envelopes and, with each name, wondered how the "guests" who had become friends would feel.

I'm one of the last remaining people on earth who still enjoys writing three-page letters to friends, but I found it difficult to find the right words for this one.

How do you phrase the end of a dream? How do you tell people that the "home" they had so warmly adopted no longer was there to welcome them?

For the people who came to *Aux Trois Saisons,* it was always a haven of peace; everything ran smoothly, there were no rough edges. But how could they understand how hard it had been to make it all look easy—the eighteen-hour days seven days a week, the constant shopping, cooking, cleaning, ironing, etc, and the uncertainties and problems of existing and trying to succeed amid the confines of the Social State which modern France has become. And then, when Dierk fell and injured himself and I had to assume his half of the burden as well as my own, it had simply become too much. We realized how precarious our existence really was, and how the constraints presented by the French government made it impossible for us to continue doing everything ourselves, as we had been forced to do, or even think of hiring another person to help us.

Our reasons for beginning the Inn were valid: we both wanted an easier existence than the hectic one we lived in Boston, one that could be seasonal and give us enough time off to travel and enjoy life. The name would be *"Aux Trois Saisons"* because the fourth season would belong to us alone. We both enjoyed meeting people and welcoming them into our home wherever we lived. From my earliest years, I had loved cooking, and French cooking was, and remains, to me, the standard against which most other cuisines must be measured.

Of course, France itself, which I had always loved from afar, (and then even more up close), offers an incredible variety of experiences, all unmistakably French but different enough to be interesting. We thought of all the things we would have time to do in our "off-season"…in France we could visit the Loire and its magnificent chateaux, explore the Normandy and Brittany coasts, the southern *Cote d'Azur*. We could take our time to discover in depth the rest of the Europe we had only known as tourists, and have a chance to savor other cultures and languages.

And Paris…the clincher was Paris. I was smitten, passionately and irrevocably in love with the many faces of the magical city that spoke to me when I was there and called to me when I left. So our fourth season would be spent with Paris as a base.

We were aware of all of these personal reasons, but for our guests at the Inn, *Aux Trois Saisons* was a singular haven of peace that they could return to each year and did. It represented welcome, warmth, a personal caring that is rarely found in the hotel chains of today. They recognized how special it was, and about sixty percent of them made reservations for the next year when they left.

So we had to choose our words very carefully and finally sent the following letter to the several hundred people who had entered our lives as visitors and became friends of *Aux Trois Saisons*:

Paris, 15 March 1995

Dear Friends,

We just signed papers for the sale of the house that was L'Auberge "Aux Trois Saisons to people who will use it as a private home. This was not a decision taken without a great deal of thought, because, as you know, we started the inn 7 years ago, and built it, from nothing, into a successful and enjoyable adventure for us and the hundreds of people who shared it with us. We've been able to welcome and get to know people from all over the world. Our guest-book is signed in many languages, some of which we don't understand, but they all speak of happiness, the pleasure of being welcomed and feeling "at home". The inn was what we wanted it to be: a place where people would be comfortable and, once they passed through the entrance gates, feel warmth and hospitality. It was for us, and them, a special experience.

All the factors that went into our decision are too numerous to go into here, but many things entered into it.

We're happily settled now in Paris permanently, and savoring every minute in this superb city and all it has to offer. For the weekends, we've bought a tiny Tudor-style cottage in Normandy, just 12 kilometers from Deauville. The hammering, etc., you hear this Spring and Summer will be our fault, as we get down to completely renovating a 300-year-old cottage that hasn't been improved in over 47 years. It will be a challenge and lots of fun, and, once we get the bathroom inside the house, quite comfortable, we hope.

The year has started off with several important changes, all good ones, and, while the seven years of Aux Trois Saisons will always remain an especially magical time, worthwhile and fulfilling, the future looks as if it will hold many happy and exciting things in store.

We look forward to sharing our times, and yours, in the years ahead.

With gratitude and warmest wishes,

Mort and Dierk

As we put the letters into their envelopes, the memories came flooding back, the early days of the Inn, its seven years of existence, and all the reasons for its creation and its end.

The letter addressed to Monsieur and Madame Festjens in Belgium was sealed with love. They were there when we opened *Aux Trois Saisons* and had seen us through that first nerve-wracking, problem-filled weekend as inn-keepers. Such kind people….

…The *Murder Mystery Weekend* put on by the US Embassy people from Paris, now dispersed to all the corners of the world served by the Embassy, when the two ladies impersonating nuns, still in their "habits," decided to join the others in a visit to the local gambling casino….

…The weekend when the marvelous artist LeRoy Neimann and his wife visited the Inn. We have the warm memories of sharing time with two gracious people as well as the treasure he presented to us as they were leaving, a lovely sketch of the Inn dedicated to us both.

The memories came back. And we remembered the birth of what would become Aux Trois Saisons, our decision bolstered by another letter, one of encouragement from that venerable lady and delightful author, M.F.K. Fischer. I had written to her with our plans for opening an Inn in the France immortalized so charmingly in her books, and, surprisingly, she wrote back, beginning a correspondence that lasted until her passing. I explained to her exactly what *Sauce Aneth* was, and so it began.

I remember that other letter so well....

AUX TROIS SAISONS

April 9, 1990

Dear Dr. Sobel:

Your letter gave me great pleasure and I hope you'll forgive my long silence and write again soon.

The life you've chosen sounds perfect to me. I can't imagine being a dentist even at Harvard and I'm thankful you escaped when you did.

I speak from the heart about dentistry as I lost four teeth at the age of ten and spent much of my life in dentist chairs since then.

I'll tell you my secret for surviving this awful path: I've fallen in love with every dentist I've ever had. Of course this began early on with dear Dr. Wanberg, a Dane who landed somehow in Whittier, California. He was an enormously fat man and his wife made shirts of pongee silk and I remember to this day how good it felt to lay my head against his fat, silky tummy. He was devoted to me, too.

And when my four teeth got knocked into my jaw by two fat boys riding down a hill on one bicycle, Dr. Wanberg went to night school to study the mouth of children, which was long before periodontics. And my good fortune still holds almost eighty years later. And my present dentist is a dear man, too. In other words, that you were once a dentist and now are a French innkeeper!

Would you please tell me what Sauce Aneth is, and anything you'd like to.

I have a thousand questons to ask you so I'll close abruptly.

With all good wishes, mixed with some envy, as you understand.

M.F.K. Fisher
to Dr. M. Sobel
L'Auberge "Aux Trois Saisons"
Le Premoy - B.P. 6
Dracy Le Fort
71640 Givry
PARIS

MORT SOBEL

Part I
Awakenings

Chapter 1
Awakenings

Catherine was a tall, big-boned girl, befitting her position as the captain of the Chalon-Sur-Saone ladies' basketball team. Her cheery smile and infectious giggle made us single her out to be our Burgundy *agent immobilier* in the search for just the right property to turn into an inn. She had done her job well, even contacting us in Paris, to which we returned between forays into the real-estate market, whenever she had a potential property to show us. She had telephoned us early that morning, so we made the three and a half hour trip from Paris to inspect these latest offerings, hoping that one of them would be perfect.

The dream of creating an inn had taken hold several years before that day, and been nurtured by photos in a magazine called "Demeures Et Chateaux" which showed magnificent old homes—enormous castles to my American eyes—just begging to be bought for amounts of money which seemed ridiculously low by American standards. Our tiny apartment in Paris, fortunately bought when the French Franc was at an all-time high of about ten Francs per dollar, served as a home base while we did some in-depth searching.

Catherine strolled us through the grounds first, probably hoping to delay our reaction to the interior of the house itself. It was the third house Catherine had shown us that morning. We were beginning to lose hope that we could find the right property for a potential inn. Either the house was lovely and the grounds awful or the other way round.

She led us through the darkened rooms, threw back the huge wooden shutters and the room sprang to life, awakened from the slumber of abandonment.

Two years of investigating France's many *departments*, during vacations from the university, had for many reasons narrowed the search down to the Burgundy wine region, but discoveries made along the way had been worth the effort. France is an incredibly varied and rich country, and each part of it has something special to offer. Normandy, with its charming thatched-roofed, plaster-and-beam houses, and its closeness to the seacoast, had been an early choice, and I remember particularly falling in love with a house called "Bourgainville" in a little village way off the beaten path. I can picture it to this day: a lovely paneled entrance foyer, beautiful formal salon in shades of light blue, dining room with tall doors leading out to the garden, and a large park offering lots of privacy. A bit too much privacy to be easily found, unfortunately. Normandy has a lot of rain, and is too-often merely passed by as people travel between Paris and the seacoast. I wanted the inn-to-be to offer a place for people to come, relax and enjoy, for *itself* as well as for what the area had to offer. Au revoir, "Bourgainville."

Another strong contender was the Loire valley, with its breathtaking chateaux, but the Loire valley was filled with an abundance of hotels with which our budget couldn't possibly compete.

On another excursion, about one hour and a half outside of Paris, we saw an eighteenth century chateau with its original clock dating from before the French Revolution set into the roof-line. Absolutely gorgeous, it sported dozens of enormous rooms on four levels, three reception salons—a Hollywood dream. There was a long *"allée"* leading up to the front of the chateau, which had a magnificent stone staircase. Attached to the property, but not being sold with it, was a working farm with several small farm-buildings, chickens running around in the yard, vegetable plantings, all undoubtedly much as they had been when the farm belonged to the chateau (as did its farmers). Being inquisitive, I opened the gate and knocked on the door of the largest farmhouse. The scene inside was from an eighteenth century painting: an old woman stirring a large pot over an iron stove with a (genuinely) *"rustique"* interior that would drive the editor of *Country Living Magazine* wild with envy. Yes, those things still do exist in rural France, as does the lack of indoor plumbing, as we'll see later on. Now for the bad news: on the top level, there was a stone "throne" which had served as the sole toilet to countless generations who, undoubtedly, considered themselves fortunate that it was *inside*. There were no other bathrooms in the chateau and modern plumbing was almost an impossibility to install in three-foot thick stone walls. It also had no modern kitchen facilities, of course, no heating system, but did have a basement with an inch of water permanently sitting there. We came to understand various other reasons why so many similar, incredibly beautiful, properties lay abandoned in France until they either fall down or are demolished for their paneling and fireplaces or for the land they stand on. It's prohibitively expensive to restore these old buildings, and it's heartbreaking how many irreplaceably beautiful paneled rooms have been removed whole from France. They turn up in Japan, despite French laws forbidding this.

The French government, blessed as it is with so rich a history and with so many architectural masterpieces, can't possibly keep up with maintaining all of them, so some are simply left to fall apart. The choice must be a difficult one, when faced with hundreds of magnificent buildings falling into ruin, and is made, more often than not, based on the architectural "purity" of the structure and whether or not it has suffered disfiguring alterations over the centuries. And, to be honest, the government itself is partially responsible for the problem. One of the earlier houses Catherine showed us that morning in Dracy le Fort was an elegant chateau that had been turned over by the government to one of the trade unions to use as a vacation spot, undoubtedly to keep them from going on strike. When they finally vacated the building, the destruction the union occupation had caused was shameful. A few years after we moved into the village, a developer bought it all and subdivided the house and the land. At least it's now not an eyesore any more, but it's sad that its original beauty is gone forever.

Burgundy, with its gently rolling hills dotted with chateaux and covered with neat vineyards, the soft golden honey hue of its stone buildings and walls, made me want to linger rather than move on. Each sunset, the stone buildings turned a shade of gold that I've seen in only one other place, Jerusalem. Burgundy offered everything we wanted. It was the perfect stopping-off point, convenient to the A6, the main north-south autoroute of France, which everyone must travel to go anywhere. Actually, this region stood as the crossroads and the geographic center of this part of Europe. It was an easy three and a half hour trip from Paris (in case there was an emergency during the time it would be closed), and boasted a wealth of places of historic and religious interest for visitors to discover and enjoy, as well as the finest wine in the world there for the *dégustation*. In short, the perfect place for our inn-to-be. The wine harvest, already in progress on that September morning with Catherine, filled the air with activity and the rich smell of the first pressing of the grapes. Decision made. Now to find the right property.

When we saw it, on that clear, crisp autumn morning, the two-acre park was breathtakingly beautiful, covered with a carpet of golden-red leaves leading down to the trout river which meandered along the property border. It was so much like the New England scenes repeated every year, scenes I treasured during those years of living and teaching in Boston, with leaves of colors almost too vivid to be real. I was soon to learn that each variety of wine has leaves that also change to a different color after the harvest has stripped them of their grapes. With all of the grape varieties, this can make for a marvelous palette. The grape-ivy covering the house's original tower, dating from 1622, had already shed its leaves anticipating the hard Burgundy winter ahead.

The gravel courtyard was sadly deserted on that day, and the huge iron gates were joined together by a thick chain, as well as the usual several locks, which opened with the most enormous keys I had ever seen. The property consisted of the main house, up a flight of stone stairs, and three *dépendances* attached to the main house but unused. After groping her way through the damp, tiled foyer, feeling along the moist walls for the latch to the shutters, and, finding it, swinging them open, Catherine turned to us expectantly. We had to wait a few moments for our eyes to become adjusted to the sudden burst of sunlight and for the dust to settle. She said nothing, just went about the work of opening all of the shutters and letting light and fresh air into the house.

Catherine had learned early on that we would not be easy to satisfy, but, with her robust good humor, took it all in stride and put up with the Americans' strange ways. Besides, there really weren't that many other people on the horizon who were searching for large houses, so, between basketball tournaments, we were the best game in town. She tried to fulfill the list of requirements we had set out for her at the beginning: a large park offering privacy and peacefulness; within easy reach of the major autoroute but not too close to it; a house offering some character to work with; potential space for at least five guest rooms, each with private bathroom; and, of course, an affordable price tag.

I took to Catherine immediately and we kept in contact in the years to come. I met her in town for coffee one day, several years later, and she was wearing a rather silly little hat with frills and tassels bouncing off it in all directions. It was St. Catherine's day, and on that day it is customary for all unmarried ladies over the age of twenty-five to wear a hat in honor of St. Catherine, the patron saint of unmarried ladies, and also, I suspect, to do a bit of harmless advertising.

The day we first saw the house that would become the inn, she wore no hat but was suitably bundled up against the cold, damp September chill in the air. What we saw, when the dust settled, was a main salon, with two sets of tall doors leading out to the front terrace, and fourteen-foot high ceilings with lovely carved moldings, which were chipped and peeling, a smaller salon to its side also with tall doors leading outside, and two rooms towards the rear of the house, which had been used as bedrooms. The kitchen was, as is the case with homes of this sort, very large and very outdated.

The ancient tower was actually a stairway that wound its way up to the second level with two good-sized bedrooms and a third room that at one time might have served as a child's nursery. Although the bones were excellent, in terms of physical condition, the house was a disaster. My partner Dierk and I exchanged glances that said "Later! Don't say anything!" and we told Catherine that we would think about it and call her that afternoon. We spent several hours in a café in Chalon-Sur-Saône and discussed what we had seen that morning. Comparing notes, we discovered we both had allowed imagination to overcome reality and looking past the peeling wallpapers, stained ceilings, chipped paint, scarred floors and all the rest, we saw the main salon as it would look with people in it, logs burning in the now boarded-up fireplace with a marble mantel, the Empire chandelier I had inherited from my mother twinkling, its crystals reflecting the flickering light. The smaller salon, off the main one, would be the library, with comfortable chairs, floor-to-ceiling bookcases, lit by another chandelier bought many years ago for my first home in New York.

We had both mentally removed the wall between the two bedrooms on the main floor and they became one large new dining room, boasting two fireplaces, not one. It led off the kitchen, which had lots of space for a center island for food preparation. It all seemed to fall into place so easily. Renovations would be a challenge, but it could be done. Too excited to return to Paris immediately, we continued talking and planning and finally decided to stay over at the *Hôtel St. Georges in Chalon-Sur-Saône* that night. We took another drive out to see the house by ourselves and made the decision.

The sales offer was signed in Catherine's office that afternoon.

A few words of introduction to French formalities and bureaucracy, the first of many in the pages to come: The French government employs five people to do the work of one. Of these five good people, at any given time, two are on vacation, two are inevitably on strike, and the fifth one can't do anything, bien sûr, until the other four come back.

If you buy a property in France, it takes two to three months from the day papers are signed until the actual closing date when the property becomes legally yours, and this was only the first *offer* not the "official" agreement. This offer is then subject to the usual negotiations, and only when the definite selling price is decided upon can the *promesse de vente* be signed and submitted to the government.

This three-month period is the counterpart of our "escrow" period in America, the interval between purchase agreement and actual sale, during which the title and legal ownership is verified. All the title work is made more complicated in France since this search can cover a few hundred years' history. It is also the time during which bank loans are firmed up, and, in the special case of France, during which time the government, legally, has the option of buying the property out from under you for whatever reason they wish. It's called the right of "pre-emption" and still exists from the King's time when all property as well as anything on it belonged to the Crown.

A few years ago, in modern day France, there was an example of how this law can be abused when the far-right mayor of a town used this law of pre-emption to legally keep out "foreigners." Whenever a house was in the process of being bought by someone from North Africa, for example, the town simply bought the house itself. Eventually, the "foreigners" gave up and stopped trying.

We are blessed, in America, with fairly straight-forward property laws: your lawyer or escrow company does a title search, which takes a few minutes at the local tax office, you pay the money, sign on the dotted line, and it's yours.

Once our offer had been accepted by the seller (immediately, since she was undoubtedly delighted to have the house off her hands) we made a date to assemble in the notaire's office the next day to sign the *promesse de vente*, the official first step in acquiring what would become *"Aux Trois Saisons."* A few signatures on totally incomprehensible documents, the down-payment check handed over to the notaire, and it was done. When you come down to it, risking your life's savings is really quite easy.

Having made the decision and signed the papers, we were free to return to Paris and give the French bureaucracy the chance to shuffle the papers around for three months from one side of the desk to another. But while in Chalon for the day, we decided to meet with a friend of Catherine's, who was an architect, to talk about the necessary renovations. The first step, *Monsieur l'architecte* informed us, was for him to draw up a *plan d'état* showing the existing house *before* any changes were made. This then had to be followed by the architect's official plan for the proposed renovations, which then had to be submitted to the proper authorities for the *permis construire* (building permit). It all sounded reasonable, if somewhat involved.

Monsieur l'architecte was a jittery, nice-looking, fast-talking man in his twenties, in love with his own voice and possessed of eyes which somehow allowed him the luxury of looking at Catherine and us at the same time even though we were seated at opposite ends of the desk. He arrived clutching the ritualistic paper-stuffed *dossier*, the portfolio which is to the Frenchman what the automobile stick-shift is to the Italian: an extension of his you-know-what. We were, as you might suspect, duly impressed.

Monsieur could also, he happily informed us, offer us the services of his very own team of workmen to perform the renovations, which seemed an excellent idea, since our command of French at that time was less than fluent. Even better since, after renovating three houses in various parts of the U.S., I still had recurrent nightmares about dealing with plumbers and electricians in any language.

"*Parfait,*" I said. "The final house sale "signature" is scheduled for three months from now. When can you and your team begin work?"

"*Pas de problem,*" Monsieur cheerfully informed us. "No problem. We're ready to start immediately," as he deftly pocketed the check for 10,000 Francs, which was, *bien sûr,* merely a retainer for his services and would be put toward the *plan d'état* charges.

We returned to Paris and a celebratory dinner at *"La Frégate,"* the restaurant on the quai Voltaire near our flat. We always dined there on our first and last nights in Paris and when we had something special to celebrate. The usual table near the large picture window overlooked the Louvre on the other side of the river, with the *bateau mouches* periodically passing and lighting the trees along their way. There was a lot to celebrate: house found, architect engaged, the first faltering steps of the journey had been taken and there was no turning back now. So much for the doubts, all the misgivings of the two years since the idea of the inn had been born, the shaking of heads and incredulous looks that had greeted the announcement of our intentions, the long search for just the right property. All was forgotten, as *Monsieur's* encouraging "*Pas de Problème*" still rang in my ears, and I waited for the three months to pass and the closing date to arrive.

It was going to happen: the dream was really going to come true!

Chapter 2
Pas de Problème, Papers and Partners

As the days dragged by, my own dossier was slowly growing, until I was beginning to feel confident that I could hold my own in any French official meeting. It was filled with Monsieur l'architecte's *plan d'état,* and an assortment of important-looking documents.

One of these was from the local farm cooperative which, irrespective of the fact that we had never *offered* it to them, informed us that they had decided *not* to buy the land on which the house sat. This was a surprise to us, as well as a relief, and, in answer to several frantic telephone calls to Catherine, turned out to be a "routine" event. Just as any property in France can be pre-empted by the state, any land which is conceivably farm land can be pre-empted by the local farming cooperative. It was a "presumed" fact that they would not, in fact, buy the land since they had no money and could scarcely turn the existing farms into profitable enterprises. Still, it was a formality that was observed.

We did not hear from the King (currently known as the "government"), so we assumed that we were safe on that account and that he had no intention of buying the property out from under us and starting his own inn with Marie Antoinette.

There were, however, several letters, back and forth, from the mayor of *Dracy le Fort*, the village where the house was located. When we signed the *promesse de vente*, we had asked the *notaire* to stipulate that the sale depended on our receiving permission to create an inn out of what had been a private home. As a result, instead of the usual ten percent closing fees, we had been charged twenty percent, the fee charged for a commercial sale. It was, therefore, tacitly understood that the property was going to be used for *commercial* purposes since we were being accordingly charged. However, the days passed without any official word from the local authorities on this critical point. So, in my best French, I had sent a registered letter to *Monsieur le Maire*, politely and officially informing him that we would be creating a small, five-room inn, and wanted him to be fully aware of our plans. We also assured him that he would be kept informed as to its progress, that we were pleased to be joining the community, that we hoped we would make a positive contribution to community affairs, etc., etc. All of the things that officialdom might like to hear from new-comers. The letter we received in return stated that he, *Monsieur le Maire*, personally, was "not averse" to having a small elegant inn in his commune. Not "pleased," mind you, just "not averse," which was neither a "yes" or a "no," just an easy, safe way for a typical French bureaucrat to say nothing and not be forced into making a decision. This, we learned with time, is par for the course.

As it later turned out, the inn was politely, though not overly enthusiastically, welcomed into the community. Its existence became a source of local interest and, eventually, pride. But that was after the mayor and his wife were invited, along with Madame Turner, an *adjoint* to the mayor, for coffee and cake, and they were personally shown what the inn would be like and how elegantly appointed the rooms were. We were, in effect, installing a five-star-quality hotel way beyond their imaginations.

Hearing that *les americaines* had decided to open a hotel in their quiet little village had probably raised fears in local minds of a Las Vegas, neon-lit affair, with flashing arrows along the road. Strangely enough, and sadly, that's exactly what the mayor himself allowed to happen with a printing establishment at the entrance to the town five years later. But the owner was the son of a friend, so…

Another letter in my dossier was from *Macon*, where most of the area's official government bureaus were located. We had been summoned to a meeting of the Historic Preservation Board to explain exactly what we intended to do. The architect, sensing an impending slaughter, volunteered to come along and plead our case. We entered a room with a long table around which were seated twelve people, two of them in wheel-chairs. After we had made the rounds of the table, with the obligatory hand-shaking, they got down to business:

"Do you have access for the disabled? How can disabled guests reach the rooms on the second floor? Do you plan on putting an elevator into the house?".... The questions shot out as fast as they could. The two gentlemen in the wheel-chairs glared at us all the while.

I am convinced to this day that, if the architect had not been in the room to argue our case, it would have all ended right then. He pointed out to them that it was completely *against* Historic Preservation policy to install an elevator in a 350-year-old tower, and, besides, at least one of the rooms (therefore, twenty percent of the available rooms) was on the ground level and was completely outfitted with wider than normal entrance and bathroom doors, hand-bars, adjustable mirrors, etc., etc., specifically designed for the disabled. If the architect hadn't affirmed all of this in the authoritative rapid-fire French that seems to satisfy officialdom, we would still be sitting at that table feeling guilty for no reason at all and being grilled like criminals.

There is nothing in this world as officious as a French official.

The letter came a few weeks later from *Macon* saying that our plans to create an inn had been accepted. My own dossier, by this time, had reached respectable proportions.

On the long-awaited day in January, we all gathered in the notaire's office for the signature. A description of the cast of characters:

Madame F., the seller, was a tiny lady of eighty-four years, who was dressed elegantly and followed the proceedings wordlessly. She gave us a half-smile when she arrived, fashionably French-late, and sat stone-faced, bolt upright in her seat throughout the proceedings. Although probably relieved to be rid of the expense and worry of maintaining the house, she was, I imagined, also probably sad to close this chapter of her life. After all, she had lived in the house for forty-five years, her children were reared there and had then gone off to create their own lives in Lyon, Paris, all over France, and Monsieur F. had long since passed on. And now the house was en route to being opened up to strangers as a public inn. But at the age of eighty-four, she found the house too much to handle, and a flat in nearby *Chalon-Sur-Saône*, within walking-distance of the shops, seemed to offer an easier existence. She had moved out, put the house up for sale, and turned the page.

Monsieur le Notaire, a bespectacled, cadaverous gentleman, served as Madame F.'s notaire as well as our own. They are obviously not as concerned about conflict of interest in France as we are in America. It was an uncomplicated sale, so we decided to use his services, even though his name sounded something like *"Huge Misery,"* which is not the most comforting name for a lawyer.

Catherine was there, cheerful and smiling as always, carrying her own dossier and helping us through the procedure.

Mademoiselle was there, as well. She was thirteen years old, making her seven years older, in people-years, than Madame F. Our Mademoiselle went everywhere with us, despite the fact that she was rather deaf, rather blind, and rather rheumy. She entered the office, was greeted with the customary *"mignon,"* and promptly curled up under the *notaire's* desk, going to sleep and snoring contentedly while we nervously initialed stacks of documents.

The other two people in the room were Dierk and myself. Two very different paths had brought us to that day. I was born in New York to parents who had come to America from Europe. They worked hard in their adopted land and loved it passionately. Their son, the fellow who sat nervously staring at the stack of papers on the *notaire's* desk, had gone to university and become a dentist, eventually ending up as an Assistant Professor at Harvard University in Boston. When I decided to move to France, Mama, who had spent so much of her life trying to forget Europe, could never understand what made me want to go back. I never understood it fully myself, but I felt comfortable and it just seemed right.

My teaching career brought me to South Africa. I accepted a position in Johannesburg at the University of the Witwatersrand, which I loved, and then was hired to go to the University of Capetown, where, one day, I was invited by some friends to a picnic at the beach. The word "picnic," to me, has always meant food, so I offered to prepare a little something to bring along. The day of the picnic, that "something" had evolved into five large plastic containers filled with fried chicken, various cold meats, potato salad, pasta salad with pesto, and assorted home-baked rolls.

As I entered the picnic area, loaded down with two gigantic shopping bags of food, I caught sight of a stranger seated with my friends. He had short-cropped blond hair, a smiling, friendly face, and turned out to be someone they had known for years.

He and I chatted, laughed at the same things, found out that we both spoke German as well as English, and that we shared many interests, including a love of travel. Dierk was born in northern Germany, trained as a textile designer, accepted a job in South West Africa, now Namibia, remained there for two years and then moved to Capetown. He'd been living in Capetown for nine years when we met.

Our mutual friends had arranged for us both to be there because our senses of humor are so similar. We both can laugh at the ridiculous and, most of all, at ourselves, which came in very handy in the years to come. The friendship just seemed natural and right. Neither of us has patience for wasting time, or game playing, or dishonesty. A friendship that has endured for many years was forged.

We returned to America, settled in Boston and, after about five years, an idea began to take shape that would allow us to do something that made use of our talents. Between us we were proficient in several languages, I love cooking, he has a talent for turning any garden or home into a showcase, we are avid do-it-yourselfers, and we both love meeting people. Where I'm outgoing and can get up in front of 200 strangers to give a lecture, he is much more reserved and would die a thousand deaths if he had to do it, but he has a giving nature and an innate ability to make people feel comfortable. We're also able to imagine what something will look like when it's finished.

What would allow us to use these talents, and, even more important, to work very hard for part of the year and to have several months of the year free? It became obvious that a seasonal activity was the answer, and even more obvious that opening an inn was the best solution, given the abilities we could contribute individually and collectively to the project. Doing it alone was absolutely unthinkable. It took some convincing on my part, and hours of discussion and practical figuring on his, but then came the day when we finally found ourselves in the office of *"Huge Misery"* signing stacks of papers filled with words we didn't understand.

Dierk was outwardly calm and in control of himself, but, I knew, as nervous about the whole thing as I was. I moved through the formalities in a state of excitement, chomping at the bit to get back to the house and get going! Mademoiselle snoozed on.

Less than half an hour later it was done. On the way out of the office, I thought it only polite to say to Madame F., *"Soyez le bienvenue, Madame":* "You are always welcome," although I knew it would remain, to her, the family home of memory. She half-smiled, softly said, *"Je ne crois pas,"* "I don't think so," turned and walked slowly away.

Chapter 3
Surprises

With the massive keys to the courtyard's huge iron gates and assorted other house keys clutched in my hands, we left the *notaire's* office and headed for the house along with a bored Mademoiselle, who had, it seemed, found "huge misery" fascinating and had to be torn away from under his desk.

Dierk stopped the car long enough for me to hop into one of the *patisseries* in Chalon-Sur-Saône for a baguette, into a *charcuterie* for some paté and cold-cuts, and a *fromagerie* for some cheese, and we arrived at the house with the makings of our first meal "chez nous." (The wine had been brought from our growing "cave" in Paris, especially for the occasion.)

I had pretty much talked Dierk into the whole inn idea. Doing it alone is impossible. If you're lucky enough to have a partner and friend who is as hard-working, serious, and easy to get along with as him, with the sense of humor without which you'll both never survive, you have a *chance* of success…a remote one, but, at least, a fighting chance. If you intend to depend on hired strangers, forget it!

Madame F., we discovered, once she was alone and safely installed in town, had used the house only for the summer months, when heating was not necessary. There was no central heating but we assumed that the gas-heaters throughout the house, when used in conjunction with the fireplaces and electric heaters as needed, must have been sufficient when it had served as a family home.

We returned, however, to a house in which we could see our breath. It was cold, damp, and the only heating devices she had left were an ancient gas-heater in the kitchen in front of the boarded-up fireplace, with a suspicious crack down its side, and a similar device in the main salon. They were both turned off and no tell-tale hiss accompanied movement of any of their dials. We traced the fuel line from the kitchen heater to two huge cylindrical containers located at ground level one floor below the kitchen, turned the spigot of the one that was connected to the pipe counter-clockwise, and a reassuring "shush" in the line indicated that it wasn't empty. Racing up to the kitchen, we sniffed for any tell-tale gas odors, especially coming from the crack, and listened for any sounds of life. Nothing. With what I feared might be a last look at Dierk, then at Mademoiselle, and, praying that the adventure wouldn't be over before it began, I slowly turned on the gas, struck a match, held it to the pilot-light area, and awaited the explosion. The heater sprang to life and we crouched over it to thaw out.

We unpacked the car, brought in the suitcases loaded with winter clothing, and unrolled the four-inch thick rubber foam mattress that would serve as a bed until the furniture could be delivered. The tile floor was cold and clammy, amplified by the condensation from the outside, once the windows had been opened for a few moments to let the air in and the gas fumes out. Mademoiselle, undaunted, curled up on the mattress and began snoring.

Nudging Mademoiselle to one side of the mattress, and with nothing else to sit on, we enjoyed our impromptu picnic and toasted our good fortune with some wine. *La vie est belle!*

She remained untroubled later when we discovered that, in addition to no heat, there was no water. No water?

Have you ever pondered the fact that the word "panic" is almost identical in so many languages? I look upon that fact as yet another indication of the common emotions that basically unite all human creatures.

In my case, it usually manifests itself as a voice, way deep inside, that says, "You idiot! What have you gotten us into *now*?"

Since moving to France, I've heard the voice most often when I'm sitting in some terribly official (and/or officious) personage's office, clutching my dossier for dear life, wondering which important document I forgot to complete. The voice was just starting to clear its throat when there was a knock on the front door.

The elderly gentleman who stood there was Monsieur P., Madame F.'s gardener, who just wanted to know if he could continue to work for the new owners. I practically pounced on the poor man, dragged him inside the house, all the while babbling, "Water! Water! There's no water!"

"The well might be dry."

"What *well*?"

"That one in the garden." He pointed to a large, spoke-wheeled, hand-turned thing that you see in old movies or antique stores at outrageous prices. "But for that you have to get the pump started up."

"Pump? You mean that thing's not just for decoration?"

"She had trouble with it last year, so I'll see what I can do."

"Isn't there a main water line that we can use for the hotel we're going to start? A well's not going to give enough water."

"Baaaaah, oui." (More about "Baaaaah when we meet Arnaud.) "I think it's over there." He thumbed in the direction of the far end of the adjoining field.

Why *our* water line might be on someone *else's* cow pasture didn't occur to me to ask at the time.

"Please, please show it to me so that I can show it to the architect."

The cows in the field regarded me with interest as I followed Monsieur P. over the barbed wire fence separating the two properties, tearing my new gray corduroy trousers, especially chosen to be worn for the first time that day for the *"signature."* Through the cow patties, slipping and sprawling and feeling inordinately stupid as the cows stared at me, I ran after Monsieur.

"Well, I *thought* it was here," he said, scratching private parts which responded symphonically. (We were, fortunately, outside, but this recurred frequently in the weeks to come, sometimes in painfully closer quarters.)

Monsieur P.'s bodily functions, however, were far less important on that day than was the fact that, after fiddling around with some wires in the basement, and after many attempts, shortly before it became dark he managed to get the pump to work and we actually had running water in the house.

Now for the bad news: it was running down the dining room wall from the upstairs bedroom where a pipe had burst. Whether this was a legacy from Madame F. or had just happened, I never really discovered, but I'll give the lady the benefit of the doubt.

"Stop the pump," I screamed. "Where's there a plumber?" This on a Friday evening.

"I'll call Monsieur Pellat. He lives in town and he knows the house."

"Thank you, thank you. THANK YOU!"

Monsieur Pellat could not come until the next morning, of course, so that first night was spent on a mattress on a cold, damp tile floor, with no water, on the alert for gas odors, listening to Mademoiselle's snoring and a voice from way deep inside me saying, "You idiot...."

On that first night in our inn-to-be, January 15, 1988, wearing every piece of clothing I possessed, teeth chattering, back hurting, lying on a thin, rubber foam mattress on a cold tile floor, in a silent room listening for hissing sounds while I tried to convince myself to sleep, Panic had a field day.

Things have to get better...they can't get worse...my last thoughts as I drifted off into an exhausted sleep. *Pas de problème.* The three most terrifying words in the French language....

In retrospect, I have two bits of advice for anyone contemplating major renovations in France, a country which is infinitely blessed with beauty, variety, and people I have grown to admire and, in some cases, to love. The first is that, as I've inferred, whenever you hear the words "Pas de Problème," you can be sure there's trouble ahead, so beware. The second is that you should never hire a cross-eyed architect to draw up your "plan d'état."

Charming as he was, animated as he was, all the telephone calls for requests to see the famous document, since time would be costing us money, were met with a cheery *"Pas de probleme."* When the "plan" was finally presented to us, many weeks later, I should have suspected trouble. The 1622 tower, which, at three stories high, was the tallest part of the building, ended up somewhere between the first and second floor on his drawing. Granted, I'm only a dentist without any previous experience with *"plans d'état,"* but it still seemed rather unusual. To me, at least. He, on the other hand, was very proud of what he'd done.

Then the fateful question: "When can the workers get started with the renovations? We're scheduled to sign the final papers on January 15th."

"Pas de probleme," he replied. "We're ready to start immediately."

Not entirely true.

He might have been "ready," but the rest of the story, (as he well knew), was that the plans for actual renovations, along with this *"plan d'état,"* had to be submitted first for approval, and only then would an official *"permis construire,"* or building permit, be approved. Issuing this building permit took, on average, if *everything* went well, a minimum of, as you've already guessed, three months…and since when does everything go well?

We had visions of signing the final papers on the morning of January 15th and Monsieur and his merry band of *"ouvriers,"* hammers poised, arriving on that afternoon.

That's not quite the way it happened. Renovations did, indeed, eventually begin, after delays, meetings, further interviews with appropriate governmental institutions, visits to the *Mairie,* the *sous-préfecture,* the *préfecture,* the *sous-ministre,* the *ministre,* the *chambre de commerce,* the *bureau des impôts,* countless telephone calls to countless *functionnaires* who all somehow managed to schedule their *"vacances"* for that week, Monsieur, and could I please telephone again *"le fin de la semaine prochaine,"* the end of next week…but they definitely did *not* begin on January 15th.

In all fairness, I must add here that the entire procedure was bound to be a lot more complicated since we were attempting a *commercial* enterprise. I'm sure that if we were ever to try creating a hotel in America, we would have the same problems to contend with: the fire department, also, would come out to check the fire extinguishers to see if they were to code; the building department, also, would come out and check the structural changes for public safety; the electricity inspectors would also come out to see if all was in order. It's perfectly natural and necessary to protect the people who might one day stay at the hotel.

On May 2nd the "team" finally arrived to begin work. Dierk and I had spent the intervening weeks doing the demolition work. The wall between the two rear rooms came down, the huge ceiling beams were stripped of layers of cement, the future kitchen was divested of the huge flowered wallpaper growing grotesquely all over the walls and ceilings, the fireplaces were opened up and proper fire-brick installed. In the upstairs bedrooms, unnecessary partition walls were removed to enlarge the spaces and make room for two additional future bathrooms. The walls were constructed of concrete-like bricks, which, if they fell the wrong way during demolition, could do some permanent damage to anyone in their way. We both have scars to prove it.

Unused spaces were recuperated to form little sitting areas in each room, the *"dépendances"* were cleaned of hay and debris so that the workers could come in and build them up again into habitable spaces, and it began to take shape in reality as well as in our imaginations.

I was learning some of the basic differences between the American and French approaches to problem situations. For example, if you ask the average American whether something unusual or different can be done, he or she will probably say, "Sure, why not? Go for it!" The approach is positive, the sky's the limit! If he or she later discovers that the difficulties truly make it impossible, well, at least you've given it a try.

If you pose the same question to the average French person, the reaction will probably be eyebrow-wiggling, shoulder-shrugging, forehead-wrinkling, and hand maneuvers worthy of a Philharmonic conductor, followed by a head-shaking, *"Non, c'est impossible!"* Of course, after some cajoling, a little chatting-up, maybe a café and some talk of the family or the last vacation, or a cigarette, they will find a way to do it. And what the French do, they usually do very well, indeed, often superbly. But the initial approach is, usually, negative. Or, at the very most, hesitant.

The best solution to this negative approach is to arrive at a meeting with an impressively bulging *dossier*. The actual contents of the dossier don't matter because those papers are never the ones needed anyway, but it's the dossier that counts so I've gotten into the habit of never leaving home without one. I walk into the bank or the electric company with my yellow (a favorite color) dossier firmly planted between my elbow and my love-handle, and, immediately, heads perk up, backs straighten and I get the VIP treatment I deserve. After all, I've got a DOSSIER! I once filled it with the day's complete edition of *Le Figaro* newspaper and got even better service. A safe equation would be "service equals thickness of dossier." Try it.

I once asked a French exchange student at Harvard, shortly after he arrived in Boston, what he noticed most about the differences between French and American mentalities. He said that he was impressed by the fact that the Americans discuss something at length, then decide, and then do it. The French first make a decision, then they discuss it endlessly, and they may never actually get around to doing it.

Another thing I've gotten used to is the French love of shaking hands. Each time a worker arrived, there was an elaborate hand-shaking ceremony with everyone present involved. Everyone shakes hands in France, from the postman to the baker to the workmen who come to fix the plumbing. If you don't take the time to shake hands, you are considered somewhat of an oaf and, certainly, beneath further respect or attention. I've caught many a hand mid-air before committing this unforgivable breach of French etiquette.

It wasn't easy, at first, because in Boston I was accustomed to asking the local grocer for some carrots, broccoli, or whatever, paying for it, and getting out of the way so as not to hold up the next customer. In France, unless I want to be regarded as a philistine, I preface these requests with a handshake, some small talk about his health, the weather, perhaps some news of his recently-married daughter, and only then do we get down to the business of what brought me to pay him a visit in the first place on this "beau" (or "mal") morning. The person behind me in line never seems to mind the delay and waits patiently for the ritual to end and for his or her turn to perform. This, of course, can turn a few routine errands into a full morning's outing, but I think it's kinder to the facial muscles and the blood pressure.

Chapter 4
Les voisins

*D**racy Le Fort* was a village in Burgundy that got its name from the Roman general Dracon and had enjoyed great prosperity, in ancient times, because it lay along the salt route. Salt was, in those days, a most valuable commodity. When we visited a nearby chateau, the owner, whose family had owned the chateau for centuries, showed us a tall chair with a rather wide seat covering a hidden hollow space. This was where the lady of the house, in centuries past, would seat herself during the visit of the local salt-tax assessor whenever he arrived, literally perched on the family's wealth.

Our house had been there since 1622, according to the inscription on the tower, at which time it had probably been a station along the salt-route. Its exact origins lay locked away in musty documents in the archives in *Macon*, all in ancient French, which is not at all like the modern language. Hidden they would remain, sadly, and we never formally documented the house's long history as we would have liked.

With each passing day, we became more familiar with the area's offerings and things became less and less strange. We took the time to investigate the chateaux, the vineyards, the religious sites, such as Cluny and Taizé, amassing information to enable us to create itineraries for future guests. But most of the time was spent with being one step ahead of the workmen, working alongside them, and buying the things we would need for the inn. The furniture that was shipped from the States was delivered from storage and remained, still unwrapped, in one of the *dépendances*, waiting to be put into place.

There were new things to buy, as well. We didn't have dining room furniture, beds, enough lamps, in short, all the trappings of a hotel. So we ventured out, each day that we weren't busy knocking down walls, did some shopping, and learned all we could about the "neighborhood."

According to our neighbors, we had, fortunately, and without planning, chosen an area that was the Beverly Hills of *Chalon Sur Saône*. The magnificent home across the road was a restored mill owned by the Neyrat family, who had, for generations, been making umbrellas in a huge factory in *Chalon* for all of France (and for the haute couture houses in Paris, which then put their own labels on them). On my next visit to Paris, I saw the name Neyrat on a number of umbrellas displayed in *Au Bon Marché*, the huge department store on Rue du Bac.

Shortly after we arrived in Dracy le Fort, we returned from one of our shopping sorties to find an invitation, stuck in the locked gate, from Monsieur and Madame Neyrat. They were giving a party and wished to invite us. We dressed up for the event and strolled across the road. The ancient mill that had become their house was straight out of a magazine, magnificently furnished with antiques, and the party was held in an outdoor *dépendance* and under a huge open tent. Among the several hundred guests were the mayor and a gentleman who was a very high-up local politician. (He later had several ministerial posts under President Jacques Chirac.)

We were introduced all around by the Neyrats as the new neighbors, *les americaines,* who had moved from America to live in France and had chosen their little corner of France in which to open an inn. Raised eyebrows all around us, smiles of agreement that yes, indeed, France was beautiful, and lots of explaining on our parts as to why we had made the decision.

The Neyrats couldn't have been more gracious or welcoming and over the years they became good friends, Monsieur Neyrat even surprising us with three superb yellow outdoor umbrellas and, as a welcoming gift, several every-day smaller ones displaying our special logo of *"Aux Trois Saisons."*

The work continued and all of the villagers strolled by on their weekly Sunday outings, pushing baby carriages and staring at the newcomers, us, and at all of the frenzied activity inside the gates.

Another invitation arrived, shortly after the Neyrats' party. Rather, it took the form of an announcement of the annual "Fête Patronale" of Dracy le Fort. It urged "all Draciens and Draciennes to join in the village's two-day celebrations and thereby show their civic *spirit* and *support* for the community".

The town square, when I went to the office of the *Mairie* to pay the thirty Francs per person luncheon fee to *Monsieur le Maire's* ever-helpful secretary, was already filled with amusement rides and fair-ground booths. It hummed with excitement.

By this time, Madame Barriere, the secretary, and I were old friends. This pleasant lady and I had plowed together through the mountain of forms and petitions needed to bring the inn to life, the permits to build, to renovate, to install a window in a classified building where there was none before, not to mention the stack of personal documents required to make me a legal resident of France.

The only other people I had really gotten to know, at the time the announcement arrived, were the people from whom I bought my meat and fish, the people at the weekly *marché* from whom I bought my vegetables and fruit, the friendly man from whom I bought my *tranches* of paté and cold-cuts, the cheese lady, and, of course, *Monsieur et Madame LeFavre,* the young couple, with two children, who ran the local post office.

While *Monsieur Le Favre* was out on his bicycle delivering the mail, his wife handled the office. Then when he came back, she retired to their living quarters behind the post office to prepare his lunch while he handled the office. Quite a nice arrangement, and my daily trip to pick up the mail was always an opportunity to chat with one or the other about the weather, the kids, the inn, in fact, any excuse to dawdle for a few moments' respite from the day's chores.

The day of the *Fête Patronale* rolled around and, all decked out in suits and ties, we arrived, on time, outside the town's meeting hall where pre-luncheon drinks were to be served. Now, "on time" for me means, indeed, the hour stated. "On time" in France means quite another thing, anywhere from being "fashionably" late—ten to fifteen minutes after the stated hour—to sometime during the following twenty-four-hour period.

The music, as we stood there with drinks in hand, smiling at lots of people we didn't know, was provided by five teen-agers who, miraculously, played music meant for enjoyment not mind-numbing escape. There were recognizable songs: javas, waltzes, old Piaf favorites…what a joy! Smiles all around, several glasses of pre-luncheon warm-ups, and my "civic spirit" began to surface.

Monsieur le Maire made a point of coming over to shake hands with us and to, very graciously, say how pleased he was that we had joined in the *Fête Patronale* celebration, especially since we were the *newest* residents of Dracy le Fort!

Our name cards were set at a table which was reserved, it seemed, for dignitaries such as the local schoolmaster, schoolmistress, and the mayor's *adjoint*, Madame Turner. Their smiling *bon jours* did the trick. No strangers here, just warm, kind people who were probably as relieved to find that we were human, friendly, and pretty much like them—except for our accents. Why is it that we spend so much time in life being either scared or sorry?

With no formal dance floor, my fellow Draciens and Draciennes still did Piaf and the old melodies justice, waltzing between tables, exchanging pleasantries with one and all as they twirled by. The meal consisted of a superb chicken dish prepared with grapes, baskets of hot freshly baked bread, and some of the fine local wine from the Deliance family vineyards. It was a sheer delight.

A most welcome luncheon companion was the mayor's *adjoint*, Madame Turner. She was well into her seventies, at that time, an elegant lady whose English name came from her late husband, a distant relative of the English painter.

Madame Turner had endeared herself to us several weeks before the *Fête Patronale*, when, as the mayor's representative, she had arrived at our inn-to-be along with representatives from the fire department, the building authorities, the police department, and heaven knows which other dossier-laden stalwarts of officialdom. All of them had descended on us that particular day to check us out and make certain that we met with all of the hundreds of regulations their colleagues had dreamed up over the centuries.

Madame Turner had arrived at the door before the others. She was the only one on time, so we had a while to get acquainted with this wonderful lady. Introductions made, in French, she then switched to flawless English, explaining that she and her late husband a distant relative of the painter, Turner, had spent their married life as much in England as in France. We were relieved and thought that, perhaps, the day would not be as much of a catastrophe as feared, with Madame as our interpreter. As she soon made clear, she was also our ally.

She informed us that we had developed a good reputation in town because we always paid our bills on time. This came as a surprise because we just assumed that it was the right thing to do, and not an unusual subject for discussion among the townspeople. But they, obviously, thought so. The day had started well.

The gentlemen with dossiers and their assistants with clip-boards arrived and joined the three of us in the salon, shook hands all around, and, turning to me, asked what that large puddle of water in the courtyard was.

"What large puddle of water?"

"That one," the fellow with the thickest dossier replied, escorting us all outside, pointing to a rapidly rising miniature Hoover dam.

Hardly ten minutes before, the courtyard had been dry as a bone, and Dierk and I had carefully raked the gravel free of leaves that morning so that the inspectors might have a favorable first impression. Now, some mysterious water-source threatened the recently completed *Suite de Jardin* with destruction.

Madame Turner and the Monsieur Dossier saved the day. He calmly investigated the source of the inundation and found that it was the water pipe which had evidently burst at that point where the town water enters our property and where the ditch traversing the courtyard had recently been filled in.

Madame Turner, equally calm, asked which *"enterprise"* had done the work and then asked Monsieur Dossier to get on the telephone himself, after I, hands shaking, and obviously in no condition to explain *anything*, had dialed the number. Monsieur, obviously a gentleman of some importance, explained the seriousness of the situation to the *entreprise*. We were, I might add, by this time, well on the way to becoming an inland waterway, and I had a fleeting vision of a courtyard stocked with trout.

We continued with the tour through the house, showing them the fire extinguishers (specific ones for the kitchen and others for the living areas), the requisite *sortie* and *privé* signs where indicated, the alarm boxes, the circuit-breaker boxes, and anything else they wanted to inspect, stopping short of my bedroom closet, which was the only truly dangerous thing in the house.

They were very nice people, not at all difficult, extremely polite, who happily made their notations in their dossiers, all the while smiling and chatting among themselves and with Madame Turner. Perhaps the earlier excitement had disposed them more kindly toward us, or, perhaps, Madame Turner's gentleness had smoothed things over. We'll never know, but, in our estimation, simply having her there as an island of comfort in a sea of disaster—literally—had consigned her to the immortals. The official papers, covered with stamps from each inspector indicating their agreement to our project, arrived a few weeks later, and we immediately telephoned Madame Turner to tell her.

Madame invited us to visit her, but it was difficult to arrange. With our own days filled with finishing touches on the rooms, and Madame's busy schedule, filled with visits to her Parisian apartment and her own family's visits to Dracy le Fort, there never seemed be enough time. Finally, a date was set, Madame casually mentioning that she would also invite her friend the *Baron de Villard*.

Monsieur le Baron owns a magnificent chateau near Dracy le Fort, which has been in his family for many generations. The chateau boasts its own tiny chapel along the road at the entrance gates. Madame and the Baron had grown up together and had remained friendly for well over seventy years.

When the day arrived, Madame greeted us at the door of her home, gracious as ever. We entered a foyer whose walls were covered with a hand-painted Chinese wallpaper depicting in soft and lovely hues the four corners of the world.

Her "workroom" revealed some extraordinarily beautiful drawings of flowers and animals. Madame's drawings, it seems, were well known to Parisian galleries and much sought after. One such work in progress was perched on an easel, a bouquet of flowers coaxed to life by her skillful artistry, so real that their scent seemed to fill the room.

The dogs started barking and, shortly afterwards, he arrived: the *Baron de Villard* himself. If you were to call Central Casting at any Hollywood studio and say, "Send me a French Baron," I doubt they could do justice to what centuries of breeding have produced.

I glimpsed him at the entrance door, as he bent to touch Madame's hand to his lips in the old manner, and noted that they still, after all those years, addressed each other with the formal *vous* rather than the familiar *tu*. This is a distinction that exists in most other languages. We have it much easier in English with the all-purpose "you," but that doesn't really tell you how well you know the person. *Vous* and *tu* are subtle ways of being able to say that neither one of you is sure yet how far to go.

Instead of memorizing all of the verb conjugations in both familiar and formal forms, I simply say vous most of the time and everybody thinks that I'm very polite. When pressed by people I've known for years, I will make an effort to say tu but if vous slips out, I'll explain that it's my lack of grammar and, although "it's vous on my tongue, it's tu in my heart." That usually gets me off the hook.

Monsieur le Baron strode into the salon, not seeming to really need the walking stick he carried. He stood erect as we were introduced, like some great military leader inspecting his troops, and shook hands with us. The steel-blue eyes were keen, the handshake firm, the smile open and friendly.

We sat down to chat while our hostess went into the kitchen to organize the afternoon's refreshments. The Baron speaks no English, or, at least, professes not to, but understands quite a bit. I discovered this when he came up with the word for rainbow, *arc en ciel,* which had completely eluded me.

The conversation flowed easily, although I can't remember what we actually talked about. In France, communication is the very essence of life. It's that indefinable French capacity to reveal warmth beneath the formalities, to convey volumes with a ripple of laughter, a wink, or a raised eyebrow. The Baron also enjoyed the Oatmeal Lace cookies and individual carrot cakes I'd baked that morning and brought as a gift for Madame Turner, so he's obviously also a man of superb taste.

Monsieur and Madame Neyrat, Madame Turner, and le Baron de Villard had, each in their own way, made us feel comfortable.

POULET PATRONALE

Ingredients:
- 1   chicken part per serving (either breast or thigh)
- 3 tbs   shallots, chopped fine
- 1 c   mushrooms, sliced
- 3 tbs   butter
- 1 c   white wine
- 1/4 tsp thyme
- 1/4 tsp salt
- 1 tbs   lemon juice
- 3 tbs   flour
- 1/4 c   water
- 2 c   seedless grapes (whichever you prefer, green or red)

Preparation:
Heat the butter in a large skillet. Sauté the chicken parts in the heated butter until cooked golden brown on all sides. Remove to another skillet and keep in a warming oven. Add shallots and mushrooms to the heated butter in the skillet and sauté for about 5 minutes or until just golden brown. Add the white wine, all of the seasonings, and the lemon juice to the skillet. Dissolve the flour in the 1/4 cup of water and slowly add this flour-water mixture to the skillet and continue cooking until the sauce becomes thickened. Put the chicken parts back into the sauce, add the seedless grapes, and simmer all together for about 10 minutes more. Serve hot.

Note:
I've used both the green grapes and the red grapes for this recipe, depending on which one is fresher, more readily available, and more reasonably priced. I prefer the red ones for the color they add to the dish, but it's tasty with either variety. Enjoy it at your own Fête Patronale.

Chapter 5
La Fin De La Semaine Prochaine

If the French say that something will take three months, believe them. It will take three months no matter *what* you do.

The architect, after much prodding and pleading on our parts, had finally completed the plans for the prospective renovations sometime around February and we submitted the official forms for the necessary *permis construire*. My weekly telephone calls, to find out the state of the building permits, turned into twice-weekly conversations with assorted anonymous voices, and then into almost daily calls. The nameless unreachables taught me another useful phrase: *"La fin de la semaine prochaine."*

"Please call back," the voices said.

"When?" my plaintive plea.

"Baaaaaa, the end of next week."

Everything would happen the end of next week…which gave them at least another week to shuffle papers around as they awaited their retirement, the high-point of the average French person's life.

I can't be judgmental about it, because they're obviously doing something very right, considering the pleasure they take from life. But one very basic difference between the French and Americans is that we, in America, identify ourselves with our work. To the French, work is just something that kills time between meals or vacations.

In America, seated beside a perfect stranger at dinner, we consider it perfectly reasonable to ask: "What do you do?" or "Where do you work?" That is *never* done in France, or, indeed, anywhere in Europe. It's considered too forward and a terrible breach of etiquette. If the person doesn't do anything particularly impressive or interesting, you run the risk of embarrassing them and *that*, in Europe, is a cardinal offense. An acceptable ice-breaker would be to ask about an upcoming vacation, or last year's vacation, or, even better, could the person recommend a good restaurant. Then just sit back and they'll take it from there.

My repeated telephone calls to the assorted government offices in *Chalon Sur Saône*, therefore, had to be polite and discreet and make absolutely no mention of the fact that I, in any way, questioned the competence of that particular agency or person. The calls, I might add, also had absolutely *no* effect.

Dierk and I continued our labors, and the demolition work yielded some marvelous discoveries. Behind dozens of old doors and broken windows, cartons of dried apples, and 360 years of debris and dust, we found the original kitchen. It lay on the ground level, near the entrance to the 1622 tower. Hours of work spent chipping away concrete revealed the old fireplace and bread-baking oven, which had been walled-off during one of the many changes made to the house since the seventeenth century.

That original kitchen became our candle-lit wine tasting room, and off to another side of the tower was the dirt-floored wine cellar, *la cave*. The old stones around the door, when cleaned, were found to have markings chiseled into them that looked very much like the round Pennsylvania

Dutch hex signs in America. I conjured up images of evil spirits being barred from the house in some seventeenth century equivalent of our American Salem witch hunts. The truth, as we found out later on, is a little less romantic. These chiseled symbols were the signatures of the stonemasons who built the house and could neither read or write, a lack which did not prevent them, however, from being master craftsmen whose work would survive the centuries.

On the main floor, when we removed the wall between the two rear rooms, we discovered enormous hand-hewn beams, measuring about twelve inches square. They had been covered over with plaster during the last century when anything made of wood was considered *rustique* and *passé*. Three weeks of meticulous removal of plaster, wire-brushing, and, then, two coats of wax brought them back to their original splendor and gave the dining room the warmth we sought. There was more than enough room for the five tables we planned, with plenty of space between them for privacy.

The garden was sadly neglected, and, hidden under ivy and moss, I found the ancient carved stone benches that, when the property had been properly cared for, had been placed along the stream at particularly beautiful and secluded vantage points. I cleared away the overgrowth and, over the following years, sat there for many hours trying to imagine the lives that had played out there over the centuries.

Above the door of the tower, I found a stone plaque with some interesting markings: a crescent moon, a star-form, an "M" and the date, 1622. We had many tries at deciphering the meaning, and one guest, an archeology buff, came up with the version I liked best. He attributed the crescent and star to the Crusader voyages of one of the home's previous owners' families.

He said that a similar marking existed at the *Musée de Cluny* in Paris, which adds plausibility to his interpretation, since the Abbey of Cluny is not far from the house in Burgundy. It was from Cluny that Saint Bernard departed for Citeau, when Cluny became too "worldly" for him, and founded the Cistercian order of monks. They are still in Citeau, and if you ever have the opportunity to visit them, try to be present for one of their prayer sessions to hear their haunting Gregorian chants resonating in the spartan chapel. And don't leave without buying one of the delicious cheeses made by the Monks. It's a delight and well worth the trip itself.

One day in April, while we were covered in plaster, *Monsieur LeFavre* came by on his bicycle and brought us the *permis construire*, which now proudly boasted all the requisite stamps.

The architect and the workers arrived on May 2nd, since May 1st is a national holiday in France. The "team" consisted of the architect, the chief electrician, the chief plumber, and the masons. Much hand-shaking, eyebrow-raising, and shoulder-shrugging later, they actually got down to work.

We had completed all of the demolition ourselves, so their job was to *re*build, *re*wire, *re*plumb, in short, *re*create a new house with six bedrooms, seven bathrooms, and a modern kitchen, within a 360-year-old ruin. Without, we insisted, destroying the character of the house.

The walls of the house were made of two-foot thick stones, so their task was a formidable one. To bring in new lines, the electrician had to drill through all this. I learned some interesting new French words.

How different from our previous house in Marshfield, near Boston, where I had simply taken out my trusty electrical jig-saw, cut a hole in the wood fame and installed a new pre-fabricated bow-window in the kitchen.

The water lines had to be tied into the town supply, since the existing well would never be enough for the inn's needs. A long and deep trench was dug from the house all the way through the gravel courtyard to the main water lines in the street outside the entrance gates. *Not*, as that fund of misinformation, *Monsieur P.* had indicated, at the other end of the adjoining field!

The property looked worse every day, which is the case with renovations, but the work progressed.

One fine summer day, about the middle of June, I looked out the window and there they were, in the garden, with a few boards resting on wooden work-horses acting as a make-shift dining table. *Monsieur le plombier* had invited *Monsieur l'électricien* as his guest for luncheon.

And there we were, in the soon-to-be-kitchen, hungrily looking down on them as they spread out the tablecloth, uncorked the wine, allowing it to breathe, *bien sûr*, carefully set out the dishes and utensils, and then slowly unpacked the meal, both hot and cold courses, which the plumber's wife had prepared and sent along in a wicker basket and appropriate containers.

We, on the other hand, had no refrigerator, indeed, no electricity, in our kitchen, a fact which did not seem, in any way, to disturb the electrician as he sat down to his twelve noon to 2:00 p.m. luncheon.

You can set your clock by French tummies. I've seen the antique merchants at the famous *Marche aux Puces* in Paris inform a potential buyer that it was noon, that the store was closed and the customer had to leave, and then completely ignore passing customers as they happily spread their lunches and wine bottles on the nearest seventeenth or eighteenth century table and munched away for two solid hours.

We lunched on a can of tuna, a few slices of cheese, a baguette, and enough wine to convince ourselves that it wasn't at all unusual. I just didn't have the heart to see what they were eating, but they kept at it for two hours, laughing uproariously, probably at us, and having a grand old time.

Monsieur Lagrange and his merry band of plasterers left an undying impression on me—and their footprints on everything else—as they went about their tasks. They spent their days putting up walls, happily splashing plaster, wet and dry, over 150-year-old parquet floors, which we spent our nights scrubbing clean.

I noticed *Monsieur Lagrange* in the garden one morning, stuffing something into a plastic bag. It turned out to be one of those beautiful *escargot* which abound in Burgundy and which spend their last hours viewing the light of day from a gorgeous garlic-butter bath.

I joined him in the garden and, while he gathered them up, *Monsieur* exclaimed in rapid-fire French exactly how his wife would prepare them in several days, after they had been fed lettuce and properly purged themselves. I will spare you the exact details, primarily because they remain a mystery to me, and, out of context, they sound perfectly disgusting. I always end up with the bought ones and concentrate on making the sauce.

While French electricians and plumbers are just as exasperating as their American counterparts, they certainly do set a nicer table. But the French stone-masons are the last true artisans. Perhaps, since there's less call for the art of masonry, we really have no idea, in America, of the quality of stone work still done in Europe. These men are absolutely a joy to watch.

I observed them for hours, as they chiseled away, turning a window into a doorway which, when they were done, looked as though it had been there for centuries. I was enthralled by their craftsmanship, and when they finished, I felt compelled to tell them how beautiful their work was. They seemed pleased by the compliment, even more so by the fact that I had taken the trouble to deliver it.

As the workers departed each room, having completed their contributions to the renovation process, we followed them, putting in the finishing touches and decorations.

I can only imagine what they were thinking when they glimpsed the crazy American perched on the closed toilet seat, deciding on the exact position to put the toilet paper holder so that getting to it wouldn't cause a sprained back.

Or the *robinets!* Oh, the *robinets!* The plumber arrived each morning with his cheery *Bon jour, Monsieur,* and his trusty lunch basket. To this greeting, I invariably replied, *Bon jour, Monsieur. Ou est le robinet?* That's the French for cut-off-valve.

Monsieur le Plombier would probably have put just one in the whole house: on/off.

"If I ever have to fix a faucet in *Suite de Jardin*, I don't want to have to turn off the water to *Bellevue!*" I patiently insisted.

He grumpily gave in to the crazy American, and put a *robinet* under each sink, each toilet, each bathtub, amid much muttering, forehead-wrinkling, and head-shaking. After all, *everybody* knows that the Americans have a fetish about plumbing!

"Why do all the water pipes show?" I demanded to know.

"So that you can get to them to fix them!"

"Doesn't show much confidence in your work, does it?"

No response, just some more muttering, forehead-wrinkling, and head-shaking. But the best was yet to come.

One day, we had to go into *Chalon Sur Saône* to see *"Huge Misery"* to rectify a slight *erreur* someone made on the final deed, which arrived, naturally, three months after the day of sale.

On the deed, in just a quick read-through, I noticed that the land-parcel numbers somehow didn't seem right. According to this "official" document, and after three months of *meticulous* attention on the part of countless *functionaires*, no doubt, we had officially bought the *town road* and the town officially owned *our house.*

"Une petite erreur," *misery's* secretary informed us on the telephone, so we left the house and drove to *Chalon Sur Saône* to drop off the deed at his office so that it could be corrected. This would take, of course, another three months.

We returned to the house to find the electrician in the entrance. He was up on the tallest ladder imaginable, snipping wires at ceiling height, a full three meters from the floor, and screwing the fuse box into place.

"What are you doing?" I asked.

"Putting in the box," he replied as if I were the village idiot.

"Why up there? If there's a problem, how am I supposed to get to it?"

"But the wires are already cut."

The box stayed up there. If he had taken the trouble to go one meter further, around the corner and down the wall with the wires, he would have ended up with the fuse box at normal ceiling height where it could be reached in an emergency. It would also not have been the first thing your eye was drawn to when you entered the foyer.

Sure enough, on April 10, 1993, a day that will live in infamy in my memory, there was an electrical storm that blew out all the telephone and electrical lines. In the middle of a raging storm, I had to traipse out to the barn and drag in the tallest ladder we had. Precariously balanced on tip-toe with a candle in one hand, and in complete darkness, I tried to replace the burned-out fuses. I was too preoccupied to remember that I have vertigo.

It happened just when the guests were in the salon having their pre-dinner aperitif. There was a crashing wall of fire and everything went dark. The guests were unbelievably good-natured about it, turning it into a romantic candle-lit adventure, while I continued preparing dinner on the gas stove in the kitchen.

The mishaps, eventually sorted out, now seem amusing. Just to give you a short list, since a long one would fill three books the size of the one you're reading:

When the "master" electrician finished his labors, somehow the fire-alarm went off whenever the bathroom light switch in the *Tour Sud* room was turned on. We, therefore, would have quickly gotten to know our guests' toilet habits, which, at three o'clock in the morning probably would not have interested us.

The "master" *menuisier*, wood-worker, managed to crack a specially ordered double-paned window that had taken five weeks to arrive and which took another five weeks to replace. He also, after very careful measurements, left us with doors that just barely missed closing.

The "master" builders somehow miscalculated the thickness of the doors and the thickness of the door-knobs, an error which led to a noticeable degree of incompatibility.

The "master" plumber put the sinks and bathtubs in so that traps were completely hidden and unreachable. However, I must admit that he did, indeed, put in the robinets.

Lest I leave you with the impression that I am being unduly harsh with French workmen, I've had some equally frustrating experiences with their American counterparts. As an example, an American "master" plumber, I'll not tell you where, installed the water faucets so that, instead of turning the handles toward me to turn the water on, I had to turn them *away*. What's more, he used the faucets on several occasions and never mentioned that they were installed backwards.

There are still fine and conscientious workmen all over the world. Incompetence, too, knows no geographic boundaries.

Chapter 6
Le Départ

After a frenzied flurry of activity, and, not coincidentally, just before our building team disappeared to their respective vacation destinations, by the end of July we had the house pretty much to ourselves. The plumbers' work was done, and we installed the ceramic tile around the roughed-in kitchen appliances and bathroom fixtures. I filled the kitchen cabinets with my white Rosenthal dinner set and enough assorted glasses and pots and pans and utensils to serve the ten guests the inn would welcome each day when it officially opened.

Furniture went into place as each room was completed. There was ample closet space, the bathrooms were roomy and well-appointed. Special attention was paid to *Suite de Jardin's* ability to welcome any handicapped guests. The *menuisiers* had finally finished the wood-work, and the handles now fit the doors. Newly-installed double-paned windows banished most of the drafts, but we couldn't replace every window in the house because that would have cost a fortune, and, as well, changed the character of the house.

The masons, the carpenters, the man with the back-hoe who filled in the enormous trench in which our new water and electrical lines were buried, all were finished and gone, except for the lone electrician and his helper who were still in *Tour Nord,* the room overlooking the front terrace.

The gravel in the courtyard had to be replaced when the workers left, because it had been totally torn up during the renovations. So we went to a local gravel pit and ordered the delivery of five tons of gravel to resurface it.

The gravel delivery truck, when it departed, left us with three six-foot high pyramids of gravel. It took us two days to spread the gravel evenly over the thirty by fifty meter courtyard, barrel by barrel, but it looked great when we were done. A back-hoe could have done it in an hour, of course, but there was none available until *la fin de la semaine prochaine,* and our friends were due to arrive before then so we did it ourselves.

The garden was in full bloom, the Wisteria on its second time around, which happens if you cut off the old buds after they've finished blooming.

The salon and library furniture was polished, chandeliers suspended from freshly painted ceilings, and the ornate flowered medallions of the ceilings were painted more in the colorful Italian style than the French. I pleaded vertigo that time, so Dierk spent hours up on the tall ladder, à la Michelangelo, painting the flowers and leaves with delicate paintbrushes. The result was magnificent.

We gave each of the five bedrooms a name rather than a number. *Tour Nord* was the first of the rooms actually completed, so it was to be the one in which the friends from Boston would stay. The double bed was made up with linens bought in New York, as were the sets of towels. In later years, we replaced the double bed in *Tour Nord* with two single beds, which seemed to be preferred and requested by European guests. It has nothing to do with whether or not they love each other. It's just customary.

It was too late to expect it to be a true "season" that first year, so it was a time for visits from family and friends from America and the handful of people who had heard of the inn in Paris. We wanted it to grow *de bouche à'oreille,* word-of-mouth, anyway, so it seemed a perfect way to begin learning the art of formal inn-keeping, something they had neglected to teach me in dental school.

Our friends were to be a trial run for us, so we tried to think of everything, and I carefully planned the Menu. They had followed the inn's progress through the letters I regularly sent back to Boston. When we heard their car enter the gravel courtyard, we went out to welcome them, took their suitcases up to *Tour Nord,* and then showed them around the house. Their reaction was ample reward for the months of work. Their faces showed how special they found the place. We all sat on the front terrace and had a cup of tea while the electrician hung out of the window above, calling out orders to his helper below. When they finally left, *"Aux Trois Saisons"* was ours.

We wanted this visit to be a dress rehearsal for the inn, so we asked Maryann and Howard, who have been friends for years and share our love of France, to be honest in their criticism if they found anything that could be improved. The next morning, Maryann mentioned something that we had overlooked: full-length mirrors for ladies to see themselves in.

It had never occurred to us. All I ever really need to see is my face in the mirror in the morning when I shave. The rest sort of takes care of itself. But Maryann was right—and we were learning—and full-length mirrors were bought for each of the guest rooms.

The cocktail hour was set for 7:30 p.m., and, at the appointed hour, we gathered in the salon. Candles were lit, soft music played in the background; the traditional Kir was the cocktail, as it would be each evening except when something else was specifically requested. At exactly

7:45 p.m. I disappeared into the kitchen to put the final touches on dinner.

The complimentary cocktail served three purposes: it was a nice gesture of welcome; it gave those people who wanted to mix and to meet other people an opportunity to do so under ideal circumstances; and last, but, to be honest, most important from a practical point of view, since the complimentary cocktail was free, it got everybody down for the cocktail between 7:30 and 8:00. This insured that, when dinner was announced at eight o'clock, everybody was present and we could begin serving all the guests at the same time.

It would have been impossible, with just two of us, to prepare and serve dinner twice or to serve the dinner courses at different times to different people. It happened, but only on very rare occasions.

One such occasion, years later, was during one of France's many strikes. That particular strike was staged by disgruntled truckers who had simply parked their trucks on the nation's roads and turned off the ignitions. They took their keys, walked off, and left the trucks right there in the middle of all the major autoroutes, thereby totally paralyzing France. Guests already enroute to us searched out telephones wherever they were stranded and called us in desperation and frustration to say that they were blocked for hours on the road. They would, they assured us, arrive somehow and we should not, please, give away their rooms. I felt obliged to provide them with dinner when they arrived. They were understandably exhausted and furious. By the time I was getting dinner ready for the third time at 11:00 p.m. I was a wreck. It was proof that the system of one-service-per-night we had decided on for the inn was the only one that could work for us.

On that first night, however, everything went smoothly and we all sat in the library and had *digestifs* afterwards to talk about the evening. Innkeeping, it seemed on the basis of that first night, was hard work but still fun. The performances of the future were not always as smooth as that first dress rehearsal had been.

The next day, we all went to some local vineyards for *dégustations*. We had plenty of time on our hands, those early years, and enjoyed Burgundy along with our guests. In between samples of each wine, we "cleared our palates" with either the small, round *"gougères"* typical of Burgundy, or chunks of baguette.

We decided on a formal closing date of October 15th, after the *vindange*, the wine harvest, is over and the tourist season begins to wind down. The harvest usually lasts from mid-September to early October, and is estimated to be 100 days after the first flower appears.

Keeping the inn open beyond that date was impractical. Heating costs, in a house the size of ours, would have amounted to far more than we could have earned. And, besides, one of the purposes of creating the inn was to have plenty of time off between seasons.

The final weeks of September in Burgundy are special. It's a time of excitement, backbreaking labor, high hopes, and shared expectations. One can smell it in the air, sense it in the quickened pace, and hear it in the rumblings and rattlings of grape-laden trucks, tractor—indeed, any means of conveyance hastily enlisted to transport the precious cargo to the pressing machines.

It's an exciting and exacting science, wine making, open to chance as well as technique. What happens during those critical 100 days determines the quality of the year's vintage. Too much rain and the grapes will expand and burst; too little and they don't mature properly.

One night of *gel*, the dreaded frost, and an entire harvest can be destroyed. A few years ago, a hail-storm swept through the Bordeaux area and demolished eighty percent of the crop. Burgundy was nearly as hard hit that year but survived. It all happened in the space of ten minutes.

The storms are so capricious that one year a sudden hail-storm, with pieces of *"grêle"* the size of golf balls, completely leveled a nearby vineyard. It passed us by and our house was untouched.

But then, after all the hard work and uncertainty, come the harvest days, in the good years, when the mountains of purple and yellow grapes, picked by hand, loaded into baskets, are trucked back to the crushers. There the superb, rich, first pressing, the "featherwhite," can be sampled by those lucky enough to be on hand.

The pickers, in those years, were mostly family and friends and local students trying to earn a little extra money. Then came the itinerant workers from Poland or other eastern countries. Whoever the pickers are, they're well fortified. Pick, drink, pick, drink. The bent-over, tedious labor becomes the occasion for a *fête*, as do most things in France.

It was a marvelous time and, that first year, we were free to enjoy it, but the time had also arrived to prepare and close up the house for the winter. The family of squirrels, the red ones here in Europe, were busy raiding the walnut and hazelnut trees near the front terrace and burying their treasures for the long Burgundy winter ahead.

Each year we drained the water pipes in case of freezing temperatures, packed cherished items to be taken to Paris to pass the winter, put anti-humidity devices throughout the house, and put some things into storage because they might suffer from being left in an unheated house.

Our fellow Draciens were protective of the house while we were away. One year, in our haste to get to Paris, the door leading off the courtyard to *Suite de Jardin* was left unlocked and the wind must have blown it open.

Monsieur LeFavre, the postman, in passing, saw it open and notified the local gendarmes. They arrived, climbed over the locked iron gates, checked the house, saw that all was in order, closed the door and departed. We only found out about it from *Monsieur LeFavre* when we returned in March to open the house again.

Before leaving, we made arrangements for bill-paying and mail-forwarding. We loaded the car, made a last-minute tour of the property to see if we had forgotten anything, and set off for Paris with a list of things to be done during the coming winter months.

We had survived the awakenings—some of them rude—the surprises—some welcome some not—made some new friends, and started the learning process that continued in the years to come. All in all, much for which to be thankful.

Mademoiselle, curled up on the back seat of the car, snoozed away, conserving her energy and preparing herself for her triumphant return to Paris.

GOUGÈRES

Ingredients:
- 1 c water
- ½ c (1 stick) unsalted butter
- ½ tsp salt
- dash cayenne pepper
- 4 eggs
- ¾ c Gruyère cheese, grated

Preparation:
Preheat oven to 450°. Place water, butter (cut into small pieces), salt, and pepper in a saucepan and slowly bring to a boil, making certain that the butter is completely melted when the water reaches boiling. Remove from heat. Add the flour to the boiling water and mix with a wooden spoon, stirring very quickly. This should be done over a very low heat, so that the final mixture is a smooth, shiny pasty dough. Place in a mixing bowl, mix in eggs one at a time, stirring constantly Add cheese and mix again, stirring constantly. (The paste should be moist enough to stick to the sides of the bowl. If not, add a little more egg.) Put into a pastry bag and squeeze out onto a greased and floured baking sheet. Form little mounds and sprinkle with a little grated cheese before baking. Bake for about 15 to 20 minutes, until golden brown.

Note:
These little puff pastries are wonderful served as an hors d'oeuvre with wine, or just by themselves as an extra added dinner treat. They can also be frozen.

Part II
Between-times

Chapter 7
Mademoiselle de Paris

One of the obvious perks of owning any seasonal business is the off-season time when your life is, again, your own. Once that first winter of renovation was past, every subsequent year, between the autumn closing after the *vindange*, and the spring opening, sometime around Good Friday, could be spent traveling. Or, as I preferred, simply enjoying the wonders of the most beautiful city in the world: Paris.

I realize that admirers of majestic Rome, or picture-perfect Bruges, or lovely San Francisco will give me an argument, but Paris speaks to me. Its incredible beauty touches me as no other city ever has. I'm grateful to the German occupying general during World War II, who was executed for disobeying orders to destroy the city on his way out.

Each year, when we approached Paris after the drive from Burgundy, the car laden with packages, I experienced the same exhilaration as I spied the tower built especially for me by *Monsieur Eiffel*. I was home again.

Mademoiselle must have felt the same stirrings. She invariably woke up as we drove over the bridge leading to the *Assemblée Nationale* and turned left on *Boulevard Saint Germain.* She had returned to the closest thing to heaven on earth for a dog.

In my next life, I want to come back as a dog in France. All the things you've heard about the English being dog-nuts can be multiplied ten times over and you will still not even approach the level of devotion the French, particularly Parisians, feel for their pampered pets.

At last count, there were over 500,000 dogs in Paris, all of whom are welcome in most department stores, restaurants, and hotels, even in the Metro. Only stores which sell food have discreet signs requesting that *nos amis les chiens* wait outside.

Cleaning up after *nos amis les chiens* also costs the taxpayers of Paris a fortune each year. Paris is the only city I know of that had a team of gentlemen, wearing their official *Propreté de Paris* clothing, who patrolled the streets on "Pooper-Scooper-Scooters." I say "had" because these fine gentlemen have been abolished by the present mayor of Paris, a move that has resulted in a far dirtier city.

When we had our first apartment on *Rue de Lille,* we made our daily rounds on *Rue Allent.* Very often, as I was being taken out for my morning or evening stroll by *Mademoiselle,* one of these gentlemen on a scooter, in a marvelous display of French patience and gallantry, would wait discreetly nearby until Mademoiselle, in no hurry at all, had finished her *toilette.* Then, as she trotted away, he would sail by on his portable vacuum cleaner and wordlessly remove the evidence.

Mademoiselle Corinne, while she was still plain old "Corrie" in her American life, was not even allowed into any hotels or restaurants in the land of her birth. All of that changed in France.

She arrived in Europe via boat, a canine Grace Kelly ready to assume her role as hostess at the soon-to-be inn. Actually, it was a freighter, since, at her advanced age, we were worried about her crossing the Atlantic in the uncertain climate of an airplane luggage compartment. So, we three embarked at Baltimore, Maryland, on board the "Egon Oldendorf" along with many, many tons of iron ore. Twelve days later we arrived in Ghent, Belgium.

When we boarded the freighter, its laborers were unloading iron ore from Brazil. *Mademoiselle*, who had spent her life up to then as a white dog, was soon covered in dark red dust. We watched as they proceeded to unload the iron ore and reload the freighter with coal bound for Ghent, at which point *Mademoiselle* became dark gray. She was oblivious to the changes in her appearance, but a nice long bath was in order before we met the other passengers.

Mademoiselle had a marvelous crossing, aside from a three-minute siege of *mal de mer*. It happened one night when the boat was stopped for repairs in the middle of rough waters. She awoke from a sound sleep, sat bolt upright in bed, looked at me quizzically, turned green, waved her head to and fro very slightly, and then promptly went back to sleep.

The freighter's instructions told us to come aboard with enough dog food for the trip, so she had her own little suitcase filled with a variety of foods, brushes, combs, shampoos, toys, and anything else we thought might come in handy. It turned out to be unnecessary.

When we entered the dining room for our first meal, the captain, whose table was directly behind our own, bent down to meet *Mademoiselle* and tell her how beautiful she was. It was mutual love at first sight, so she ignored her regular food, and us, in order to save herself for her captain. He fed her from his own plate and then ordered the cook to come up with special *plats du jour* for his new love. The suitcase full of dog food we had lugged aboard at Baltimore came ashore with us, untouched, at Ghent, much to *Mademoiselle's* annoyance. By that time, she was used to better things.

I heartily recommend freighter travel to anyone wanting a restful, informal way to get somewhere. Freighters are, usually, quite comfortable, not quite so posh as the commercial ocean liners. Our cabin was simple and clean, with a private shower and toilet.

We had the misfortune of having an Austrian chef, so the meals were a bit heavy on the meat and potatoes. We certainly didn't go hungry and you can get used to anything if you know it's not forever.

On board were seven passengers and one spoiled dog. Three of the passengers were a father and his two teen-aged sons, who were being home-schooled by the father. They were travelling to Sweden for six months to hook up with other home-schooled children. I had never met youngsters who were being schooled in this manner. I was struck by their politeness, their innocence, and, disconcertingly, their immaturity. Everything seemed new to them, which was charming at first, but it made me wonder if the lack of interaction with other young people of their own age would prepare them for functioning in the real world. They were nice boys and I hope the world has treated them well.

Another passenger was a lady from New York who was absolutely delightful. Full of fun, sweet-natured, and a pleasure to be with, Terrance was the perfect seaboard companion and we corresponded for years after the trip.

The last passenger, who shall go unnamed, was a gentleman who was retiring from his position at the United Nations and was returning to live in Europe. If the ship had been sinking in shark-infested waters and I was faced with the prospect of spending time with him in a life boat, I might seriously have considered swimming.

Dierk, *Mademoiselle*, and I completed the passenger list. We spent our days reading, scanning the horizon, and counting the dolphins and flying-fish frolicking alongside the freighter. We even tracked a hurricane from the captain's bridge. It was a thoroughly enjoyable voyage.

When we arrived in Ghent, we were ready to produce our own passports and *Mademoiselle's* dossier, which was filled with papers certifying *Mademoiselle's* obvious good health, her medical and rabies inoculation records, and some forms from the FDA certifying that she was, indeed, a dog and not a cow.

Naturally, nobody asked to see her papers and *Mademoiselle* brightly stepped onto European soil without a backward glance, with us carrying a suitcase filled with dog food and waving her dossier.

Once in France, *Mademoiselle* adapted with delight to her new home. She was welcomed at her preferred restaurants where, without even being asked, the waiters brought over her bowl of water. A plateful of croissant pieces for breakfast was *de rigeur*. She attended a jazz concert at the *Café de le Danse,* which she slept through, and was welcomed at hotels that offered special meals if requested.

She was admired and fussed over by people wherever she went. At street corners, waiting for the little green man in the traffic light to tell me to walk, people would ignore the baby in the carriage at one side and bend down and coo about how *"mignon"* Mademoiselle was.

Her manners were impeccable. In restaurants, she took her place under the table, folded her hands and went to sleep. I had to wake her up when it was time to leave. It was then that fellow diners who hadn't seen her arrive were surprised to discover she was there all the time. Except for those who had heard the soft snores and contented sighs coming from under the table, and they smiled.

Walking with *Mademoiselle* was a great way to meet people in Paris. Otherwise stern-faced neighbors, once they've seen you with a dog, will drop their reserve and begin smiling.

The huge canine population, in the absence of strictly enforced litter laws, has led to the creation of a dance I call the "Paris Shuffle." Mademoiselle had nothing to do with this, thanks to her impeccable manners and her friend on the scooter. The "Paris Shuffle," unlike the "Tango," can be performed by a single person and anyone can learn it. It begins with a surprised look on the face, followed by a look of pained comprehension, which then gives way to an imploring look towards heaven. There follows a rapid brushing of the soles of the shoes against the nearest hard surface, all done while leaning your weight on the other foot.

This one-legged variety of the old soft shoe routine became less popular under previous Parisian administrations, as the *Propreté de Paris* people became more aggressive. With the unfortunate disappearance of the "pooper-scooper-scooters," everyone who has been in Paris recently knows the dance well. Parisians are, after many years of practice, extremely adept at the "Paris Shuffle" and bear it, as they do almost everything else, with stoic acceptance and good humor. French dogs trot merrily along, secure in the knowledge that they are mignon and truly have the world by the leash.

Chapter 8
Native Customs

The Japanese eat very little fat and suffer fewer heart attacks than the British or Americans.

On the other hand, the French eat a lot of fat and also suffer fewer heart attacks than the British or Americans.

The Japanese drink very little red wine and suffer fewer heart attacks than the British or Americans.

The Italians drink great amounts of red wine and also suffer fewer heart attacks than the British or Americans.

Conclusion: Eat and drink what you like. It's speaking English that kills you.

Perhaps what makes my French friends so special to me is that they relegate nothing to being routine. Whether it's in dressing up or dressing a festive table or addressing each other, they take the extra time to make an event, a special happening, out of the most ordinary of circumstances.

Having mastered the intricacies of the handshake in Burgundy, I found that, in Paris, the only people who *don't* shake your hand when they greet you are the gendarmes. These impressively stern looking policemen, whose faces crack into a smile after you've been sufficiently convinced of their ferociousness, do not shake your hand. They salute you.

Since I have absolutely no sense of direction, I seem to spend an inordinate amount of time searching for places, even armed with that handy little book of *Paris par Arrondissement.* So I march right up to my closest gendarme, get saluted, and feel immediately as if I'm the most important person in the world.

The French have also elevated the simple kiss to an art form with a language all its own. It is a highly choreographed practice which must be mastered if you are to spend any time with French people. The kiss protocol begins with a gentle brushing of your own right cheek against the right cheek of the kissee. The other cheek is then, literally, turned and the same brushing motion is performed with the left cheek.

One or two kisses are basic for the first meeting, but the second time you meet the person, it is permissible to proceed to three. If you know the person well, it becomes four. I am on four terms with all my friends in Paris.

This presents several potential dangers, the foremost being the hitting of noses and clinking of eyeglasses. This is totally unacceptable and requires careful synchronization between kisser and kissee. The lips never touch, although they may be pursed, and there is absolutely no sound made at all. The cardinal sin is to leave the other person mid-air without your being there for the anticipated contact.

It is considered perfectly acceptable and natural for men to kiss. French men are sure enough of their own masculinity to openly embrace and touch cheeks with other men without fear of being considered effeminate. They *know* what they are so they don't even think about it.

This is awkward for some Americans, but I've also lived in Muslim countries and seen two fellows walk down the street arm-in-arm, worry beads happily clicking, without anyone raising an eyebrow. It's a perfectly innocent local custom.

How odd it is that in America it's perfectly all right for basketball or baseball players to hug each other and pat each other's rear ends. That's considered macho, but two brothers, reunited after not seeing each other for three years, may not feel comfortable, on meeting again, if they walk together on the street with arms interlocked. Native custom, too, but rather sad.

The French, male and female, kiss, cry, laugh, pout, raise eyebrows, shoulders, and voices, as the mood hits them. It's perfectly all right to be as the good Lord made you and to use the heart He gave you.

If you have the occasion to watch French television, littered as it is with re-runs of old American series, you will notice that on the *French* shows the performers, for the most part, are not in the first blush of youth. Mature women, and, even, middle-aged, bald men can be stars and croon love songs without being laughed off the stage.

In France, it's no sin to grow older. Youth is looked on with a loving, knowing, wry smile by those who have been there already and come to terms with themselves, their strengths, their weaknesses, their own mortality, and the beauty and fragility of life. But maturity is appreciated for the extra dimension life has bestowed upon it.

I observed this one evening at *"La Coupole,"* one of the oldest restaurants in Paris. This was, of course, in the days before they decided to renovate this Paris landmark and turn it into a slick, glorified cafeteria.

We were a party of six people, one of whom was Marcelle. She is a delightful lady, with a son well into his forties, but her mischievous sense of humor and her warm and captivating smile are ageless.

Marcelle was dressed, as always, elegantly. That particular evening she wore a beige Chanel suit and her blonde hair was combed straight back off her face and bound into a chignon. The effect was stunning.

The restaurant was filled with an assortment of pretty young women, some of them of the nubile, voluptuous variety, and most of whom were one third Marcelle's age. I watched the reactions of the other gentlemen in the restaurant, young and old, when Marcelle left our table to go to the ladies' room. Their eyes followed her movements with appreciation, silently acknowledging that grace and beauty can't be counted in time.

The French do not temper their lives or calories with guilt or regret. Last year, the experts said that caffeine was bad for you; this year other experts say that decaffeinated coffee can kill you. And, suddenly, red wine is good for your health, which the French have known for centuries without NIH grants totaling thousands of taxpayer dollars.

I'm quite used to living in France and there are a number of things I heartily admire about the French. They have been, and still are, in the forefront of medical research and can be compassionate to those often rejected by other societies. They have an infinite capacity for savoring all aspects of life, and their artistry in food preparation is unmatched.

But there are, also, some things I do not, and never will, understand about them. For example, I cannot understand how people who are endowed with such a keen esthetic sense—who are justly famed for their food, fashions, art, history, and so on—are *not* bothered by seeing all sorts of exposed plumbing pipes and electrical circuit boxes cluttering up magnificent architecture.

I cannot understand why the French will line up and wait for hours, without complaining, for everything from a *baguette* at the *patisserie* to buying a stamp at the post office. They won't utter a word of protest when the salesgirl in a department store chats away with another salesgirl and the line keeps getting longer and I become more and more impatient and angry. They won't lose their tempers and storm out of the store. Yet these same people become maniacally impatient on the highways, tail-gate and blink their lights, and pass on hairpin curves just to get one car-length ahead of you. However, to be fair, I must admit that the sound of an automobile horn is rare in Paris, despite the sometimes horrendous traffic.

The French will combine colors so beautifully in their fashions and will use colors so elegantly in other areas yet, until recently, it was almost impossible to find any plain white toilet paper.

The French created *Versailles, Fontainebleu,* and countless other large and small superb examples of architecture and interior decoration which have inspired us for centuries; yet, for their own homes, most of them will inevitably choose some absurdly hideous wall-coverings with flowers large enough to devour Chicago.

The French will spend millions of francs to save the old *Gare D'Orsay* and turn it into a magnificent, soaring museum and then turn around and say that they find an abomination like the *Centre Pompidou* "*amusant.*"

They will settle for only the finest food and wine but will pay far less attention to the way the table looks. Almost all of the beautiful table settings we used at the inn came from Germany, where the food itself is presented in an almost utilitarian way rather than designed to please the senses. The useful and pretty little heaters *("stöfchen")* we placed under coffee pots and teapots came from Germany, and quite a few of our French guests asked where they could buy them.

They are marvelously patriotic, almost as much as Americans, yet they put up uncomplainingly with the fact that, at one time or another, *everything* in France is either *en greve* (on strike), *en panne* (out of order), or *en vacances* (on vacation). They just live with whatever inconvenience this fact of French life causes.

It will take me a lifetime of discovery to understand these and other things about the French. That's just fine with me. It's great fun learning, so *Vive la difference!*

Chapter 9
Le Syndic

Most apartments in Paris are individually owned, although some are owned by the government and become the object of occasional scandals when it is discovered that they have been rented to family and friends of politicians for practically nothing. An indignant article appears in the newspaper one day, is forgotten by the next, and French bureaucratic life goes on as usual.

Many privately-owned apartments are rented out by their owners. Since there are two separate real estate taxes, the proprietor's and the occupant's, it means that, if the apartment is rented out, the occupant is responsible for one tax while the owner is responsible for the other. If the apartment is *not* rented, the owner must pay both taxes. You even have to pay the occupant tax for a parking space you may be renting.

As the owner of an apartment, actually a condominium, since you own not only your apartment but a certain percentage of the common areas, you will periodically be summoned, by the *syndic*, to a meeting of the owners. The *syndic*, or building management company, is hired by the owners association, and is held responsible for seeing that the building is maintained properly.

In our first apartment building, the deterioration, in the five years we lived there, was shockingly noticeable. There was still a concierge when we first moved in, but, as has happened in many buildings in Paris, this became prohibitively expensive as the result of an unfortunate combination of reasons.

The government's penchant for involved and expensive employment requirements and the fact that people simply don't want the job any more, has led to there remaining only about forty percent of the concierges there used to be in Paris. There are so many costs in addition to salary, the *"charges sociaux"* you have to pay if you employ a person, that it is more expensive, per hour, to hire a cleaning person in France than it is in the U.S. The records that must be kept and turned in to the proper governmental agency, and the forms to be regularly completed, sometimes monthly, make it more of a chore to hire someone than to do it yourself or, simply, do without.

For financial reasons, the concierge had been asked to leave at #15 *rue de Lille*, our first apartment, much to my regret, because the hallways were immaculately clean when she was still there and the 350-year-old floor tiles in the stairway and entrance gleamed and smelled deliciously of wax. After she left, a man arrived on a rather haphazard schedule several times per week. He mopped the five floors of the building with the same bucket of water, succeeding only in rearranging the grime.

Once, when we arrived back in Paris, there were two sacks of plaster sitting near the staircase. I assumed they would be removed with the rest of the garbage. They weren't, and three weeks later, when I collared the man who was paid by the *syndic* to take the garbage out to the street for pickup, I demanded that he get rid of them. This was met with the usual shrug and the "it's not my job" response. I put them out myself.

In Paris, you'll find many apartment buildings with dingy entrance foyers that have paint chipping from the walls, electric meters stuck out at eye level, and dismal lighting. Yet these same buildings also contain apartments which are immaculately clean and beautiful beyond description, with carved ceiling moldings and architectural details of incredible elegance.

In New York, on the other hand, I have friends who live in an apartment building in the east 70s. Their apartment is small, dark, low-ceilinged, with a marvelous view of a brick wall which they can reach out and touch, but the entrance lobby has crystal chandeliers, bolted-down lamps and pictures, is lavishly appointed, and is the size of a football field.

The choice is yours to make in Paris, since the city offers both extremes and everything in between. But if you choose a building with lovely, ornate winding staircases and marble floors, and a nice apartment as well, just be prepared to pay for it.

On *rue de Lille*, we, like the other owners, were unhappy with what was happening to the building. "You're coming to the Assemblée meeting, *n'est ce pas?*" Madame Gillot asked one morning when we met in the hallway. "We must get rid of this *Syndic*. They do nothing, *rien!*"

The registered letter arrived, stating time and date of the next meeting, and the three of us—Dierk, myself, and Mademoiselle—were officially invited to take part in this exercise in Parisian democracy as only the French can practice it. It is known as *L'Assemblée des Copropiétaires*.

We doubted our ability, at that point, to make points well enough in French to be effective, but Madame's insistence overcame our hesitation.

The *Syndic's* office was on the *Ile de la Cité*, the oldest part of Paris, where it all began so many centuries ago. It was a long walk but we gave ourselves and *Mademoiselle* plenty of time for a leisurely stroll.

We arrived at the appointed time to find Madame Gillot in heated discussion with three other women, each clutching a dossier. They obviously meant business!

We introduced ourselves, everyone *"mignon"*ed *Mademoiselle*, and then all four ladies began telling us, all at once, with fire in their eyes, that things *had* to change. When they realized that they had allies in us, they seated *Mademoiselle* and the two of us in the front row.

The gentleman representing the *Syndic* entered the room, and, with an arrogant and condescendingly sweeping glance around the room, began the proceedings. He seated himself behind his desk with us in front of him like children at school. I disliked him immediately.

Our four women, oozing ice, sat in a group behind us and we were surrounded by about thirty other tenants, all silently gearing up for the kill.

Monsieur Arrogant must have sensed trouble when one of our ladies raised her hand and sweetly announced that we all wanted to get rid of him because he was taking our money for nothing. *Rien!*

As the other people in the room nodded and voiced agreement Monsieur began to turn a strange shade of purple-green, which actually made for a very interesting Monet-like color combination with his pale blue eyes. We were delighted. Mademoiselle began snoring. It had been, after all, a long walk.

He retaliated by giving us a polite lecture on parliamentary procedure, pointing out that we needed a president and other officers before we could proceed with something as important as a proposal to get rid of him.

A formidable lady who lived on the fourth floor, walk-up, was elected and promptly raised her hand and announced that *now* we wanted to get rid of him. Monsieur A. turned still another shade of green and tried to stall for time by turning on the charm and suggesting that we first clear up the budget and take care of old business.

He had gained only a few minutes' reprieve when Madame President raised her hand and began to recite the grievances against the *syndic's* management of the building. I was so carried away by her eloquence that I raised my hand, caught up in the excitement, and added my complaints.

"The building is not clean," I said, encouraged by the others, "and I am embarrassed to invite friends to visit!"

I felt slightly awkward about being a foreigner and being so critical, but they seemed pleased that I cared enough to take part and pretended not to notice my grammatical sins.

Around me I saw the same kind of democracy at work as we have in our Town Meetings in America, so I really wasn't that much of a stranger. We shared a common belief that things *can*, indeed, be changed by ordinary people, although we in America are a bit more reluctant to remove their heads.

I glanced around the room, smiled at the four ladies taking notes for their dossiers, and imagined their ancestors sitting in the *Place de la Concorde,* knitting away, or perhaps taking notes, too, as the Revolution wrought its vengeance.

I was relieved that we were on the same side. Never underestimate the strength of a group of ladies who feel unjustly wronged. They're a lot more ferocious than their husbands could ever be.

Monsieur A., having run out of options and colors, suggested a vote. Much to nobody's surprise, the *syndic* was relieved of its duties and the vote was, except for two obviously misguided—or paid-off—proprietors, unanimous.

We all filed out of the office, each giving a perfunctory smile to the quivering remains of Monsieur Blue Eyes behind us, and gathered outside to celebrate the victory of democracy.

There was still time for a late dinner, so we found the small restaurant that we knew, from past experience, served a superb *Cassoulet* and a marvelous dessert called *Iles Flottante,* or floating islands. Fortified spiritually by our exercise in democracy, and needing a little exercise after polishing off the *Cassoulet*, we left the restaurant.

Mademoiselle, feeling rested, was ready to begin the walk back to *rue de Lille*. We crossed the oldest bridge in Paris, called the *Pont Neuf*, which means "new bridge," past the spires of Notre Dame Cathedral, and over to the other side of the river.

We've called this side of the river home ever since we first came to Paris. It's known as the *left* bank, although it's really *south* of the Seine and neither left or right. The area is also part of the *Quartier Latin*. People originally started calling it this centuries ago when the language of the Sorbonne University, nearby, was Latin, and the name has stuck.

One of the best cups of coffee in any café in Paris, and a perfect view of Notre Dame, can be had at *Le Café du Petit Pont* at the corner of the *Quai* and *rue Saint Jacques*. We've been going there for years, ever since we rented an apartment around the corner from Shakespeare and Company, the oldest English language bookstore in Paris.

The next time you're there, please stop in and say hello to the young owner of the café, Georges, and give him my regards. He looks more Spanish than French, sports a handsome pony tail, and is charming.

CASSOULET

Ingredients:

2 lbs	(1 kilo) of white kidney beans
1 lb	(500 gm) of smoked bacon cut into 1/2 inch thick slices
2 lbs	(1 kilo) of pork loin cut into 1-inch slices
2 lbs	(1 kilo) of lamb cut into chunks
6	pieces of goose (or duck) already cooked
2	large smoked sausages
6	onions
4	tomatoes
4	carrots, cut into 1/2 inch slices
1/2 tsp	cloves
	bouquet garni
5	garlic cloves, crushed
1/2 tsp	thyme
	salt, pepper

Preparation:

Soak white beans in water overnight. Drain beans and set aside. Add pork loin, cut into thick slices. Put slices of bacon in the bottom of a large casserole dish and heat until transparent. Cover bacon with the drained beans. Cut 4 onions into quarters, arrange them over the beans, and sprinkle with cloves. Add sausages, bouquet garni, 3 crushed garlic cloves, carrot slices, salt and pepper. Add water to cover, bring to boiling, lower heat, cover casserole and simmer for 2 hours. Meanwhile, fry the lamb, goose, and pork in the olive oil in a deep frying pan until just done. Add 2 finely chopped onions, 2 finely chopped cloves of garlic, thyme, finely chopped tomatoes, salt and pepper. Add enough water to pan to cover the ingredients and simmer for about 1 hour. When the beans in the casserole are cooked, remove the pork loin pieces and the sausages. Cut pork loin and sausages into small pieces, return to casserole. Add goose pieces. Remove and discard the bouquet garni. Combine ingredients from frying pan with the casserole ingredients and simmer together for about ½ hour. Serve hot.

FLOATING ISLANDS

Ingredients:
- 6 eggs
- 90 gm powdered sugar
- 2 c milk
- 1/2 tsp vanilla
- 1 tsp brandy

Preparation:

For the meringue "Islands":
Beat 3 egg whites until stiff. When egg-whites are stiff, gradually beat in 60 grams of the powdered sugar until the mixture will stand in very stiff peaks. Heat the milk in a sauce pan. Drop the beaten egg-white mixture in large spoonfuls on to the simmering milk and continue to simmer gently for about 4 minutes. Turn the egg-white mixtures over on their other sides and cook for another four minutes in the simmering milk. Using a slotted spoon, remove the cooked egg-whites from the simmering milk and drain on paper towels. Continue until all of the egg-white mixture has been cooked, setting the "islands" aside while the custard is made. Strain the milk and set aside.

For the custard:
Beat the 3 egg yolks with 30 grams of the powdered sugar until they are light and fluffy, mix in the strained milk, and return to low heat. Cook the custard gently until it begins to thicken and will coat a spoon. Add the vanilla and brandy to the custard. To serve, strain the custard into a large serving dish, "float" the meringues on top of the custard, and put into the refrigerator to chill. Serve chilled.

Note:
Be certain that the egg whites are stiff before adding the sugar or the end result will not be stiff enough, and cook the custard very gently or it can curdle. It's a light and delicious dessert, very easy to make, and very impressive when you bring it to the table.

Chapter 10
Au Café

Between 8:00 and 8:30 every morning, a procession of children is escorted to school by their papas. I've watched them from my regular table near the window at the *Café Pré Germain* on *Rue du Four*, and some of them have become my favorites.

There's the tall thin young man with two sons who are now about ten and seven years old. The older boy is the image of his father and all three usually hold hands as they cross the street. Then the younger one, obviously less the hand-holding type, sets off on his own and explores doorways, shop windows, and the tiny round tables set on the narrow sidewalk outside the café. The older boy never lets go of his father's hand.

This morning, the younger boy did a Gene Kelly dance around the lamppost while his father and older brother continued on their way. After a while, having deposited his charges at their school, the father walked back the same route, his head buried in *L'Equipe*, the sports newspaper he'd just bought.

Another threesome consists of a father with son and daughter in tow. They never let go of each others' hands. This father is shorter than the other one and the son is rapidly catching up in height, seemingly before my eyes. But it's the children's hair that first caught my attention.

The girl, younger than her brother, skips rather than walks, and fashions her nondescript brown hair in a pony tail. The boy has platinum blond wavy hair, worn long, and is so incredibly beautiful that, even at ten years of age, he's already turning heads. His sister skips merrily along, not yet aware, I presume, of the difference in beauty between her and her brother.

They come in twos, as well, papas and daughters or papas and sons, each ready for the new day. They, on their way to school and I, in a way, also on my way to school, but as a teacher in the *Université Paris–7 Ecole Dentaire* which I did each winter when the inn was closed.

What were the mamas doing during this daily procession? Were they getting ready for work, after spending a hectic hour preparing breakfast and getting the papas and kids out of the house on time? Or were they still comfortably snuggled in their beds, the papas having done it all?

It's none of my business, of course, and there are, I should add, the occasional mamas who do the escorting. In one particular pair, the mother and daughter are almost identical, both sporting long bangs over perfectly shaped faces, one in miniature. Two porcelain dolls, holding hands and laughing over some shared secret.

In all cases, the children carry over-sized backpacks laden with school books and supplies. One newspaper recently carried results of a physicians' survey which found that French school children are prone to back problems later in life because their spines are being deformed by these heavy burdens. They do seem to walk with a forward tilt, giving an air of anticipation to their movements.

I take my morning café seated by the window in the *Pré Saint Germain*, and I arrive there long before my work at the university begins each day, just to sit over a *café crème* and watch the city come alive. The same people pass my vantage point each morning, strangers bound together by circumstances, not speaking, just scurrying along avoiding direct glances.

The Metro puffs out another gaggle of muffled people, scarves wrapped tightly around their necks, and the dog lady passes the window of the café while I dawdle away the first hour of the day. That's all I know of her, the "dog lady," because we've never done more than nod at each other since that first morning years ago when I smiled at the frisky little puppy who's now a full grown blond Labrador.

He walks her along the same route each morning, reading the letters left on each lamp post and tree by generations of other dogs leading masters on their rounds. The dog lady and I once exchanged silent *Bonne Année* New Year greetings through the plate glass window, as well as our regular morning smile and head-nodding, so I guess our acquaintanceship is firmly established.

This particular morning, the soft dusting of snow had created a stillness and calm, unusual for Paris even at this early hour. The city seems to sleep between two and four in the morning, then slowly stir itself awake, prodded by the sounds of garbage cans being emptied, streets being washed down, and the first young men on their high-volume mopeds varooming madly past red lights on their way to their own favorite cafés. All this while shopkeepers and other Parisians sleepily go about the business of beginning a new day.

The taxi driver who parks outside and comes in for his morning coffee and croissant pauses to brush the snow from his car, then enters, rubbing his hands together, exclaiming about *"l'hiver, l'hiver"* as if this was the first winter ever. After the hand-shaking ritual, the nods and obligatory *"monsieur/dame"* to all, but to no-one in particular, he sidles himself into position at the bar, dunks his croissant in his coffee, chatters away to the lady who sits at the cash register, and then rejoins his taxi to begin the day's voyage.

During the course of his day, he'll pass down the same streets that the horse-drawn carriages of another day bobbed along, past the same buildings, past countless other cafés containing other people sipping their coffee as the city lives out the day.

All things change, yet there's a permanence here that I feel part of now, during my own passage. It didn't take very long to reach the point of not even having to say more than *petit* or *grand* to the waiter as I pass him on the way to my table.

The *café crème* arrives soon after, piping hot, with the glass of water and the usual *"Ça va?"* and *"Oui, Ça va"* and a few words about the weather and accompanying head-wagging and shoulder-shrugging.

The waiter at the *Pré Germain* is a pleasant middle-aged man, who doesn't really like to smile and I suspect it's because of his not having very many teeth, but he's a nice way to start the day. One day he wasn't there and his place was taken by a hipless, high cheek-boned young fellow, which could describe most of the male population of France. It just wasn't the same.

I take my café, on most other days, at the *Solferino*, which is the café just up the street from our present flat. It's on the corner of *rue Solferino* and *Boulevard Saint Germain* and is typical of all neighborhood cafés, the type of establishment where you feel as if they've been keeping the coffee hot just for you. It's a convenient drop-in place for a cup of coffee, a beer, a *Croque Madame,* or a chat. The lunch-time bustle finds all sorts of people from the *quartier* rubbing elbows while the inevitable sandwich is munched, washed down by a *vin de table.*

The elegantly coiffed and costumed ladies who run the antique shops, the workmen who are busily tearing up the streets or renovating an apartment nearby, the thin, handsome, dossier-clutching young men, also high cheek-boned and hipless, who work in the government ministries which abound in the 7th *arrondissement,* the elderly women who shuffle along on their way to and from the market, all crowd along the brass counter. They somehow find space and companionship in an oasis of belonging surrounded by the anonymity of the city outside.

The tiny tables offer limited seating for those, like myself, with time enough and the inclination to sample the *plat du jour* or one of the lovely freshly baked *tarte tatins*.

It's there that I go to recuperate after a visit to the market, or a shopping expedition to *Dehilleron*, the doyenne of all cooking-utensil shops in Paris, or to the third floor of the huge *Samaritaine* department store, which is filled with gadgets enough to satisfy any food lover.

Or just to daydream, which is a perfectly acceptable way to pass the time in Paris.

TARTE TATIN

Ingredients:
6	apples	(preferably Golden Delicious or a similar variety)
1 3/4 c	sugar	
1	lemon	
1/2 c	Calvados	
	puff pastry	

Puff Pastry:
1 lb	(450 g) butter
1 lb	(450 g) cake flour
1 tsp	salt
3/4 c	ice water

Preparation:

Puff Pastry:
Put flour into a large mixing bowl, add a little of the ice water at a time to form a firm ball of dough. Knead the dough ball on a floured surface for about 10 minutes, until it is very smooth. Wrap in plastic wrap and refrigerate for 30 minutes. Roll chilled dough out on floured surface until it is a rectangle about 6 inches by 12 inches. Slightly soften the butter and form it into a rectangle just slightly smaller than the dough. Place the butter in the center of the dough so that it covers the middle third of the dough, fold the bottom third over the butter, then the top third over that. Seal the margins. Turn the folded, sealed dough 1/4 turn, so that one of the narrow ends is facing you. With a rolling pin, roll the folded dough out to its original size. Repeat this entire process of folding and rolling, then wrap the dough in plastic wrap and put into the refrigerator for 30 minutes. Repeat the above process of folding and rolling at last another 3 or 4 times. Wrap and refrigerate overnight or freeze for later use.

Tarte Tatin:
Preheat oven to 375°. Peal and core apples, and cut into slices, or wedges, if you prefer. Place the slices in a bowl and cover with the juice of one lemon, the 1/2 cup of Calvados, and about 1/2 cup of the sugar. Let stand for at least one hour. Drain the apple slices. Put the rest of the sugar into

an oven-proof skillet, heat until the sugar begins to melt. Stir until all of the sugar is melted and begins to caramelize and turn light brown. Remove the skillet from the heat, arrange the drained apple slices closely together in the bottom of the skillet. Remove the puff pastry from the refrigerator, roll out on a lightly floured surface until it is just a bit larger than the skillet. Lay the dough over the apples, tucking the dough in so that it completely covers the apples. Put the skillet into the preheated oven (375°) and bake for 35 to 40 minutes or until the pastry is golden. (The time will vary according to the oven, so keep constant vigil.) Remove the tarte from the oven, cool slightly, then place a plate over the skillet that is larger than the skillet and invert the skillet so that the tarte sits on the plate with the apple side facing up.

Chapter 11
Père Lachaise

It may seem like an unlikely way to spend a lovely Sunday afternoon, but you couldn't prove that by the dozens of young couples pushing baby carriages along the paths of *Père Lachaise* on that sunny day in early April.

Père Lachaise is the oldest cemetery in Paris, named after the confessor of King Louis XIV, and has the atmosphere of a park. The other cemetery, also on the must-see list of Paris landmarks, is the *Cimetière de Montmartre*.

The two are very different, in spirit and content. *Père Lachaise* is the resting place of such famous people as Oscar Wilde, who has finally found peace, and Jim Morrison, the rock star, whose fans won't let him find his. Morrison's memorial is covered in graffiti and is littered with debris.

If you go around behind Gertrude Stein's monument you will find the much smaller one dedicated to Alice B. Toklas. It's a poignant reminder of her fate: to be eternally relegated to playing second fiddle.

And although he strayed far away from her during his lifetime, Yves

Montand will spend the rest of eternity faithfully lying next to Simone Signoret.

Balzac, Piaf, Chopin, Seurat, Modigliani—all are among the famous people who lie along the winding paths of *Père Lachaise*, and, before she was moved to Greece, so was Maria Callas.

I first discovered, or, rather, came close to discovering, *Père Lachaise* when friends from Boston came to visit Paris and announced their intention of seeing it. I bundled *Mademoiselle* into the carry-bag that had become her means of transportation for long trips, and we all boarded the Metro.

We arrived at the entrance gates to the cemetery, and passed the vendors selling the *Plans du Cimetière,* showing where the most famous residents lie, lending a festive rather than somber element to the visit.

The guard at the entrance spotted *Mademoiselle's* head peaking out of the carry-bag, and began *"non-non"*ing excitedly. Canine people are usually welcomed everywhere *dans les bras,* held in one's hands or in a carry-bag, but this fellow was having none of that.

Mademoiselle, who had seen the insides of the chateaux of the Loire valley, whose favorite restaurants welcome her warmly, who had been invited to attend jazz concerts and theaters in France and Germany, and been told how *mignon* she was, endlessly, was not pleased.

I tried the *"Chien, quelle chien?"* routine, hoping that a sense of humor would be the password, as it usually is in France; but that, too, fell on deaf ears. As did my pointing out that Mademoiselle, borne as she was, presented no greater problem than an infant. Less so, in fact, since she could not be expected to wail if the bottle was late.

Rather than ruin everyone's afternoon, Mademoiselle and I decided to wait in a nearby café while the others went on with their visit. The afternoon turned out to be a fascinating experience in local color for us both, far more fun than *Père Lachaise* would have been.

Père Lachaise lies in an area of Paris which has seen better days. The apartment buildings are as elegant as ever from the outside, but the whole area is run down and it has not undergone the gentrification of, for example, the *Marais*.

Its residents are a mixture of all the people who have come to Paris from other areas and are worlds removed from the chic, sophisticated *Avenue Montaigne* crowd. The café was decorated with photos of Marcel Cerdan and other boxers and the owner's nose indicated a familiarity, perhaps closer than planned, with the fists in the photographs.

The welcome, as it is in most cafés in Paris, was non-committal but not unfriendly, so *Mademoiselle* and I seated ourselves at a table near the window.

Mademoiselle got a very friendly smile from the child, no more than six years old, who was seated at the bar near her proud father. She was sipping daintily on a red liquid which, giving them the benefit of the doubt, I assumed was the French equivalent of a Shirley Temple.

The pinball machine behind us, undoubtedly primed to liven things up, erupted at intervals with the sound track of a John Wayne World War II movie, whether or not anyone was playing the machine. The other source of entertainment was a large billiard table around which were assembled gentlemen who, between them, could have satisfied the graduation requirements of every dental student in the western hemisphere. And then some.

After two hours and two cups of coffee, nature no longer simply called, it fairly screamed. But the one place where I have *not* seen any dogs in France is in a public toilet. I wasn't inclined to leave her alone at the table, or, worse, trust her to a smiling, tipsy six-year-old. Decision made, we marched—as unobtrusively as one can with a furry, white canine in tow—past the billiard table, smiling at the gentlemen all the while, and into the, as it turned out, communal W.C.

I have nothing against what are referred to as "Turkish Johns." I first became aware of them years ago when I was stationed in Turkey for two years with the U.S. Air Force. My apartment in Ankara, since it was a very modern building, boasted the regular Western-style toilet as well as the Turkish-style.

For the uninitiated, let me explain that a traditional Turkish toilet consists of a slab of concrete, or marble for the more affluent, with two raised footprints where your feet are supposed to be implanted, surrounding a hole, whose purpose is obvious.

My Turkish friends would take great pleasure in pointing out to me how much more hygienic this arrangement was than the Western sit-down variety. In the two years that I lived in Turkey, the little room was used only as a broom closet.

Imagine my delight, then, when *Mademoiselle* and I, having gotten past the quizzical looks coming from the billiard table, entered a room with a sink in it and, to one side, the concrete footprints I had avoided for so long.

Mademoiselle looked up at me, I looked down at *Mademoiselle*, we both looked at the hole. She turned up her nose and was, quite obviously, mortified. I tied her to the pipe leading from the sink, for once happy that the French simply *love* exposed pipes.

When we emerged, the table next to us had been taken by two very friendly young ladies, who, in sequins and spiked heels, were somewhat overdressed for that time of day. They proceeded to consume two packs of Gitanes, several beers, all the while *mignon*'ing *Mademoiselle*, much to her delight, and then, consulting their social diaries, departed hastily.

Their places were taken by a young lady with a harmonica and three of her friends, one of them a fellow with orange hair, earrings in unexpected places, and eyebrows last seen on Marlene Dietrich. This group turned out to be British and, after the harmonica recital, began pumping coins into the juke-box.

I have the greatest affection for my British friends, most of them people I've known and loved for years, and some of the most wonderful guests at *Aux Trois Saisons* were from England and Ireland. Delightful, friendly, and with marvelous senses of humor, they were a joy to be with. This group, undoubtedly on a pilgrimage to the final resting place of Jim Morrison, paid no attention to Mademoiselle or to me, or to the billiard players, who stared at them incredulously. They raucously ordered beer after beer, sadly justifying the continent's less than flattering opinion of some young British tourists who, like some wines, simply don't travel well.

Three and a half hours, three cups of coffee, a beer, and another visit to the facility later, my friends retrieved us at the café. I reluctantly bid farewell to barman-owner, pinball machine, billiard table habitues, harmonica, earrings, and eyebrows. I can see them all if I close my eyes now. *Mademoiselle*'s thoughts remained unspoken.

I have since returned to visit *Père Lachaise* on several occasions. Each time I discover more, and it's like reading a history book of France.

The *Cimetière de Montmartre* is in a much nicer part of town and is more recent, having opened its doors on January 1, 1825. It lies in a park containing over 800 trees right in the middle of a bustling *arrondissement*, and it's worth a visit just to see the statuary done by famous artists. It's also the place where the friend of a friend of ours was laid to rest, so it has special meaning for us.

Chapter 12
Renato

The front page of *Le Figaro* caught my eye a while ago. It had a photo of Renato and his officially gowned lawyer, *Maître Bureau,* who was stroking Renato's back fondly. *Monsieur Severin,* Renato's proprietor, held him and looked proudly on. Renato himself was staring straight into the camera, looking as bewildered as only an innocent chicken can look.

Renato, a typically handsome French coq had only been doing what comes naturally to French cocks. His neighbors had taken umbrage and subsequent legal action at his natural instincts, because Renato ushered in each new dawn with a bit too much gusto for their tastes. So here he was, the caption explained, a perfectly normal four-year-old cock who had to travel up from his native Périgord region to be judged by the tribunal at Bordeaux.

The photo had been taken after both sides presented their cases. How I would have loved to hear Renato's defense testimony. The verdict was now going to be deliberated by the presiding judge, who remained nameless, undoubtedly out of fear of public reprisal if things went bad for good old Renato.

Why they call lawyers in France, of all professionals, *Maître* is beyond me, since they're no more "masters" than anyone else, and often a good deal less. At any rate, *Maître Bureau* and *Monsieur le Propriétaire* were, it seemed to me, doing what lawyers and clients all over the world do and simply trying to get a little public sympathy with some well-placed publicity.

From the look on his face, Renato himself wanted to get on with things and back to doing what comes naturally for French cocks.

It's for the best that Renato was unable to read the last sentence under the photo. It said that "he will have to wait until February 29th to find out in which sauce he'll end up."

I think that's a rather insensitive way of describing Renato's anxious moments until the judge's verdict comes in.

Even for a French cock, that's pretty humiliating!

ON JUGE BIEN LES COQS A gauche, Mᵉ Pascal Bureau, avocat. A droite, Bernard Van Severen, propriétaire. Au milieu, Renato, venu de son Périgord natal pour être jugé au tribunal de Bordeaux. Ah, oui ! Renato est un coq de quatre ans. On lui reproche de chanter au lever du soleil. Le jugement mis en délibéré, Renato devra attendre le 29 février pour savoir à quelle sauce il sera mangé. (Photo J. Morin/AFP.)

Chapter 13
La Baptême

The tiny one-room church is in Rambouillet, a town outside of Paris. It lies to one side of the property which has been in Dominique's family for many years. Unheated and cold in the winter, the ancient church is eerily beautiful in its simplicity. There is a long rope, pulled by whoever is closest to it, which rings the bell announcing a service.

It was the occasion of the baptism of Alice, the second daughter of Dominique and Serge, and I was to become Alice's godfather. The service was short, Alice behaved impeccably throughout, and I stood before the assembled family and friends to read the short passage assigned to me by Dominique.

"Je crois en Dieu," it began, "I believe in God," and as I held this fragile new little person named Alice in my arms, the words, although spoken in a language new to me, and in a church of another religion than mine, never meant more to me.

I had accepted the honor with pleasure, knowing that, in asking me to be Alice's godfather, they were saying that I was more than just a friend. I signed the old church registry, adding my name to those going back hundreds of years.

After the service, we all returned to the house and had a typically delicious Sunday feast which Serge, a cinematographer, preserved on film.

It seems strange that the day in Rambouillet really had its origins on the beach on the Greek island of Hydra some years before. We were there on a vacation, soaking up the marvelous Mediterranean sun and chatting away in English. The young French couple next to us seemed friendly and, eventually, Dominique chimed in and told us that she and Serge were on *their* honeymoon and lived in Paris.

My American puritanism took quite a beating that first day. Try as I might to be sophisticated about it, I wasn't yet really prepared for the topless sunning and bathing which is so taken for granted throughout Europe. Dominique, hearing my American-accented English entered our conversation, bless her, and I summoned up all of my latent worldliness, and focused my eyes unwaveringly on her face.

I've since become almost as blasé as the Europeans about nudity. Their nudity, that is, although one evening in Hamburg, Germany, when friends produced photos of their last vacation and passed them around, I had to restrain myself from flinging my hands over the eyes of their teen-age children sitting on either side of me. The kids, of course, were far more interested in the meal at hand and would have thought me insane.

I have a history of running for a towel when faced with the possibility of having my body, love handles and all, too closely scrutinized by what might be less than sympathetic eyes. When I lived in California, I, of course, joined the obligatory health club. The Adonis assigned to me as my "personal trainer," and who I fully expected to resemble at the end of my three-week free trial period, took my vital statistics, which I altered slightly.

To his credit, he didn't even blink an eye when I answered the height question with "six foot five" instead of the more truthful "five foot six." He just stared down at me from his Olympian height, pen poised mid-air, and then continued writing. The exercise program he designed for me required that I perform, in fifteen minutes, more physical activity than I had done in the previous fifteen years.

As my fellow "athletes" passed the enormous mirrors placed everywhere to deliberately intimidate me, they flexed and postured. I avoided eye contact with the mirror, retired to the whirl-pool bath and spent the rest of the afternoon exchanging recipes with an absolutely charming seventy-four-year-old lady whose doctor had talked her into joining for her arthritis. We met regularly in the whirl-pool bath for the next three weeks, I put on eight pounds as a result of the exchanged recipes, and from then on my body and I have kept a pact not to embarrass each other.

That day on Hydra, wearing my regulation all-covering T-shirt, I was delighted to meet two new Parisian friends. We met again, later in the day, at the sea-side restaurant and, when we parted, exchanged addresses, as people in those circumstances often do.

The difference is that when I exchange addresses I really mean it. It's not just an automatic or polite gesture. I wrote to Dominique and Serge, they wrote back, and the birth of Audrey, their first daughter, was cause for more happy correspondence. So it went until, years later, we moved to Paris.

Since moving to France, and as my awareness of French customs has grown, I've discovered that one way of knowing that you have "arrived" with French people, is when they invite you to their homes. Restaurants are the usual meeting places until then, for several very practical reasons.

Most Parisian apartments are small, sold by the square meter at horrendous prices, and most French kitchens are minute. European kitchen appliances are tiny by American standards, although I prefer the

European idea of having the refrigerator *above* the freezer compartment, rather than the other way around. It makes sense to me because you go to the refrigerator far more often than you go to the freezer.

With space at a premium, the restaurant becomes, in fact, an extension of the home, where the *habitués* are warmly greeted and treated like part of the family. We're on this basis with *Le Fregate* on the *Quai D'Orsay*. Even after a seven month season, while the inn was open, each time we returned to Paris, *Le Fregate* gave us a greeting that suggested that they had been sitting there all that time waiting for us. It's a good feeling.

It's also part of the changing pattern of modern life. The two-job family has become far more prevalent in France. Most things are very expensive in France, primarily due to the taxes the government adds to the price tag. I can't imagine Americans paying over five dollars per gallon of gasoline without a minor revolution; yet the French do it uncomplainingly, and eighty percent goes to the government in taxes. Paying these prices, however, means that one income may just not be enough.

So, with both husband and wife working, the days where a modern, working French housewife can afford three hours a day to go shopping and prepare dinner are fast disappearing. Take-home meals, beautifully prepared and delicious, are becoming the mid-week choice, and going out to a restaurant, especially one where you are made to feel at home, seems a quite reasonable alternative to cooking at home.

The weekends can be another matter entirely. We've had countless enjoyable hours with Serge and Dominique and other friends, always impressed by the incredible knowledge and joy that goes into the preparation of the meal.

Serge usually does the weekend cooking and is a superb chef. One Sunday he prepared Stuffed Quails in Calvados that was superb. He is also a true connoisseur of wine. In fact, he can smell a wine, taste it, and then tell you not only exactly where it *came* from but its *recolte*, the *year* it was bottled. I will never reach that level of expertise, but I've learned a lot from Serge and how he puts food and wine together and that knowledge helped me at the inn. On another occasion, around the Christmas season, he prepared the traditional *foie gras,* with fresh figs and just a touch of cognac. It melted in our mouths, and was enhanced by its "marriage" with a great Sauterne wine that, by itself, is too sweet but was perfect when served with the *foie gras.*

When they rented a chalet in *Megeve* in the French Alps for their winter skiing vacation, they invited us to join them. The date happened to fall on our American Thanksgiving holiday, so I insisted on preparing the traditional Thanksgiving meal. The Turkey, bought at my favorite *boucherie* on *Rue Cler* in Paris, made the trip with us to *Megeve* and I stuffed it with my favorite apricot, sausage, and herb stuffing, and served it with the cranberry sauce and sweet potatoes and mashed potatoes and pumpkin pie I look forward to all year.

It was Serge and Dominique's first real Thanksgiving dinner and they loved it. We gave thanks in both languages for the friendship we shared then and still do. The language of the heart transcends all others.

The tiny church in *Rambouillet* was one of many shared memories, and as I held little Alice I wished for her, too, a lifetime filled with experiences and good people with whom to share them.

STUFFED QUAIL IN CALVADOS

Ingredients:

Stuffing:
2 c	bread crumbs
1 c	whole chestnuts, chopped fine
1 c	chicken broth
1	egg
1/2 tsp	salt
1/4 tsp	pepper
1/4 c	butter, melted

Quails:
1	quail per serving (game hen)
1/2 c	Calvados
1/2 c	chicken broth
1/2 c	white wine
4	shallots, chopped fine
1/2 c	carrot, chopped fine
1/2 c	celery, chopped fine
1 tsp	Herbes de Provence
2 tbs	flour

Preparation:

Mix stuffing ingredients together, stuff each quail and close the openings with a wooden skewer. In a large covered skillet, heat the 1/4 cup butter. Brown the quail on all sides. Add the Calvados, the chicken broth, and the white wine to the skillet and heat gently. Add chopped shallots, carrot, and celery, and the Herbes de Provence. Cover the skillet and cook for about 1 hour. Remove quail from the skillet and keep warm. Remove about 1/4 cup of the liquid in the skillet and stir in 2 tablespoons of flour. Slowly stir this into the simmering liquid in the skillet and serve this thickened gravy over the quail. Serve hot.

Chapter 14
Á Pied

When we first moved to Paris, Sabine and Erik presented us with two enormous volumes called *Dictionnaire Historique des Rues de Paris*. Erik is a well-known architect and Sabine is a sculptress who has shown her free-form sculptures internationally. Both share our love for the city. Those two books have given me more hours of pleasure than I can tell you.

They list, alphabetically, *every* street in Paris, its history, who lived at particular street numbers, in short, everything there is to know about Paris. As in any other large city, of course, there's the high cost of living, the noise, and the pollution you could complain about if you chose to. But they're minor complaints compared to the joys that are there for the taking, the sensory delights which, in Paris particularly, tantalize without terrifying.

When I'm in Paris, I feel as if I'm more than I really am, more clever, more sophisticated, or, at least, the city coaxes me into believing it.

New York, where I was born, is exciting and vibrant, but it can be intimidating when compared to Paris, perhaps because it's built up rather than out. The only really tall building on the skyline of Paris is the ugly *Tour Montparnasse*.

In Paris, I'm surrounded by beauty, so beauty becomes the norm. I'm surrounded by culture, so culture comes as easily as breathing. Countless plaques placed on various buildings attest to the past presence of artists, musicians, scientists, poets whom the city refuses to forget. Each day is a discovery, not merely a span of time.

Paris is a city made for walking and finding new places. And Parisians truly love their city and are proud of its beauty and history. If you say to a New Yorker, "Your city is the most beautiful in the world," he or she will usually laugh, shake his or her head, and begin cataloguing all of the city's faults.

Say the same thing to a Parisian and you'll get a simple *"Oui,"* with a look that says *of course it is, everybody knows that!*

An unusually warm late February afternoon brought us, along with the rest of Paris, it seemed, out onto the streets. We paraded and marveled and drank it all in, the avenues and side-streets of this most magical of all cities.

Our promenade was carried out at a slower-than-usual pace because, at age fifteen, *Mademoiselle* tended to walk with less enthusiasm than in earlier years. We began on the *Quai Voltaire* which borders the Seine, directly across from the Louvre.

We walked along the *Quai Voltaire* and then crossed the river and passed to the left of the glass pyramid designed by Mr. Pei, a fellow American. I remember when the pyramid was first constructed and was the subject of heated arguments between Parisian friends and myself. They loved it from the beginning, calling it *amusant*. I thought it was sacrilege to place it where it is: smack-dab in the middle of the courtyard of the Louvre. Of course, I've since caught up with my friends and now I, too, point to it proudly when I show visitors around Paris. Especially at night, when it is all lit up and glows like a jewel. It also functions superbly as the main entrance to one of the world's finest museums, and creates an open and luminous space.

The inverted pyramid area, which came later, has become a subterranean city of shops surrounded by the newly-discovered and preserved foundations of the original Louvre palace. I feel almost as if it belongs to me because I watched the excavations, going three stories down, below where the *Tuileries* gardens are located. Then they covered the whole thing up with a park and created absolutely gorgeous seasonally planted gardens. Nobody would ever suspect what they cover.

We walked on to the *Rue de Rivoli,* mobbed with people, the souvenir shops selling their usual kitsch, mostly to Japanese tourists who seem to travel only in clusters. They're easily located because, with an average of 2.6 cameras per person, all you have to do is listen for the clicks. They've been a boon to the French economy. They buy everything in sight, since, with the cost of things in Japan, it's cheaper for them to buy a Japanese camera in Paris than in Tokyo.

The *Rue de Rivoli* was a bit too crowded for *Mademoiselle's* taste, so we doubled back to the Seine and walked along the *quai*, inspecting the books, posters, and antique postcards of the stalls.

I've never understood how these *bouquinistes* make a living. They're usually reading, not selling, and will often ignore potential customers. Most of the stuff they're selling isn't really worth buying, not old enough to be truly "antique" but just old enough to be thrown out of the attic as junk in a few years.

If your pleasure is simply browsing, as mine is, then this is heaven, with the occasional postcard or print purchased for no good reason, simply for fun. I enjoy wandering and looking, and it's certainly an inexpensive and relaxing place to do that, so I hope they're around for as long as I am, and long after.

We crossed back over to the Left Bank via the wooden, romantic *Pont des Beaux Arts,* just pausing to sit on one of the benches to give *Mademoiselle* a chance to rest and enjoy the scenery. From this vantage point, high above the Seine, one can look toward *Notre Dame* and the *Ile de la Cité,* with the houses narrowing to nothing around the *Place Dauphine,* one of my favorite little Parisian hiding places.

In the other direction, there's the old *Gare D'Orsay,* now the incredible *Musée D'Orsay,* and the *Tour Eiffel's* peak, and the *Grand Palais* and the *Petit Palais.* Such beauty in every direction, all there to be seen at no cost except the effort.

Mademoiselle's pause over, and both of us feeling rejuvenated, we crossed the street to the *Quai Conti.* We walked down *Rue de Seine,* past the *café La Palette* which is a student hangout, since the *Ecole des Beaux Arts* is very close. It's one of my least favorite cafés in Paris, not particularly friendly the few times I've been there, but it reminds me of the Greenwich Village of my youth. All of the girls still seem to look like Audrey Hepburn.

On to the end of *Rue de Seine to Boulevard Saint Germain,* a right turn, and one of my favorite places for people-watching, *"Aux Deux Magots."* Along with *"Café Flore,"* its neighbor, these two are probably the most famous, most photographed cafés in Paris. Hemingway has a plaque behind his favorite table in *Deux Magots,* and Sartre, Bouvier and other famous authors and thinkers are immortalized accordingly. The prices are very touristy at both cafés, but the show is worth it.

We seated ourselves at an outside table on the Boulevard, *Mademoiselle* taking her usual place under the table. We ordered beer and a dish of water, and followed our favorite pastime in Paris, observing.

On another afternoon, we trekked out to an out-of-the-way place called the *Musée Français du Pain.* Paris must be the only city in the world with a museum consecrated entirely to bread.

The Bread Museum, at *25 bis. Rue Victor Hugo* in case you ever decide to visit it, is near the Metro station of *Charenton-Ecoles,* and is literally crammed with anything having to do with bread and its history.

There is a letter from Marie Antoinette naming a new chief of her bread-pantry and a bread box which belonged to Louis XVI. There are stamps used to mark and identify breads and cakes from the fifth and twelfth centuries, along with countless molds, serving dishes, baking pans, centuries-old written edicts setting down the type of flour to be used as well as the price of bread, and vouchers good for bread, which were issued during the French Revolution. Even that old revolutionary Danton got into the act with a decree he signed on the 26th of July 1799, which promised death to anyone found hoarding bread. The French, it seems, have always taken food very seriously. I decided to try my own hand at bread-making as soon as possible.

My favorite display cases were the ones filled with tiny figures, called *fèves,* no more than an inch high, which are baked into the *Galette des Roi* cakes available only around January 6th, Three Kings Day. These are delicious puff-pastry concoctions filled with almond paste and one of these little favors. If your wedge of the luscious *Galette* contains the porcelain figure, you win the honor of wearing the golden paper crown on top of the cake and you're King or Queen for the day. I was lucky one year and still to this day carry my good-luck charm around with me.

I've discovered a lot of practical things, as well, during my wanderings in Paris. For example, if you ever need any hardware, the best store for that in Paris is the huge basement of the BHV department store.

Each year, when we returned to Paris from the inn, I invariably spent the first week repairing things in the apartment that had either ceased to function or awaited my return to immediately do so. One year, it was a broken electrical wall socket.

There is absolutely no standardization of electrical materials or supplies in France. By my third visit to assorted little hardware stores and electrical supply shops, I discovered that the broken socket, which was a triple one with two on/off switches and one actual socket for plugging in an appliance, belonged to a special series called "Europa 35." The series, naturally, had been discontinued, and, unfortunately, was the only one designed to fit the long, narrow receptacle in the wall.

Changing to another series would have entailed major alteration to the wall, so I prepared to set off for BHV's *sous sol* on a lovely Monday morning in Paris that boasted a clear blue sky and a gently invigorating autumn wind. The sort of morning when the city throbs with new life and anything can be accomplished. Almost anything.

I gave *Mademoiselle* a larger than usual breakfast and took her on a slightly longer walk than usual, and then, once she was happily snoring away, I snuck out of the flat, tip-toeing so that she wouldn't know I was leaving.

Since *Mademoiselle* was hard of hearing, this was really quite unnecessary, but, although she had adjusted beautifully, I still hadn't. She was 115 years old in two-legged people's years and slept a lot at that point in her life, but she still got frantic if she picked up her head and thought she was alone.

With her hearing loss and only a little peripheral vision left, her world had really become very limited. For fifteen faithful years she had filled my life with such love and joy, I figured that the least I could do was to make her as comfortable as I could and not cause her any unnecessary upset. So I tried not to leave her alone for any length of time and scheduled my necessary shopping excursions for her post-breakfast snooze period when she was literally "out."

I quickly left the flat, and walked up the quai, crossing over the bridge to the other side and past the spectacular Paris City Hall and entered the BHV department store directly across the street. BHV stands for

Bazar de l'Hotel de Ville, and I expected to be out of there in record time.

The salespeople at BHV, however, seem to be specially trained to unsmilingly shake their heads from left to right and say "Non" at the same time, that is, if they deign to acknowledge your presence. After several tries, I found one salesperson who divulged, as if it were a State Secret, the name of an electrical supply store near the *Place de la Bastille* which might still carry some remnants of this now-defunct "Europa 35" series.

The salespeople in BHV are not representative of all French salespeople. Very often, if I approach a French salesperson, or any other French person for that matter, with a polite smile and preface my question with a simple *"S'il vous plait,"* they will respond graciously and often go out of their way to help me. To some, in fact, it seems as if they almost consider it a sacred duty to have been chosen at this moment in time to uphold the national honor and won't let me go until they've helped me or found someone else who can.

I raced out of BHV, continued up the *Rue de Rivoli* to the new Opera House at the Bastille, nicknamed by disgruntled Parisians "the concrete croissant" because it's so ugly, and turned right onto *Boulevard Henri IV.* Time was becoming important with poor *Mademoiselle* at home alone and likely to wake up at any time.

Finally, there it was, the electrical supply store, at number 34 as promised, but closed up tight. I'd forgotten that it was Monday and in France those stores which are open on Saturday, even for a few hours, close on Monday for the entire day, in most cases, or in others just half a day. This was obviously one of them. It's one of those things you get used to if you live in France, and I should have thought of it.

I started the long walk home. On *Rue Saint Antoine* I saw a magnificent courtyard behind huge doors. An incurable looky-loo, I quickly dived through the portals and found myself in the courtyard of the *Hôtel de*

Sully.

The word *"Hôtel"* in French doesn't necessarily refer to a place which rents rooms to travelers. The *"Hôtel de Ville,"* for example, means, simply "City Hall," and the *"Hôtel de Sully"* means, simply, the house of Sully. Don't ask me why this is so, and don't bother asking a Frenchman either. All I can tell you is that Mr. and Mrs. Sully had quite a house!

As I paused there in their cobbled courtyard, I could almost hear the horses' hoofs over the centuries as they brought the carriages through from the *Rue Saint Antoine* to deposit Monsieur or Madame or their visitors or their descendants. There was another portal beyond that opened onto a lovely large, square formal garden. The sounds of birds chirping away actually blocked out the sounds of Paris traffic on the busy street outside.

The *Hôtel de Sully* is a museum now, open to the public only on certain days, and I made a mental note to return on a day when I didn't have a possibly frantic 115-year-old waiting for me at home.

I chose the most direct route home to *Mademoiselle* and crossed the bridge over to the Ile Saint Louis, surely one of the loveliest parts of Paris as well as one of its most expensive real estate districts. The Rothschilds have their home there, the *Hôtel Lambert*, and, not being certain which one it was, and somewhat in a hurry, I chose one of the most beautiful, at random, and decided that it was theirs, imagining the soirées and galas and the notables who had filled its rooms.

There were plaques over the entrances of some of the three- or four-story buildings, which I noted as I hurried along. One of them stated that the house was "in 1695, the property of Louis Joseph de Playbault" who was *"Seigneur de Villars,"* Lord of Villars, and *"Capitaine au regiment de la Reine,"* captain in the queen's regiment.

What did Louis look like, as he hurried along this same street in 1695? Had the queen summoned him for some special purpose? After all, if he was a captain of her regiment, he must have been pretty high up. What secrets did he carry with him?

No more time for Louis. Further on, at #19 *Quai de Bourbon,* a small plaque proclaimed that "Camille Claudet, Sculptress, had a studio at the end of the courtyard" where she worked from 1899 until 1913, at which time, the plaque continued sadly, "her brief career ended." I felt sad for Camille Claudet and imagined her chipping away at the end of the little courtyard, giving form and life to her shattered dreams. For that brief moment, I hated Auguste Rodin, the fellow who had made Camille's life so unbearable.

Each house, each courtyard, each plaque and the moment in time and someone's life it commemorates—each can fuel the imagination and stir the heart if you just let it. The electrical outlet could wait until Tuesday. This was Monday and I was in Paris and I could feel and dream and savor life just as the French, bless them, do so well.

A bit out of breath, I unlocked the door to the flat and opened it to find a somewhat bleary-eyed *Mademoiselle* sitting in the center of the room, head bobbing up and down. I like to think she missed me.

GALETTE DES ROIS

Ingredients:

Puff pastry:
225 g (8 oz.) flour
5 g salt
200 ml ice water
225 g (8 oz.) butter

Filling:
200 g finely ground almonds
100 g softened butter
200 g sugar
4 egg yolks
2 tbs rum
1 tsp vanilla extract
1/3 ltr milk
50 g flour

Preparation:

Puff Pastry:
In a bowl, mix the flour, salt, and iced water until it forms a ball. Place butter between two sheets of waxed paper and flatten into a long rectangle with a rolling pin. Knead dough on floured surface until smooth. Chill for 15 minutes. Roll dough into a long rectangle (1/2 inch thick) which is 1 inch wider than butter rectangle. Place butter rectangle in center of dough rectangle, fold both ends of dough over the butter, and knead out again into a rectangle the size of the original rectangle. Repeat this folding and rolling procedure five times. Chill after final fold for 30 minutes. Cool for 10 minutes before using.

Filling:
Preheat oven to 240°. Beat egg yolks and sugar until well blended. Heat milk and add flour to thicken. Add the ground almonds and the butter to the milk mixture to obtain a smooth creamy consistency. Add the rum and vanilla extract. Divide the puff pastry into two halves, roll each half out to form a circle of about 24 cm in diameter. Place one circle on a slightly

buttered pan. Spread the filling mixture regularly, leaving about 1.5 cm around the edge. Place a fève in the filling cream. Moisten the edge of the first circle, cover with the second circle and seal edges. Paint the entire surface with beaten egg. Bake 10 minutes and then lower temperature to 210° (#7) and bake for another 20 minutes, until the Galette is golden in color.I hope that you get the wedge of Galette with the fève in it and that you're king or queen for the day.

Chapter 15
Le Retour

The winter months passed quickly, and the longer days and milder temperatures meant that we would soon be returning to *Dracy le Fort* to open up the house, burn the fallen leaves, and prepare for the Official Grand Opening of *L'Auberge Aux Trois Saisons* for Easter.

An excerpt from my diary during one of those last few weeks before leaving Paris says, "Last night, at dinner at Françoise's home, around a table where mostly French was spoken, I realized a basic fact about the French people. They really don't expect you to speak their language or pronounce it as *they* do. After all, they're FRENCH! Just so long as you make an effort and speak quickly, they're quite content and will congratulate you on your proficiency and assure you that they wish they spoke English as well as you do French. The French also love provocateurs, people who shake up the establishment and are eccentric. They will applaud behavior that, to us, seems outrageous, as long as it's done with style. The worst thing one can do, to the French, is to be silent or boring."

That still holds true as I read it today. With great effort, I may someday speak French at about the level of a ten year old, but I never let that stop me.

Don't depend on dictionaries entirely either. Invariably, the first definition given in the dictionary will turn out to be the wrong one in conversation.

I found this out the hard way when *Mademoiselle*, shortly after her arrival in France, managed to pick up, as dogs are prone to do when they are puppies, a case of worms. How she did it at age thirteen remains a mystery and one that caused us to panic for fear that it could be dangerous for a "mature" dog.

I grabbed for the telephone directory and the dictionary, dialed the local veterinarian on *Rue Saint Dominique*, and, while the phone was still ringing, searched for the word for worms.

I found the word, and excitedly sputtered, *"Ma chien…elle a…SERPENTS."* There was a long silence from the other end.

The veterinarian turned out to be very nice and *Mademoiselle's* health was soon restored. My faith in dictionaries hasn't been the same since then, but my vocabulary has, indeed, improved.

French grammar, on the other hand, still escapes me, even after all these years. English refers to everything as "the," but in French everything has a gender. The street is feminine, *la rue*, while the restaurant is masculine, *le restaurant*. There's no special reason to explain which is what and it's a question of memorization.

To compound my confusion, many of the words that are feminine in French are often masculine in German, so my French friends just smile at my mistakes, and cover my embarrassment, and, possibly, theirs, with constant reminders that my accent is trés *charmant!*

It most certainly is not charming; in fact it's horrible. After all these years, I still can't pronounce the word *"rue"* as the French do. No matter how I distort my lips, it still comes out *"roo"* or *"ruh,"* anything but "rue."

One of the first purchases we made at the inn was a telephone answering machine. I recorded the message in French, German, and English. I thought the French part sounded wonderfully authentic until I played it back. Our French guests professed not to mind.

Regardless of what you've heard, the French are unbelievably polite. They have endured their undeserved reputation for rudeness as they do almost everything else, without complaint. What is often interpreted as rudeness is, in reality, simply an innate formality.

Part of this natural gentility must stem from the French language, which lends itself to flowery and beautifully phrased expressions. This makes French the perfect language for diplomacy since French politicians can speak for hours and say nothing, a talent they have developed into a science.

Some traditional habits, such as the obligatory *"Monsieur-Dame"* that you hear when a French person enters or leaves an establishment, are said to no-one in particular, and are just a courtesy. It may be as meaningless as "Have a nice day" has become, but it certainly doesn't hurt.

A prime example of both the politeness and political flexibility of the French language is the art of letter writing. Much more formalized than even our most formal American business letter, each letter sent out in France must adhere to some very strict rules.

The content of the letter may range from important to utterly trivial, and it may contain the most belligerent, libelous intimations. But the *last* sentence must assure the recipient that he or she, indeed, his or her ancestors, are, nevertheless, the noblest people ever put on earth, and please be assured that the writer is honored to breathe air on the same planet as them.

For example, I recently received a letter from one of the many government agencies that reside in, and periodically emerge from, the woodwork. The letter, on official stationery, advised me that I was, in essence, a cad, a malevolent shirker, etc., in that I had not, as expected, complied with some regulation, the expiration date of which was not, of course, previously made known to me.

Only of importance was the undeniable fact that the expiration date had arrived and duly departed and, as a result of my noncompliance, I was seriously in danger of forfeiting my first-born child or some such unspecified punishment.

What truly fascinated me, though, was the fact that this incredibly offensive and intimidating letter concluded with the sentence, *"Je vous prie de croire, Cher Monsieur, à l'assurance de mes salutations les meilleures,"* which translates as "I pray that you believe, dear sir, in the assurance of my very best greetings."

Charmant!

Letter writing is much more difficult for me than speaking, since, with suitable slurs and mispronunciations, hand motions, and my American accent, I can get away with a lot. With a letter it's out there in black and white, to be red-penciled for grammatical and spelling mistakes.

So I sit with my dictionary, searching for each word's gender, for the—hopefully—correct meaning, and spelling. A simple letter can turn into a full afternoon's labor.

I've succeeded in memorizing several suitably flowery and embarrassingly complimentary closing lines like the one I've quoted above, in the hope that, having decided during the main part of my letter, that I am an illiterate moron, at least my parting sentence will warm their hearts.

Another item on the Do-list of that first winter, and one which may have been responsible for much that happened at *Aux Trois Saisons* in the years to come, was to visit travel guide publishers in Paris. Friends who ran an inn on Cape Cod had told us that being in a good tourist guide can make all the difference in the world, so we made the rounds.

I'll tell you the results of that in a little while.

The night before leaving Paris, we had dinner, as always, at *Le Fregate* and watched the *bateau mouches* illuminating the Louvre as they passed by, and savoring the very best onion soup in Paris. Every time I left Paris I was sad, even though I knew that in seven months, when we closed the inn, I would be back.

Every day away from Paris is a day lost from my life. I can't help feeling that way. But there was also the anticipation and the exciting challenge of making the inn a success, and the unknown adventures that would lie ahead.

Early the next morning, I took *Mademoiselle* on a long farewell walk on *Rue Allent.* Each year, on the day we left Paris to begin the months spent in Burgundy running the inn, *Mademoiselle* seemed to take just a little longer with her rounds than usual. She met Bruno, the large Boxer with whom she often chatted, then lingered with her favorite friend, a gigantic, elegantly trimmed, handsome white Poodle named Romeo, who lived with a lady who worked as a journalist for the Paris fashion showings.

Having said her *adieus*, she settled herself onto the back seat of the car, and, in royal fashion, head high, left Paris with only one wistful backward glance at Romeo, perhaps thinking of what might have been. I can only imagine what was in the letter she had left for him.

We headed out of Paris for the A6 on the road back to *Dracy le Fort* and *L'Auberge Aux Trois Saisons.*

SOUPE D'OIGNON À LE FRÉGATE

Ingredients:
4 c	sliced onions (about 1 pound)
1/4 lb	butter
1 1/2 c	chicken stock
1 1/2 c	beef stock
1/2 c	red wine
1 tsp	mustard
1 tbs	flour
	salt
	pepper
	slices of baguette
1 c	grated Gruyére cheese

Preparation:
Slice onions into thin slices. Put butter in a sauce pan, heat until melted, and add the onion slices and mustard. Gently cook until onions are slightly browned. Carefully stir in the flour. Carefully stir in the two stocks and the red wine. Bring mixture to a boil and gently simmer for 45 minutes. Add salt and pepper to taste. Toast baguette slices, place one slice in the bottom of each individual oven-proof soup bowl. Cover the bread with soup and sprinkle with the Gruyére cheese. Make certain that there is a thick layer of cheese covering the soup, place under a grill and cook until the cheese is melted and turns light brown. Serve immediately.

MORT SOBEL

Part III
L'Auberge Aux Trois Saisons

AUX TROIS SAISONS

Chapter 16
La Carte de Vin

We returned to *Dracy le Fort*, unloaded the car, and did a quick walk-through of the grounds to see if there had been any damage to the property or the house. The long, cold, wet Burgundy winter hadn't caused any major damage, but we were knee deep in leaves.

We spent our days raking the leaves into huge piles, burning them, and preparing the house for the Grand Opening three weeks away. It was actually a nice quiet time for us, despite the back-breaking work, and, with the long list of things that still had to be done before the first guest arrived, the time passed quickly.

Copies of the letters I had written during the winter, along with the responses received, were dutifully filed in dossiers bulging with documents from a number of official French organizations I hadn't dreamed existed:

There was the *Société de l"Audiovisuel,* which imposes a tax on every French person who uses their television set. Yes, you read that correctly. In France, and in many other European countries, you pay an annual fee if you *own* a TV set, and, if you're a hotel, you have to pay a separate tax on each set. We pay a sales tax in America and that's it. If you've bought it, you have the right to use it. Not in Europe, where the record of sale is transmitted to the government, so there's no escaping bureaucracy.

There was the *S.A.C.E.M.*, whose initials remain a mystery to me, but is the organization which extracted a tax from us for using our own radio and tape recorder at the inn. The reason they gave was that the guests could hear it in the dining room and we were, therefore, providing music with dinner. I wondered whether, if we played it loud enough for the neighbors to hear, we would have had to pay an extra fee.

There was the *Chambre de Commerce,* which required an annual filing of a set of useless, mostly-blank business forms and then had the *chutzpah* to demand that we pay them a tax of 200 Francs for the privilege of having them *accept* the forms.

In an effort to use the facilities of the community, we went to the local bank, which accepted our money to open a checking account and then fiddled around for three months without giving us a checkbook, at which time we gave up, demanded our money back and continued using our Paris bank.

There was the *License pour Boissons,* the liquor license, which stipulated that, as a hotel-restaurant, we could serve alcoholic beverages only with dinner, which was all we intended to do anyway. Anything beyond that would be a *License IV,* the little dark blue sign you see in bars and cafés throughout France, which gives them the right to serve liquor under any circumstances.

L'Assurance, the specific insurance policy, covered food-poisoning as well as the usual injury and fire protection, which seemed reasonable, since we would be offering breakfast and dinner. *L'Extincteurs,* the fire extinguishers, with different types for the bedroom and kitchen areas also had to be placed in specific locations and appropriately documented by the fire department.

With the above documents proving that we had dutifully complied with all of the regulations they managed to invent, our dossiers had increased considerably in thickness, and we began feeling quite important. But what made it all seem worthwhile was when we inspected the results of our work of the previous summer.

Each room was different and each had a special charm. It was worth all the effort. When the furnishing and decorating was finished, we had insisted on sleeping in each room to be certain that the bedside reading lamps were in just the right position and gave enough light; that the bathmats and soft, terry-cloth bathrobes were conveniently placed, and that the towel racks were handy; that there was enough shelf space in the bathroom for his and hers toiletries. Each room was quality-tested for any defects or oversights.

The five guest rooms each had different color schemes; the furnishings were a mixture of many cultures, American antiques blending with the European ones. There were even some from the Middle East that I had brought back from my Air Force days in Turkey and some old pieces from Dierk's family in Germany.

After their first visit, guests would often request "their" room when they returned the next year, and the inn eventually had a sixty percent return rate, which we took as a great compliment.

In *Tour Nord*, for example, the American patchwork quilts went nicely with the antique night stands found at a local *brocante* in Burgundy, and the natural wood floors were bare except for the large oriental rug under the sleeping area. The little reading alcove was upholstered in a traditional American Colonial fabric bought in Boston, and we put up a few Grandma Moses prints, bought from a New York gallery, which European guests loved.

Tour Sud had white walls, as did all the rooms, with dark green curtains and patchwork quilts in various shades of green and draped over one of the chairs was a large knitted afghan blanket that Dierk took three weeks to make. The dark green color set off the massive wooden beam that extended through the bedroom on into the bathroom. The rocking chair was a big hit, the guests pointing to it and saying, "Kennedy," because he had so often been photographed in one.

Bellevue, my favorite room, was done in shades of pale blue and pearl gray, with a paisley fabric over the round bedside tables on either side of the old wooden headboard we also found in a local antique store. The side chairs were bought in Rancy, a town known for its craftsmanship.

Lumière d'Etoile was the smallest of the rooms, up under the eaves, with a semi-cathedral ceiling and a raised sitting area that permitted a panoramic view of the garden through the window set in the roof.

Suite de Jardin, the garden room, was the last room to be completed, mainly because the right fabric had been so hard to find. It had to suggest a garden but not overwhelmingly so, since there would be so much of it. The huge, high-windowed double doors leading off the courtyard, as well as the door leading out to the back garden—the door which we had to get permission to change from its previous life as a window—and the skirt of the large table in the sitting area, *and* the bed, *and* the canopy curtains, all would be covered in the same fabric.

We finally found exactly the right fabric on our annual visit to the south of France to visit Julia, one of our closest friends in Paris. At that time, she also owned a villa in the hills of *Mandelieu-Capitou*, a town sitting in the hills overlooking *Cannes*, and, every February, we were invited—the three of us—to spend a week with her. *Mademoiselle*, incidentally, had been the only four-legged person ever allowed in Julia's home, but they had hit it off at the jazz concert in Paris and were good friends by then.

February is the month when the Mimosa trees are in full bloom in the south of France and the hills were a blaze of yellow blossoms. It's a truly beautiful sight.

Julia suggested a fabric shop in *Cannes* and our search was over. It was a perfect fabric, not too busy, but the bright colors brought the sunshine into *Suite de Jardin* even on dull days.

When we returned to *Dracy le Fort,* the first task was to open up the house, let in some fresh air, and do a thorough top-to-bottom spring cleaning.

Another task, much more pleasurable, involved choosing the wines for the *Carte de Vin,* the wine list, which would be available with dinner.

All I knew about wine before arriving in Burgundy was, basically, its color and the old rule of thumb that if it's white it goes with fish or chicken, if it's red, with meat. I soon discovered that this is nonsense and that the French drink red wine with just about everything.

They will, however, spend a great deal of time choosing exactly *which* heavy-bodied red goes with one particular dish, or which lighter one goes with another. Hours can be spent in discussion over whether the Bordeaux, which the French liken to our California wines, would be better in some instances than the rich Burgundy wines.

The Burgundies are more to my own personal taste but are too heavy for some people. They have also, unfortunately, almost priced themselves out of the market. There's no argument about their being just right to enhance a robust *Boeuf Bourguignon,* while only a really good Champagne or a fine Sauterne are worthy of a *foie gras.*

If it's a truly good *mariage,* in wine as in life, what greater joy?

When we began choosing the wines that we would offer at the inn, we thought of Serge and all he had taught us. We happily began a series of *dégustations,* wine tastings, with the purpose of selecting the entries for our *Carte de Vin.*

The inn was, after all, in Burgundy. People come to Burgundy primarily because they've heard of, and become fond of, the area's wines, so the list had to be very carefully chosen, especially since, as "foreigners" we would be expected, at least by the French, to know absolutely nothing about wine.

The French are, to be honest, rather chauvinistic about their gastronomic expertise. The word, in fact, comes from the French officer named Chauvin who was in Napoleon's army. Even when Napoleon's fortunes were at their lowest and everybody else had deserted him, Monsieur Chauvin still remained loyal and proud of his Commander-In-Chief, thus assuring himself a place in history—and the French version of Trivial Pursuit.

We made the rounds of dozens of the vineyards in Burgundy. Rough work, indeed, but somebody had to do it!

All of the fine Beaune wines, the *Meursaults, Nuits St. Georges, Pommards, Puligny-Montrachets, Pouilly-Fuissés,* and others that ended up on our wine list were carefully tested and chosen on the basis of their quality and price. In the process, we discovered the real treasures...the people who devote their lives to this ancient art and science.

We discovered one of these treasures thanks to Don and Carol Brown, embassy people who came as guests and remained friends. His name is Jean-Claude Brelière and his little vineyard is near the *Place de l'Eglise* in Rully. If you have the good fortune to be there, please meet Jean-Claude and say "Hello" from us.

Jean-Claude had worked at many things, tourism and other professions, traveled extensively and learned several languages before he decided to go into his father's vineyard and make it his life's work. But he agreed to do it only if he could do it *his* way. So he studied, took courses, experimented, took chances, and surprised everybody, including his father, by creating a wine that today is considered one of the finest of the entire region.

Jean-Claude loves his work and his wine shows it, winning prizes year after year, appearing in wine guides and consistently producing quality wines at affordable prices. Over the years, we dropped some of the more famous wines, which became prohibitively expensive, and replaced them with some of the local wines that were brilliant and one third the price. I gave up paying for labels on my clothing years ago and the same holds true for wines. I don't need an animal on my shirt, and I don't need a fancy label on my wine.

The Brelières, Jean-Claude and his wife Anna, became our good friends over the years and, happily, have remained so. Jean-Claude's father still helped out in the vineyards in those early days and he introduced us to his private stock of *Marc de Bourgogne,* a potent drink whose manufacture is closely regulated. It was superb!

Jean-Claude also speaks fluent English, which made *dégustations* a particular joy for our guests. He never tired of explaining why and how a wine is created, the various methods of storage, how the type of wood used for the casks and the age of the wood can affect the wine's taste, and the precise moments at which a vintage can be destroyed or assured.

He showed us a little gadget he uses that can analyze the grape juice at various stages of growth and fermentation to determine its sugar content and readiness for the next stage in the process.

Jean-Claude uses his barrels for only a given number of years and then discards them. The huge metal vats used for fermentation of certain wines must be pressed down from above so that the foam is distributed and it ferments evenly.

One year, while we were there on a buying expedition, we watched as Jean-Claude decided to try an experiment and do it the old-fashioned way. A young man, stripped down to his shorts (it was done naked in the old days) was suspended by chains and used his weight to press down the fermenting froth. I've got the photos to prove it.

The chains were used, in ancient times, because the heady aromas of fermentation could knock the poor fellow out and drowning was not an uncommon result. In fact, good ventilation is essential even today, because as one vintner told us, the fumes when you arrive first thing in the morning can be potent and have been known to kill any unfortunate field mice that venture in during the night.

Aside from educating us about wine, Jean-Claude and Anna showed us the human side of rural France. During the season, they and we were all too busy with our respective work to socialize much, but, before and after the busy times, the evenings spent together were a delight. Anna, of Italian heritage, makes the best lasagna I've ever tasted, from scratch, and it's beyond description. She and Jean-Claude are both lively, animated people, so times together were never dull. After the kids were put to bed, the conversation continued long into the night. Jean-Claude brought out his best wines and his father's Marc and we had every reason to be content with life.

Near the Brelière vineyard is another one which lies in front of the Chateau de Rully. The vineyard is owned by the Guyot-Verpiot family and their wines and *Cremant de Bourgogne* are excellent. *Cremant* is a champagne-like drink and I'd rather have a good *Cremant*, like the one the Guyot-Verpiots make, than a champagne that is less than excellent. Visit them, too, when you're in Burgundy. They speak no English, but the pleasure they take in what they do so well is universal.

The chateau that dominates their vineyard, owned by the *Comte de Ternay*, is magnificent, set high on a hill and straight out of a fairy tale. When one of the deans from Harvard and his wife, Ethel, who remained good friends even after I left the University, were visiting the inn, they expressed a desire to see how the chateau looked inside, so Madame Guyot-Verpiot telephoned the *Comte de Ternay* and he was kind enough to invite us all over for a visit.

The *Comte de Ternay* is a Paul Newman look-alike who is absolutely charming. He greeted us at the door, graciously welcomed us inside, turned his Gallic charm and piercing blue eyes set in an incredibly handsome chiseled face on the dean's wife, and proceeded to transport her into another world.

During the visit, the count saw Ethel admiring a magnificently carved Louis XV armchair whose upholstered tapestry fabric was, however, terribly frayed and falling apart. He smiled at her, blue eyes twinkling, and softly said, *"Oui, Madame.* It needs repair…but the roof needs it more."

As we left, after having her hand kissed by the count, Ethel calmly announced, with a far-away look on her face, "I want a divorce."

She and the dean, however, are still very happily married and great fun to be with. We've often reminisced, in the years since their visit to Burgundy, about our trips together each morning to the *patisserie* to buy the *baguettes* and *croissants* for breakfast.

When we first arrived in Burgundy, we decided to include some wines from *Beaune* on the wine list. The annual wine sales, in October, attract buyers from all over the world, and it is the wine center of Burgundy. *Beaune* is also a busy tourist area, known for its ancient *Hospice*, which was the first attempt at a hospital and is architecturally unique. The colored tile roof is magnificent and the "hospital" part looks very modern until you find out that, in times of great sickness and plague, there were two people per bed, which is why the beds are open to aisles on each side to make access easier for the nurses.

We visited the very commercial cellars of *Chateau Meursault* in *Beaune*, enjoyed many *dégustations* with them, and suggested that guests at the inn do the same for the experience. We had their wine on our wine list for the first two years. Then, even though the economy started going down, their prices kept going up, so, between their base restaurant-prices and our modest mark-up, they became so expensive that a bottle of *Meursault* would have cost twice as much as the dinner it was designed to go with.

The French will pay these prices for wine without a murmur, but the tourists won't, so we searched out and found excellent local wines, without the famous names, that were just as good.

One such discovery came from our *comptable*, our accountant, Bernard, who mentioned one day that his father had a vineyard in Beaune. Mounsier Gilbert Lucuelle produces a *Beaune Premier Cru* which is just as good as any *Meursault* wine I've ever tasted and far less expensive. Besides, Monsieur Lucuelle and his wife are kind, warm-hearted people and it's always a pleasure to visit them and catch up on the latest news. Bernard is now a proud father and Gilbert and I can now compare our hip surgery x-rays, so some things change while others, thankfully, remain the same.

As for white wines, my favorite, *Pouilly-Fuissé*, was found at the vineyards of Roger Luquet at *Fuissé*. After our first visit to this small vineyard, we were no longer strangers, and the welcome each time we returned was warm and genuine. It still is, these many years later.

The wine from our local *Dracy le Fort* vineyard, just up the road from the inn, was called *Deliance*. It's an excellent wine but of limited production, so either it had to be snapped up fast or ordered well in advance. The wines of Givry were the preferred wines of King Henri IV, who visited the area often. The fact that he also had a mistress there could have been part of the fascination, but that's not publicized by the local Chamber of Commerce.

Choosing champagne meant a trip to the champagne region since, to be called true Champagne, it must be produced there. *"Moët & Chandon,"* so popular in America, is certainly a nice enough *Champagne*, but, unless you order huge quantities, the distributors really don't want to be bothered with small outfits like *Aux Trois Saisons*, so they were eventually removed from the wine list and replaced by a superb, if lesser known, champagne from a smaller vineyard. To my taste, it was just as good and it was half the price.

Unless you're talking about a fine *"Perrier-Jouet,"* which is the preferred *Champagne* of the French and well worth the high price, you don't have to pay a fortune for a good *Champagne*. It just takes some searching. Or, as I suggested already, try to find a good *Cremant* and sit back and enjoy.

Our *Carte de Vin* ultimately offered a wide selection, and we had found all of the entries ourselves through trial and error. When you go to Burgundy, try some of these smaller vineyards and avoid the glitzy, over-priced, over-hyped labels. You're paying for their advertising and their rent, not necessarily for the quality of the wine they're offering.

Do your own *dégustations*; meet the people and the wines they're so proud of. To go with the wine, I perfected my recipe for *Boeuf Bourguignon* and, if I may be immodest, it's terrific.

BOEUF BOURGUIGNON

Ingredients:

2 lb	lean beef, cut into 2" cubes
2 c	good red wine
1/4 lb	(1 stick) butter
4 tbs	vegetable oil
6	shallots
1 1/2 tbs	flour
1/2 tsp	salt
1 1/2 c	small mushrooms
1/2 tsp	thyme
1	bay leaf
4	peppercorns
10	small white onions
3	cloves garlic, chopped
12	carrots cut into 1-inch slices
	Bouquet garni (see recipe for Canard aux Huitres)
	Cognac

Preparation:

Place the meat cubes in the dry red wine and marinate overnight. Sauté the shallots in the butter in a large deep kettle until golden. Drain the meat cubes, pat them dry, sprinkle them with flour, and brown gently on all sides in the butter. To prevent sticking, a little vegetable oil may be added while browning the meat. Add the red wine in which the meat marinated to the kettle. Then add the salt, garlic, thyme, bay leaf, peppercorns, bouquet garni, and enough water to cover the meat. Cover the kettle and simmer for 1 hour. Remove the bouquet garni and add the white onions and carrots and cook for 1 hour more. Then add the mushrooms and cook for 1/2 hour more. More water and/or red wine may be added to maintain the consistency as the meat simmers. To thicken, a loose flour/water paste should be slowly and carefully stirred into the mixture as it cooks. The final ingredient, 15 minutes before serving, is a few tablespoons of a good Cognac. The alcohol content will disappear with cooking, but the flavor it leaves will greatly enhance the dish.

Helpful Hints:

Boeuf Bourguignon is even better when made the day before, or early on the same day, and re-heated. I always served it over a bed of noodles to soak up the rich gravy sauce. And, whenever cooking with wine, be sure to use a wine that's good enough to drink on its own. The flour/water mixture is used just as a thickener. In some recipes, you will see the term roux. A roux is, technically, a mixture of flour and fat. Béchemel is a basic roux-based white sauce to which is often added chicken stock or white wine. The general belief is that this is named after Louis de Béchemel, who was the Marquis de Nointel and Louis XIV's steward. If you add some finely grated cheese to Monsieur Béchemel's namesake, you've made a Sauce Mornay . Very versatile!

The Courtyard During Renovations

The Courtyard After Renovations and New Gravel

AUX TROIS SAISONS

Our Own Harvest

The Dining Room from the Kitchen—Before

The Dining Room from the Kitchen—During

AUX TROIS SAISONS

Dinnertime

The Salon

MORT SOBEL

The Library—Before

The Library—After

AUX TROIS SAISONS

The Library—A Quiet Corner for Reading

Suite de Jardin

Suite de Jardin

AUX TROIS SAISONS

Suite de Jardin

The Original Kitchen with its Bread Oven from 1622

AUX TROIS SAISONS

Bienvenue—Welcome

Chapter 17
Grand Opening

The weekend of the Grand Opening arrived and we were expecting our first and only guests, a Monsieur and Madame Festjens from Belgium.

The week before their arrival, France was hit by another of those *grèves*, the strikes for which France is famous. This strike was against the postal system, and we had not yet bought the FAX machine and many years would pass before emails came into existence.

A letter arrived from the United States the day before the strike began, asking for a brochure and rate information. I typed the response, put it, along with the rate sheet and brochure, into an envelope, sealed the envelope, and we got into the car and drove two hours to Geneva, Switzerland, to post it. Not a very auspicious beginning, but one learns to deal with these minor inconveniences in France.

The Festjens were arriving from Belgium and had reserved a room for two nights on the recommendation of a mutual friend from Paris. They were on their way down to the south of France and *Aux Trois Saisons* was the perfect mid-way stopping point on their journey. They turned out to be well-traveled, multi-lingual, friendly, and, like so many of our Belgian guests, extremely knowledgeable about food and wine.

The finest chocolates in the world, the Neuhaus chocolates, are found in Belgium, as well as some of the best restaurants in Europe. *Bruges* is one of the prettiest cities in all of Europe and *Brussels* has a pastry shop called *"Wittamer"* that is beyond description. It's in the old *Sablon* antique district and well worth a trip to Belgium.

The Ferstjens arrived late in the afternoon and were accompanied by Beau, a beautiful, sleek, long-haired dachshund. Beau jumped out of the car, sniffed the shrubbery, and, it having met with his approval, turned his attention to *Mademoiselle*.

Beau comes from a long line of champions; *Mademoiselle* was obviously impressed, and Beau, showing a taste for older, taller ladies, reciprocated. While we helped Monsieur and Madame Festjen with their luggage, *Mademoiselle* and Beau trotted alongside. Then the two of them disappeared—simply walked off together—and the next we saw of them, *Mademoiselle* was calmly walking with her new admirer through the doorway leading from the salon to the library. Ever the perfect hostess, she had shown him around her home, both of them ignoring their two-legged families.

Mademoiselle, by the way, adjusted beautifully to life at the inn. She dutifully accompanied us, at each sound of a car in the gravel courtyard, tail wagging, to welcome the arriving guests.

Those first few "trial" months, since she already knew many of the people who arrived, I'm sure that she just felt they were visiting her in her new home. Then, in the years to come, she simply continued welcoming all of her returning friends, and made some special new ones herself.

Dinner times were busy for *Mademoiselle*, as well. She sat quietly in her corner of the kitchen while the meal was being prepared and while the courses were brought out to the dining room. Then, between the cheese course and dessert, she made the rounds of the tables, seeing that her guests were satisfied.

Breakfasts were her favorite, especially if one of her guests happened to offer a piece of baguette or croissant or breakfast meat as a "Thank You" token. Every year she received birthday cards from her admirers and, often, little gifts as well. She became an important part of *Aux Trois Saisons*.

That first official weekend at the inn was incredibly pleasant for all of us. Madame Festjen's hobby was book-binding and her husband was a well known author and collector of rare books, so the talk flowed easily during the cocktail hour. I was so fascinated by these lovely people that I sat a bit longer than I should have.

Just as Monsieur Festjen was telling me that he was a *Chevalier de Tastevin*, which means a fully recognized wine and food expert, and would be pleased to invite me to the next meeting, I smelled something.

I calmly excused myself, and retreated to the kitchen. When Dierk followed, in a few minutes, he saw his partner running frantically around, hysterically trying to re-prepare in fifteen minutes a main course that I had spent one hour painstakingly putting together that afternoon and which I had just managed to burn.

To this day, I don't know how I did it, but dinner was only seventeen minutes late that night and my *chevalier* was kind enough to say that it was good.

The Festjens became regulars at the inn and Madame Festjen insisted on re-binding one of the old books in our library that had seen better days. Monsieur autographed and presented us with his latest book, which has a place of honor on our bookshelves in Paris. It is called *"Anniversaires de l'Histoire"* and is a fascinating look at some people who share the same birthday and the important events which happened on each day in history.

They returned year after year, stopping on their way south and on their way back, despite something disastrous happening each time they stayed with us. Another year, they were our first guests of the season and the only ones in the tower that night and I had forgotten to turn on the separate hot water heater that served both tower rooms. It took only a few hours for the water to reach bathing temperature, but there was not a word of complaint about the inconvenience, nothing to indicate that we had done anything wrong. They're just, good, kind people who probably are, at this very moment writing a book about their strange experiences at an inn in Burgundy.

All of the meticulous planning, scheduling, choreographing of the inn's operation resulted in our making it look easy, but that's probably because nothing was left to chance.

The Menus were planned so that their preparation and serving could be done by just the two of us and several courses could be prepared well ahead of the dinner time. The *Boeuf Bourguignon,* for example, was made early in the day and tasted even better when it was reheated for dinner and served over a bed of tagliatelli noodles.

I devised fourteen special Fixed Menus, which we presented on a rotating basis, so that guests staying more than a few days wouldn't have the same dinner twice, and there was more than enough variety in the courses that comprised the Menus to please every taste.

Guests could make minor changes to the Menus, but no major substitutions or I would have to prepare several dinners at the same time, an impossible task for one person. We served six separate courses: usually a cold soup, like a chilled cucumber soup, or a hot soup, like my special Mozart Soup, to begin with; then a salad; fish course; main course; cheese; and dessert.

The breakfast, cocktail, and dinner hours—all were specifically scheduled for very practical reasons. It seems, now that I describe it, an operation of almost military precision. It had to be or else we both would have ended up running around in circles.

The guests were, for the most part, wonderful. They cooperated because, I think, they realized what we were trying to do, and that we needed their cooperation if we were to be able to provide the quality, service, friendliness, and assistance that we offered with just the two of us. A larger staff would incur higher charges and, also, make it a different type of operation.

Breakfast, for example, was served only until 9:30 for the simple reason that every minute from then on was accounted for. By 11:00 each day we had already completed check-outs for departing guests. Dierk had stripped the beds so that the two washing machines could be started; I cleared up after breakfast and loaded the dishwasher; we both had begun cleaning the rooms, and I would be halfway out the door on my way to do the shopping for dinner.

During breakfast, *Mademoiselle* and I would make the rounds of the tables, tell the guests what we were going to have for the Fixed Menu at dinner, and find out if they would be joining us. That way, I knew how many people to prepare for and there was no waste, which is usually a major problem for ordinary restaurants.

Fortunately, there were two of us and, between us, Dierk and I did the work of six. One of the reasons for the inn's functioning as well as it did was the fact that neither of us stood on ceremonies when it came to doing things. Whoever was free at that moment simply *did* what needed doing without score-keeping of who did what when.

A harder working, more level-headed, easy-to-get-along-with person than Dierk just doesn't exist. He is soft spoken, can do anything he sets his mind to, and do it well, and is meticulously thorough about anything he does. He also has a sense of humor only a little less outrageous than my own. So even with the eighteen-hour per day schedule we kept to, we still managed to see the ridiculousness of certain things and people, laugh about it and them, and then get on with the work.

We tried to divide the major responsibilities and each assume the responsibility for certain chores. I did the shopping and cooking while Dierk took care of the garden and seeing that the rooms were clean enough to pass his Germanic scrutiny. It wasn't enough for the bathroom faucets to be clean, they had to be wiped with a dry cloth so that they sparkled and there wasn't a spot on them or the fixtures. Have you ever checked into a hotel and discovered water spots on the faucet? It just doesn't *feel* clean, does it?

Dierk kept thirty-five vases filled with fresh flowers each day, which, with the high cost of flowers in France, would have broken our entire budget if we had to buy them. He planted a variety of flowers and kept a constant supply coming indoors from the garden.

We both did the ironing together, setting up the ironing boards in front of the television and enjoying an hour and a half of French-dubbed American soap operas while we ironed the sheets and pillow cases. Have you ever slept in a hotel bed that just didn't *smell* clean? That, we did not want.

After a few weeks of this, however, I was hooked on *Les Foux de L'Amour*, which is "The Guiding Light" in the US, I think. If the French judge all Americans by what they see on French television, as they undoubtedly do, we're all incredibly rich and beautiful creatures with buff bodies, perfectly coiffed hair, we live in mansions with enormous kitchens the size of some restaurants in Paris, and are unbelievably screwed up. Of course, some of the American tourists descending from tour buses in Paris soon dispel most of this image…or do they?

The Festjens began what would be a most enjoyable season, although a not-too-busy one. We expected that the first two years would be slow and decided to leave ourselves with enough money in reserve to cover basic expenses in case we ended up sitting all alone in a big house and staring at each other.

It didn't turn out that way at all.

CHILLED CUCUMBER SOUP

Ingredients:

2	cucumbers
1	small onion, sliced
1/2 c	water
1/4 tsp	salt
	a dash of pepper
1/2 c	crème fraiche
2 c	chicken stock
1	bay leaf
2 tbs	flour
2 tbs	dill
	(any additional crème fraiche, as desired)

Method of preparation:

Cook cucumbers (peeled, seeded, and sliced thin), water, onion, salt and pepper, until soft. Remove the softened cucumber pieces, reserving the liquid for later use to thin or thicken if necessary. Put the softened cucumber pieces into the food processor bowl and blend until very smooth. Place the cucumber puree into a pot. Dissolve flour in the chicken stock and add to cucumber mixture. Add a bay leaf, simmer for several minutes and then remove from heat. Add dill to the pot while simmering and adjust the texture of the soup with the liquid saved from step 1. CHILL for at least several hours or overnight. (Remove bay leaf). Just before serving, add the crème fraiche. Start with 1/2 cup and add any more that you want to according to your taste. Serve very cold with a sprig of fresh dill as a garnish.

MOZART SOUP

Ingredients:
- 4 large onions
- 2 tbs vegetable oil
- 6 stalks leek (only the white parts)
- 1 lb mixed chopped meat (pork and beef)
- 1 c sliced mushrooms
- 4 c beef broth
- 1 large package (16 pie-shaped wedges) of soft cheese (such as La Vache qui Rit)

Preparation:
Chop the onions into small pieces and fry in the oil just until the onions are transparent. Cut the leeks into thin slices, add to the onions, and gently cook for about 5 minutes. Barely crumble the meat and add to the onion-leek mixture. Brown slightly. Add the 4 cups of the beef broth and the sliced mushrooms. Simmer for 30 minutes. Remove 1 cup of the broth from the simmering pot. If using La Vache que Rit (the wedges come individually wrapped in foil), separate the wedges and whisk them into this hot broth until they are completely dissolved. Return the stock/cheese mixture to the simmering soup and cook for 10 minutes more. Add salt and pepper to taste. Serve hot.

Note:
This soup can be made the day before, refrigerated, and then reheated. It may also be frozen for later use. Either way, it's delicious, and nobody will be able to guess that the secret ingredient is melted cheese.

Note #2:
In case you're wondering why this is called Mozart Soup, it's because one particular year, Salzburg was chosen to be honored as the European Cultural City, and Mozart, of course, as a native son, was prominently featured all year. It's in his honor that this soup was named.

Chapter 18
Le Guide Rivage

During that first winter in Paris, we visited the office of the *Guide Rivage* on *Boulevard Saint Germain*. The *Guide Rivage,* also called the "Green Guide," was used by French-speaking people throughout Europe and considered to be the best of its kind. It featured photos and write-ups of each establishment and did not accept any payment at all for this, unlike some other guides.

The person we spoke to was pleasant and took our information and one of our brochures and we left thinking that, even if nothing came of it, at least we had tried.

I'll never know whether it was that we had made the effort and hit it right or if somebody else had told them about the inn, but near the beginning of the following year, we received a call for a reservation for one night, with dinner, from a pleasant sounding young man.

He arrived with a very pretty young lady; we showed them to their room and, as always, asked if they would like to see the rest of the house and the park. Midway between the salon and the dining room, I saw them smile at each other, and nod knowingly. We continued the tour and

I could see that Dierk was not particularly impressed with the fact that the young man's shirt was halfway out of his trousers and, although nice enough, he really didn't look particularly special.

They loved dinner, lingered over their wine in the candle-lit dining room, then sat in front of the fireplace in the salon and seemed very content with *Aux Trois Saisons* and all it offered.

The next morning, after he paid their bill, the young man volunteered the reason for their visit. He was, he explained, a representative of a travel guide; they had heard about the inn and his visit had convinced him that it was exactly what their guide was looking for. Would we be interested, he asked, in having the inn featured in their guide? We would, of course, we said, thanked him, got on with the day's work and thought nothing more of it.

During the following winter, when we returned to check the property, as we did periodically from Paris, there was a message on the telephone answering machine at the inn. When I returned the call, I asked the person, as I always did, who had recommended him.

"Oh, I saw you in the *Guide des Auberges et Hôtels de Charme en France*," was his reply.

"The what?"

"*Le Guide…*"

I made the reservation, hung up the telephone and flew out the door to find the nearest book-seller and there we were:

We never saw the young man again, but, wherever you are, "Thank You!" You literally made the inn a success.

French friends had said that *de bouche á oreille*, word of mouth, was the best way for the inn to grow as we wanted it to while allowing us to maintain the intimacy and quality we wanted. True, the word of mouth was beginning to show signs of success even after the first full season, but it wasn't until the inn appeared in that French *Guide*, also sold in

Belgium, Switzerland, Canada and Italy, that it really took off. And, in subsequent years, the *Guide Rivage* was actually translated into German, English and Italian and we got calls from all over Europe and wherever those languages were spoken.

From then on, its continued success was assured. And the nicest thing is that we never paid one cent to be in this guide. They chose to maintain their standards by doing anonymous spot-checks, but they never told us if they did, and we were in the guide every year after that. The *Guide Rivage* was eventually bought out by Fodor's.

Some British guests also wrote to the "Good Hotel Guide" by Hilary Rubinstein, and the inn was in that, too. Between the two guides, and the fact that about sixty persent of our guests were return visitors, either by themselves or bringing family and friends back with them to show off the inn, by the third year of operation, we felt confident about *Aux Trois Saisons*' future.

During the third year we also had a charming Swiss lady who arrived with her mother for two nights. They loved their room, raved about the dinner, took long walks in the inn's park along the stream, and were delighted by everything. When they left, the lady turned to me and said, "I'm going to send you a surprise next week."

A surprise it was. The lady, it turned out, is a journalist who writes for *"24 Heures,"* one of the leading Swiss newspapers. Her surprise was a story about the inn, or, as she called it, *"Le Jardin Enchanté."*

It was sheer poetry, telling of the house, the walks along the trout stream, the boxwood hedges along the paths, the nightingale's songs after dark, the sound of the owl who lived in the park, the candle-lit dinner, soft music, meticulous service and friendliness she had found in her "Enchanted Garden."

As long as three years after the article first appeared, we had guests who had clipped it out of the newspaper and saved it waiting for the day when they could call and arrange to stay at the inn themselves. Her "surprise" was one of the nicest ways anyone had ever thanked us for our efforts.

There were many others to come.

BOURGOGNE

Auberge Aux Trois Saisons

Dracy-le-Fort - 71640 Givry (Saône-et-Loire)
Tél. 85.44.41.58 - Fax 85.44.46.53
MM. Völckers et Sobel

Ouverture de Pâques à mi-octobre **Chambres** 5 avec tél.direct, s.d.b., w.c. et t.v. sur demande **Prix** des chambres simples et doubles : 400 F, 450 F - Petit déjeuner 45 F **Cartes de crédit** Carte bleue, Eurocard, MasterCard et Visa **Divers** Chiens admis avec 25 F de supplément - Parking à l'hôtel **Possibilités alentour** : château de Germolles ; château de Rochepot ; Buxy ; la vallée des Vaux - Golf 18 trous de Chalon-sur-Saône, parc des loisirs de Saint-Nicolas **Restaurant** : service à 20 h - Menu : 135 F - Spécialités bourguignonnes et américaines.

Véritable amoureux de la France, le docteur Sobel a abandonné l'université de Harvard pour venir s'installer dans cette ancienne gentilhommière. Cinq chambres ont été aménagées et décorées avec un goût parfait. Elles sont spacieuses, les poutres et les murs blancs en soulignent le côté authentique, tandis que descentes de lit en zèbre, édredons en *patchwork*, fleurs fraîches et chocolats sur la table de nuit témoignent d'un souci de raffinement. Les salles de bains, dotées de peignoirs douillets et de savons parfumés, concourent beaucoup à cette atmosphère de luxe. Autour de la maison, pommiers, cerisiers et pêchers invitent à se promener jusqu'à la rivière qui délimite la propriété. A 19 h 30, l'hôte propose l'apéritif puis s'éclipse à la cuisine afin de terminer les préparatifs du dîner servi à 20 h. Les tables éclairées aux chandelles, la qualité des plats et le fond musical discret en font un moment rare. A noter que malheureusement l'auberge n'accueille pas les enfants.

Itinéraire d'accès (voir carte n° 19) : à 28 km au sud de Beaune par N 74 et N 6 jusqu'à Chagny, puis D 981 jusqu'à 2 km avant Givry, à gauche vers Dracy-le-Fort.

Chapter 19
Good Times And Others

The people were what made it all worthwhile and the inn attracted some great ones. Hanging in our flat in Paris is a drawing of *Aux Trois Saisons* done by LeRoy Neiman, with an inscription saying that it was "sketched well rested on a full stomach." He and his wife Janet visited the inn on a detour from an exhibit of his paintings in the Bernheim Gallery in Paris.

LeRoy and Janet Neiman are delightful people and, when they made reservations, we decided not to book any other guests for the day they were with us. We took them on a tour of some of the villages and chateaux around the inn and then to Jean-Claude's vineyard for a *dégustation*. LeRoy was busily sketching all the time and found Jean-Claude's father a fascinating subject. I think he became part of a painting that LeRoy did of his Burgundy experience.

Before they left us, I saw them walking in the garden and LeRoy was, as usual, busy sketching something on his ever-present pad. He presented it to us as a parting gift and dedicated the back of the sketch to us. It was a spontaneous gesture of friendship that will always be a special treasure.

But we also brought out the artist in other less famous guests. When an English family visited us, I looked out the kitchen window to see their teen-aged son sitting cross-legged in the garden one afternoon for about two hours. He later proudly gave us the result of his afternoon's work, a beautifully detailed pencil drawing of the 1622 tower.

A woman from Massachusetts, who had been an amateur artist for all of her life, did a dream-like sketch of the house, which we also have framed in Paris. She sent a long thank-you letter to us for her visit to what she referred to as a "paradise."

The elderly, tall, distinguished gentleman who was so warm and friendly to everyone during the cocktail hour, and so genuinely interested in what they had to say, turned out to be Monsieur H. who, in his younger days, had been very high up in the Belgian government and private secretary to the king. Only when other Belgian guests recognized his signature in the guest book did we discover that *Aux Trois Saisons* had been host to a person of such importance.

His wife called frantically from the south of France, after another visit, saying that she couldn't find her ring, a family heirloom. We looked high and low for it, found it wedged between two pillows in the sitting area of their room, called her back, and gave it to her when they came back on their return trip north to Belgium.

One afternoon, two women, both in their sixties, arrived at the inn for a two-day visit. One was very quiet but both were very nice. We always had music during the dinner hour and that particular night some Pavarotti tapes were playing. While I was helping Dierk clear the dishes off the tables between courses, I started humming along. When one of the ladies—the quiet one—started humming along, I promptly stopped clearing the dishes, and right there, in the middle of dinner, oblivious to all the other guests, we both happily sang along with Luciano. The other guests laughed and applauded when we finished our impromptu concert and the lady was grinning from ear to ear.

Later, when she had gone up to bed, her friend tapped on the kitchen door as I was washing up and said "Thank you" with tears in her eyes. She explained that she and her friend had known each other for over fifty years. They had been schoolmates, remained friends all their married lives, and now her friend was in the terminal stage of her battle with cancer with not too much longer to live. It was the first time in years, she said, that she had seen her friend smile. I finished my chores that night very grateful that *Aux Trois Saisons* could have provided those few moments of happiness.

There was also the night when, purely by coincidence, we had three couples celebrating their wedding anniversaries. It was the first, the fifth, and the fiftieth anniversary for the respective couples, so I baked a large cake as dessert, decorated it with a "1", "5", and a "50", and we opened a bottle of Champagne to celebrate with them.

All three couples were delighted. One of the other guests in the dining room that night, as glasses were raised in a toast, turned toward the fifty-year couple and said, "Here's to the next fifty." Without a moment's pause, the elderly lady said, simply, "God help me!" then turned to her husband with a wink and a mischievous smile.

On another weekend, one of Switzerland's most famous prize-winning authors, a gentleman who was a distant relative of Jacqueline Kennedy's French ancestors, had reserved all the rooms at the inn for himself and his wife and their children and spouses.

The occasion was his birthday party, but the party was almost ruined. His wife caught Dierk as he was dashing about between chores and announced that her husband couldn't come down to dinner because he had cracked his dental bridge. Dierk consulted the "house dentist," me, just as I was preparing the ingredients for that evening's *Roulade de Veau* and *Timbale d'Epinard,* and I went up to their room.

The poor man was sitting there dejectedly shaking his head. All of this preparation for nothing, and the family had come in from all over for the event. I examined the wreckage, took the pieces back to my kitchen, got out the old Duco cement, had things back in order in ten minutes, and we had a great party that night, my new friend smiling up a storm.

A week later, we received a copy of his latest book inscribed to us and thanking us for a memorable visit. It's also in the bookcase in Paris, along with Monsieur Festjen's book.

The inn's reputation grew and, eventually, an article appeared in the American Embassy newsletter about these two Americans who had shown the French a thing or two about running a small, intimate inn. The article was written by a fellow named Bill W. and he came with some other embassy friends the first time, then returned with the young woman he was going to marry.

Bill and Kirsten loved the inn and decided to spend their honeymoon the next year at *Aux Trois Saisons*. Bill wanted to go hot-air-ballooning when they returned, so, jokingly, I said, "Okay, if you come back and go ballooning, I'll go with you!" never expecting Bill to say, "Book it."

I'll tell you more about this in a little while.

A comment here, in passing, about the U.S. Embassy people we met. Word travels fast on the embassy grapevine. After the first satisfied people, we had a series of Americans over the years who were, with no exceptions, marvelous. America has reason to be proud of these people and they're worth every penny we spend. They're exceptionally well trained and prepared to respect other people's and nations' customs and feelings. If America has to be judged by its representatives abroad, we couldn't ask for a finer, more dedicated group of people. They gave us many happy hours and memories too numerous to go into detail now, but they're terrific and we're grateful to have met them and still cherish many of them as friends.

The Paris Embassy people decided to stage a Murder Mystery Weekend and rented all of the rooms at *Aux Trois Saisons* for the entire weekend. It was the brainchild of Ginger Carney from Paris, who arranged it all in her inimitably effervescent way. Ginger and John came with Justin, who was then about nine years old and loved the garden. Justin is now 6'2" and starting college.

The ten guests arrived for the Mystery Weekend, in normal street dress, each one having been assigned, beforehand, the character he or she would play. Then each one changed and arrived for the cocktail hour in costume and in character. The evening's theme was the opening of "The Velvet Room," a speakeasy in the 1920s, and Dierk and I played the owners.

We set all the tables to one side of the dining room. The other side was the "bandstand" where Trixie, the slinky nightclub singer, would perform. Along the wall were the "gambling" tables. Of course, since it was during Prohibition, we couldn't serve any liquor, so we asked each guest if they wanted "tea" or "coffee" ("tea" was white wine, "coffee" was red wine) with the appropriate wink and leer, and actually served the drinks in tea or coffee cups rather than in wine glasses.

One of the other characters in the mystery was "Sister Mary," a nun, and the lady who played her had actually sewed the nun's habit and headdress herself. Then there were "Big Ed," "Pretty Boy Floyd" (who was the French fiancé of one of the embassy women and, indeed, very handsome), "Malone," the chief of police, and all the rest.

The dastardly deed was done, according to Malone's calculations, sometime between my *Roulade de Veau* with Spinach Timbales and Dessert. After Malone had solved the crime, using clues we had all dropped during the evening, everyone was having such a good time that someone suggested the evening be continued at the local real-life gambling casino in nearby Santenay. It was too late to change, so they decided to go in costume.

One of us had to stay at the inn, so Dierk took the whole group over to the casino while I stayed at *Aux Trois Saisons* to clean up. The next morning they were all still laughing. It seems that the casino's manager had almost had a fit when he saw this bunch arriving and poor "Sister Mary" was forced to check her head-dress.

I would have loved to be at the roulette table when one of our guests came out with, "Pray for me, Sister. I've got all my money on Red!"

The bridge tournament held at *Aux Trois Saisons* was another highlight, again with an embassy crowd, but this time they were from Geneva. They were very serious bridge players and would have played for three days straight, but we enticed them into visiting some local vineyards and that cut into card-playing time considerably.

Linda and Robert arrived from Paris. They are Canadian and, at that time, Robert was the Canadian Ambassador to the OECD. They were perfect guests, and we never ran out of things to say, especially since Linda and I share an unconditional love for Paris. Since she was based in Paris, she had discovered more than I about all the little hidden-away places that make the city so special.

The next winter, Linda took us on a special tour of the old covered *Passages* of Paris. This is another world hidden behind the huge archways one passes without realizing what lies beyond. Most of these *Passages* are in the area around the *Palais Royale* and were, in their day, the equivalent of today's shopping malls. People would parade through the ornately decorated corridors, pause to look into the stores, have lunch or tea in one of the restaurants, or visit the old book sellers, some of whose establishments are still there.

Linda invited us to the Canadian Residence for a memorable luncheon and we have remained in contact all through their various assignments and their return to Canada.

Just the opportunity to cross paths with someone like Helene Schaefer would have been worth all the work we put into creating *Aux Trois Saisons*. Mrs. Schaefer, widow of the gentleman of Schaefer beer fame, arrived at the inn with two ladies. They were fresh from a ballooning and barge trip on one of France's many canals. Mrs. Schaefer had given the trip as a gift to herself to celebrate her recent graduation from Manhattanville College in New York.

Mrs. Schaefer was eighty-nine years old at that time, and the two ladies with her, dressed in ordinary lay clothing, were Sister Ruth, a former Dean at Manhattanville, and Sister Eileen, one of Mrs. Schaefer's teachers and advisors. We fell in love with all three women, and, if I can mature with the grace and warmth of any one of them, and still retain my zest for life and my interest in all things, as Helene Schaefer has, I will be very grateful.

Since the late Mr. Schaefer was of the old school and, during their married life, she was busy with rearing her family and being a good wife and hostess, Mrs. Schaefer never had the time to go to college. When Mr. Schaefer died and her grandchildren came home with stories of how wonderful college was, she decided it was time to go back to school herself.

She enrolled at Manhattanville College when she was eighty-five years old and, on the first day of school, realized that she was having a hard time hearing the teacher. The next day, Helene Schaefer went right out and bought herself a hearing aid.

So much for technicalities!

The following year, when we went back to the States for a visit, Mrs. Schaefer invited us to lunch at her home in Westchester County. This incredible ninety-year-old lady greeted us at the door with an apology. She was sorry that lunch would be a simpler affair than planned. Her housekeeper, she explained, was not feeling well and she, Mrs. Schaefer, had been busy taking care of her. The housekeeper was a mere eighty-seven.

Aux Trois Saisons was also the scene of a cooking course. It started when a woman from London who is a "food stylist" called and suggested that we hold a joint cooking course, which she volunteered to advertise in England.

In case you don't know, because I certainly didn't, a "food stylist" is a person who arranges the food for the photographer to take the photos that appear in various books or magazine articles. It's actually a very interesting art because whipped cream, for example, will not last very long under hot lights, and, therefore, using something like shaving cream, which is not affected by the lights but looks like whipped cream on the photos, results in a scrumptiously photogenic dessert.

It's the same problem that exists in television, where designing things so that they look good for the camera requires great know-how and artistry. The lady in question had done similar things for various cooking publications in the past, so we agreed to let her arrange the "Cookery Course" and didn't take any other reservations for that weekend.

The ten people who arrived for the Cooking Course were all extremely nice and very happy with the arrangements, especially when we included several wine *dégustations* in the curriculum.

The "food stylist," who shall remain nameless, was indeed quite good at arranging the food on a plate. She placed the stalks of the *ciboulettes* very artistically, and dribbled the sauce so that it looked inviting. She was also positively obsessed with sprinkling substances like chocolate powder or curry powder over every spare inch of the plate, which Dierk, to this day, insists looked messy rather than artistic.

That evening at dinner, however, her only problem was that, in her efforts to create visual masterpieces, she completely forgot about the people sitting in the dining room. When I sensed another revolution brewing in France, this time on the part of hungry people waiting for their dinner, I quickly took over and, *ciboulettes* or not, served the food.

Fortunately, the "students" were all very understanding. At the graduation party, they all signed the *Livre d'Or* Guest Book and drew little cartoons of each person. It's, as you might expect, also in the bookcase in Paris. They left the inn with some great recipes and lots of tips for food preparation, so it was a success after all.

There were so many people, each with a special story. We seemed to attract people who were either themselves writers, or whose relatives were writers. I can tell you that Alex Haley and James Clavell, both of whom I never actually met, have delightful sisters-in-law, and the diplomatic and literary communities of Belgium and Holland number some very charming people.

One of the first American families to visit the inn came from Washington state and the two teen-age sons were perfectly behaved. They came to dinner dressed neatly and never complained about the dinner Menus even if they'd rather have had a hamburger than my special caviar mousse.

I finally cornered their father, who had treated his wife to the trip for their fifteenth wedding anniversary, and asked him if the boys were always so good. He smiled and said that he himself was in shock, because at home they were always arguing. Somehow, *Aux Trois Saisons* and our treatment of them as adults had worked wonders. The couple promised to return for their twenty-fifth anniversary.

The Collins family from Minnesota sends us a photo with their Christmas card each year, and we've watched the kids grow up and get married. Some other folks, from Georgia, gave us official Olympic pins, since one gentleman was on the U.S. Olympic Committee that was arranging the Games in Atlanta.

We had a group from the midwest who spent five days with us and toured Burgundy on their bicycles, pedaling from chateau to vineyard, and came home each day bubbling with excitement.

One guest, a Parisian, asked if he could take the Guest Book to his room the night before his departure. The next morning, he handed it to me, with a full two pages of poetry all about his stay at *Aux Trois Saisons*.

We had an adorable lady from Japan, first time out of Tokyo, and a young Russian couple who told the aunt from Paris who had brought them to us that Dierk and I were "heroes" for all the work we did.

We were brought candies from Sweden, waffle-cakes from Holland, and chocolate from Belgium. And all the guests from England brought us their marvelous laughter and great good humor. Very special gifts.

One more official chore, not related to the inn, had to be completed during that first full season: my French driver's license. I was allowed to use my American license for the first year but that time was almost over.

I enrolled in a driving school in nearby *Chalon-Sur-Saône*, took the obligatory course of instruction and, feeling confident that my many years of driving experience would make me a shoo-in, I took the road test. The examiner got into the car. I said *"Bon jour,"* smiled, buckled my seatbelt and took off. He grumbled something under his breath and told me to stop at the next corner.

"Hah, un arret americaine!" he shouted.

Now, I assure you, I did indeed come to a complete stop. Believe me. He, on the other hand, insisted that I had come to a rolling stop, so it was pretty evident that this gentleman had a thorn in an unmentionable place as well as something against American drivers.

I decided that if he was going to fail me anyway, which was a certainty, at least I'd have some fun. I took him for a ride he still probably hasn't forgotten. Red lights and stop signs meant nothing, pedestrians were hooted at every opportunity, and *Monsieur Instructor* was a sobbing mass of protoplasm by the time he jumped out of the car blubbering that I wanted to kill him.

The second time I took the road test, the instructor was a friendly gentleman who had an American neighbor and was looking forward to going to New York for a visit the following summer. We hit it off fabulously well, I did everything right, and we parted on good terms.

I had successfully passed the road test but I still had the written test to pass. It consisted of thirty-five slides shown on a screen, depicting various situations, and you have to choose the right answers to thirty of them then punch a hole in a little card next to the corresponding number.

The room was filled with about forty teenagers who, even if they couldn't read or write, and had never studied for another test in their entire lives, had obviously studied like mad to get their "wheels." Only one other student and I were older than eighteen.

When the thirty-five slides had been shown and we had all punched our cards, we were asked to individually bring the card up to the front of the room where the examiner had a briefcase that was actually a little computer. He passed the cards through it and it graded them right then and there, giving a short beep each time there was a wrong answer.

The first fifteen or so of my fellow "students" marched up and handed him their cards. Once in a while there was a beep, but they all marched away beaming with success.

It was my turn to give him my card. I marched up and smiled pleasantly at the gentleman. He smiled back, put the card into the machine, and it started beeping. To the amusement of the roomful of teenagers, it continued beeping and the examiner and I stared at each other in bewilderment.

This kind man leaned over and discreetly whispered in my ear, "Perhaps, Monsieur, it would be better if you take an oral examination?"

I stayed after all the others had left and he handed me a paper requesting the oral examination. As I was signing it, I read the word *analphabet*. I got out the dictionary as soon as I got home and discovered that the word *analphabet* means "illiterate." I prayed that none of my students at Harvard ever got wind of this.

I am pleased to say that I did, indeed, pass the test for the illiterate and am today the proud holder of a *Permit Conduire Français,* my French Driving License.

ROULADE DE VEAU (VEAL ROLLS)

Ingredients:

1 lb	veal, sliced in 4 thin pieces
2	sweet Italian sausages
1	small onion, finely chopped
3	cornichons (gherkins), finely chopped
½ tsp	Dijon mustard
6	capers, mashed
	paprika
	salt
	pepper
	flour
1	bay leaf
2 c	boiling water
½ c	crême fraiche or heavy cream for the sauce

Preparation:

Flatten the veal into very thin pieces. Place the meat from the Italian sausages in a frying pan and lightly brown. Salt and pepper the flattened veal lightly. Mix together all of the other ingredients. Place a tablespoon of the mixture in the center of the wider end of each piece of flattened veal. Fold sides up to filling then roll the veal up, fastening each one with a toothpick, and sprinkle with flour. Brown the rolled-up veal on all sides quickly in 2 tablespoons of oil to seal in the flavor and the juices. Add 2 cups of boiling water to the pan and one large bay leaf. Bring to a simmer, cover, and cook for about 45 minutes. Add more water if the pan begins to dry out. Just before you're ready to serve, remove the veal rolls from the pan, cut them into pieces (like a jelly-roll), and put them into the warming oven. Add 1/2 cup of crême fraiche or heavy cream to the pan liquids, stir with a whisk to form a sauce and pour over the Roulade pieces before serving.

TIMBALE D'EPINARD (SPINACH TIMBALES)

Ingredients:
- 2 c cooked fresh spinach
- 3 tbs cream cheese
- 4 eggs, well beaten
- 1/4 tsp salt
- 1/4 tsp nutmeg
- 1/8 tsp pepper

Preparation:
Wash and drain spinach, remove and discard stems. Put the spinach leaves into the food processor, add the other ingredients, and process until blended, not mushy. With a spoon, ladle the mixture into lightly greased individual ramekins to almost the top of the molds. Place the ramekins in a large baking pan and pour boiling water around them. Transfer the water-filled pan to a 400° oven and cook for another 30 minutes or until a toothpick inserted in the center of the mold comes out clean. Allow to stand for 5 minutes, loosen edges with a sharp knife and unmold onto the serving plate.

Note:
It's easier to unmold the timbales if you cut a piece of waxed paper the same size as the bottom of the mold, insert the paper in the oiled mold and then put the spinach mixture over this before putting it in the oven. This eliminates any chance of the spinach sticking to the mold and creating problems when unmolding.

Chapter 20
"Do you have any chickens?"

Lest you think that it was *all* sweetness and light, there were some genuine horrors. Before opening *Aux Trois Saisons*, we spoke with other people who owned inns and asked if they had any problems with their guests.

Most said that ninety-five percent of their guests were wonderful, on holiday to enjoy themselves and not to create problems if they're treated with courtesy and consideration. It was their own time they would be wasting.

The other five percent, they said, are just plain miserable people, whether they're on vacation or not. Poor souls, they cart around their anger and unhappiness wherever they go and spoil everything for themselves and others. Fortunately, one forgets them. Almost.

I'll never forget "Minsk and the Monster." Minsk, a lawyer from California, arrived with two other couples. All three gentlemen had ordered specially equipped European sports cars and parked them in the courtyard, which immediately made *Aux Trois Saisons* the talk of *Dracy le Fort*.

Unfortunately, Minsk, no bargain himself, arrived with a lady who was his "date" for the trip, a thoroughly awful woman he had picked up in a bar in L.A. and invited on the spur of the moment. The Monster made everyone's life miserable, nothing pleased her, and when Minsk and the Monster vacated their room, they left us with a mattress that was completely soaked through. They also departed with all of our expensive coat hangers—every single last one of them—which meant that, in between other chores, I had to rush out and buy replacements before the next guests arrived. That, Mr. Lawyer, is called "theft" in any language.

Madame W., who helped us with cleaning chores, bless her heart, just shook her head when she arrived, and we all pitched in, frantically trying to get the room clean. Getting a new mattress delivered within a few hours was impossible, so the three of us worked with hair-dryers, used two cans of room deodorant, and placed dishes of nice smelling *pot-pourri* all around the room.

It was in fine shape when the new people arrived, but we were wiped out.

I'll also never forget "The Three Graces." Those three young ladies had been referred to *Aux Trois Saisons* by one of their friend's fathers who had stayed at the inn. The girls, unfortunately, were turned off for precisely the reasons the friend's father had been turned on. They were annoyed because there was no disco on the property, no eligible young Frenchmen who would ravish them within five minutes of their arrival, and they were, quite simply, bored stiff.

On top of that, when they made their reservation, they had requested two rooms, one double and one single. When they arrived, they decided to save some money and all stay in one room and share two dinners between all three. We had, of course, forfeited the income from the second room and the potential third dinner, and probably could have charged them for it, but that wasn't the worst of it.

Let me describe The Three Graces. One of them, the one who had made the reservation that was completely different than what they really wanted, seemed like a fairly normal young woman. Stupid, perhaps, but not particularly offensive. The second one had an Ann Miller bouffant hairdo, a whining, nasal voice, and hated the inn, and us, on sight. The third one was built like a whale and had a perplexed look on her face, very much like the one I described on Renato, the chicken.

We hurriedly set up a folding bed for the third person in the room, for which we hadn't been warned, and you'll never guess who ended up on that, looking every bit as if she had been beached in a storm.

Later, during the cocktail hour on the terrace, the Ann Miller wannabe plunked herself down next to a very elegant Parisian lady, and nasally demanded, "Wotseahdudooheah?"

The lady from Paris, who along with her sister was a regular guest, looked her up and down, and, motioning with a graceful, bejeweled hand towards the park surrounding the house, said, "Enjoy."

They left the next morning, The Three Graces: Dumbo, Jumbo, and Bimbo.

I'll never forget "The Pungent Punkers." These two young French apparitions arrived with a reservation for two nights. She had her head almost shaven; he had one long pony-tail hanging from his otherwise completely shaven head. They both arrived wearing the same filthy T-shirts they had worn for three weeks and bearing an unbelievable stench. Even in the open courtyard, it could have knocked your shoes off.

Dierk and I looked at each other, gulped, and showed them to *Suite de Jardin*. We looked out of the kitchen window and saw them walking in the garden and decided that we just couldn't inflict them on the other guests. I was given the task of telling them that we expected proper dress in the dining room, which was the truth. They went out to eat that night and, to our relief, realized that they were in the wrong place and left the next morning.

It took a whole can of room deodorant to undo the harm they did to *Suite de Jardin*. Heaven knows what they've done to the ozone layer.

I'll never forget "The Strasbourg S & M"er whose check bounced three times before I threatened to contact his employer and he finally paid. He clanked into the courtyard swathed in leather and chains, appeared in the dining room in another equally fetching leather ensemble, had an animated chat with an architect from Paris who undoubtedly thought it *amusant*, and left several rather graphic magazines lying around his room that I'm certain Madame W. did *not* find amusing.

Or "Mrs. Magoo," the elderly woman with her elderly dog who simply opened doors and walked in…*any* door in sight, not necessarily the one to her own room.

Or the Swiss lady who had given us her order for breakfast the night before and then sent her husband down the next morning to demand breakfast in bed while we were busy scrambling eggs and pouring coffee and tea and hot chocolate. I told her husband that all I could do on such short notice was to put together a tray with coffee, a croissant, baguette, and jams. Madame was so furious that she put a huge gash in the shower curtain, which we discovered after they'd left.

Or "The Two Little Piggies," the American honeymoon couple who arrived with three huge suitcases and proceeded to unpack all three and throw the contents all over their room so that we had to climb over piles of clothing to be able to clean the room and make their bed. They then wore the same T-shirts and shorts for the entire three days of their visit. Madame W. told us the next day that when she saw them riding their rented bicycles through *Dracy le Fort* heading back to *Aux Trois Saisons*, she pointed to them and told her neighbor *"Regarde, les petite cochons rentrent chez eux."* "Oh look, the little piggies are going home."

Or the lady from the Paris suburbs who didn't like her room because it wasn't *"rustique"* enough. It was late in the season, I was tired, we were more than busy enough to fill the rooms with regulars who appreciated the inn, so I just looked at her and said, *"Oui Madame. The toilet is inside!"* She dragged her husband out and left in a huff.

But perhaps my favorite among the horrors was the woman from Brussels who telephoned for a reservation and asked if we accepted dogs. I replied that we did, made the reservation, and we, and *Mademoiselle*, looked forward to their arrival.

I was in the kitchen when we heard the car drive into the courtyard. I was busy washing or chopping something, so Dierk went out to greet them and help them with their luggage. I dried my hands and went out a few minutes later to meet them. I froze on the stairway.

There in the courtyard was Dierk, staring transfixed at one large dog. Near the entrance gates was a man running after another huge dog. A cat, much to *Mademoiselle's* disgust, was jumping down from the back seat of the large station wagon. Smoke was coming out of Dierk's ears.

There were, in all, three dogs, two cats, this incredibly weird Belgian woman, and her English husband, who was, perhaps, the weirdest of all.

As long as I live, I will never forget the cool calm with which Dierk, glaring at this insane woman, inquired, "Do you have any chickens?"

Fortunately, one *almost* succeeds in forgetting them because the great ones, the other ninety-five percent, are so very nice to remember.

Chapter 21
Up, Up, and Away

"Air Escargot" is the fitting name that Pierre and Christiane Bonnet have given to their hot-air balloon business in Burgundy. We first met them through Mrs. Schaefer when she and the two Sisters came to the inn and had reserved a montgolfier trip with Pierre.

The sport is named after the Montgolfier brothers, who started hot-air ballooning in France many years ago and actually took off from the Tuileries gardens in Paris on one of their first flights. If you look carefully, you'll see the plaque commemorating this near the Tuileries exit closest to the *Place de la Concorde.*

Pierre Bonnet had a passion for hot-air ballooning that started as a hobby and turned into a flourishing business. His wife Christiane is an ex-school teacher who now helps Pierre in their enterprise. Christiane is a tall, lovely woman with a beautiful smile. She drives the search car that follows along the balloon's route and always turns up at the landing site to greet the ballooners with the champagne that's been kept chilled in honor of their safe return.

I have vertigo, and, after the first two steps of a ladder I hang on to the wall for dear life. For the first two years at the inn, I resisted Pierre's invitation to take a trial flight as his guest.

I had run out of excuses by the time Bill, the fellow from the U.S. Embassy in Paris, returned to *Aux Trois Saisons* with his new bride all ready to take off in a balloon. When I had promised to go with them if their return happened to fall on my birthday in July, I never expected them to take me up on it.

July 29th arrived and the rain I had been praying for never materialized. It was a glorious morning, just perfect for ballooning. I was trapped.

I climbed into the basket of the balloon after it was partially inflated, said a silent prayer, closed my eyes and tried to avoid panic. The balloon took off, I opened my eyes, and there I was with the most marvelous bird's eye view of *Aux Trois Saisons*. The peace and calm defied description.

I had the feeling of just floating along, with the occasional noise from the burst of gas that makes the balloon ascend. The pilot can control the ascent and descent of the balloon and its rotation, but he can only control its direction side-ways by finding the proper air current. That's where the expertise comes in.

Pierre is an expert pilot so we had an incredible ride over the vineyards and chateaux of Burgundy. The people in *Dracy Le Fort* and the neighboring villages waved to us as we drifted over the towns; the dogs barked, and the cows went berserk in the fields. The chateaux, from this vantage point, were even more spectacular than up close. We barely missed the trees, scraping some leaves as we floated by. I forgot my fear and was in awe.

Pierre explained that vertigo generally only becomes a problem when a person is "attached" to the ground in some way. That's why a person with vertigo might get dizzy on a ladder but can look out of an airplane window at 10,000 feet and not be bothered at all.

After that first trip, I was hooked and went five times more, enjoying it more each time. Dierk did about fifteen trips before we became so busy that ballooning just didn't fit into our schedules while the inn was open.

But one year, Pierre and a professional photographer invited us to go along with them to the Alps in March before the inn officially opened. The photographer was doing a book about ballooning in snow country, and he was leaning out of the balloon madly snapping photos and telling Pierre to go "Higher, higher!"

We were up to an altitude of 12,000 feet with Mont Blanc in the distance, and the photographer was still precariously leaning out. When a small airplane flew beneath us, I retired to the bottom of the balloon, assumed the fetal position, crouched in a corner and, as calmly as I could, awaited impending death.

I "retired" my wings after my sixth flight, but those balloon trips were memorable. I often take out the photos and wonder at my own bravery.

… AUX TROIS SAISONS

Chapter 22
À la campagne, à Paris....

I am not, by nature, a country person. This probably stems from my earliest recollections of "the country."

When we were children, my parents, in their desire to provide my sister and me with a bit of fresh air and wide open spaces, neither of which were available in New York City, rented a small bungalow in the Catskill Mountains each summer. This was a major budgetary expense for them, but they thought it important enough, like the endless music lessons, for them to make other sacrifices.

My father would spend the week working in steamy, suffocating Manhattan, and then drive up in his 1948 Plymouth to be with us and, presumably, be revitalized for the week ahead by all that healthy air.

My sister and I hated every minute and we yearned for the city and all of our friends who were, like us, deprived but happy in their ignorance. We were bored.

In answer to our complaints, Mama's instructions were to "Go outside and BREATHE!" I dutifully did what she told me to do. My earliest recollections, therefore, of "the country" are of sitting in a field all alone, feeling guilty for my ingratitude, and hyperventilating.

Living in France, however, has taught me the value of sitting and just doing nothing special. It's called day-dreaming and I do it all the time now when I'm in Paris—without the slightest shred of guilt.

I've also, over the years, developed great respect for those people who invest their time and toil, not to mention risking their financial security, in that vast region outside of the cities, "the country," where existence can be so fragile.

Spending seven months of the year in rural France, I realized how hard and constant the work of the vintners and farmers really is, their total dependence on the elements, no vacations, long days and uncertain returns. And then I saw first-hand what one fifteen-minute storm could do to the vineyards of Burgundy.

A long time ago, for about two years, I lived in upstate New York, in that beautiful part of the northeast which is referred to as the "tri-state area." It's where New York, Massachusetts, and Vermont meet. My neighbors were the cows in the surrounding fields, and I saw the look on the face of one farmer when disaster struck his herd. It was one of the saddest looks I've ever seen on any man's face because it represented more than just the sorrow of financial loss for him and his family. It meant all the time and effort and hope that had been invested and were now gone.

The French countryside, too, is filled with the same hard-working, good people whose friendship, once given, is unconditional and honest. The difference is that the French counterpart may live in a 250-year-old stone house himself, and his neighbors may live in magnificent chateaux.

The *Chateau de Couches,* which commands the entire valley, was one of our neighbors at *Aux Trois Saisons,* and the *Chateau Le Rochepot,* also nearby, is a real-life Disney castle sitting high on a hill, its fairy-tale turrets singing a hymn to the majesty of human creativity and imagination.

As much as I love the French countryside, however, the major part of my heart remains in Paris, with its museums, theaters, excitement and vitality. *Aux Trois Saisons* gave us the chance to partake of, and enjoy, both worlds: the country and its pleasures during the time the inn was open; the city and its treasures, when it was closed.

In France, both city and country have one thing in common. The French have maintained the concept of the open *marché*, the market where local merchants set out their folding tables on the sidewalks, private cars dispossessed to side streets on those special days.

Shopping for food at these markets, although time-consuming, can be great fun and is a terrific way to meet people. There are dozens of open *marchés* in Paris, and each town outside of Paris has a weekly or bi-weekly market. Near *Aux Trois Saisons*, for example, the town squares of *Givry*, on Wednesday, *Chatenoy Le Royal*, on Thursday, and *Chalon Sur Saône*, on Friday and Saturday, are bustling and alive with sights and sounds each market day. The country *marché* may be a simple affair, with only one cheese merchant, one butcher, and one vegetable vendor. Quite different from the grand open *marché* on *Avenue du President Wilson* in Paris, where you can spend hours strolling and picking out the best food set out on the dozens of folding tables lining the center of the street. Crowds appear out of nowhere, each person toting a straw basket, or some plastic counterpart, into which go the fixings for that evening's meal.

My butcher in *Givry* knows just the size I want the chunks of meat for the *Boeuf Bourguignon* to be and carefully trims the fat away so that I have the right number of perfect pieces for each serving. The duck breasts for my *Canard Aigre-Doux* come from ducks, he proudly assures me, that were raised in nature, running freely about, not confined in some commercial factory-type establishment. And, of course, the chicken breasts, for my "Nutty Chicken" are all the blue-legged *poulets de Bresse*.

I think it's a matter of honor with him that I'm satisfied enough to return to him, trust him, and do not go across to his competitor. Madame, his wife, sits behind the cash register and finalizes each sale with a sing-song, *"Merci, et bonne journée, Monsieur."* French often seems to be sung rather than spoken and an inflection can turn an ordinary statement into a question or a challenge.

My cheese lady greets me with a cheery smile and chatter, begins poking her finger into a *Camembert* to see if it is *parfait* for serving tonight, and then with her mini-guillotine slices off however large or small chunk of *Brie de Meaux or Emmenthal* I choose. A little *morceau* of whatever else looks good and I'm off to the next merchant.

So it goes in the country and I'm certain to spend one and a half to two hours each morning as I make the rounds. It's the longest chunk of my day, not made easier by the fact that everything is bought fresh every day. The fruit bought today must be eaten by tomorrow or has to be discarded. Produce is picked and marketed at the height of its freshness because the French expect it and won't settle for less.

In Paris, I favor the *Grand Epicerie* supermarket at *Au Bon Marché* department store, even though it is a bit more expensive. It's an entire level containing just about anything you might want or need. There are several *paté* counters, exotic take-outs, very good fish and meat sections—although I buy these at my local merchants—a garden of fresh produce, and a full selection of paper goods and household needs. I visit there each time I return to Paris, stock up on some basic items, and then go to my favorite markets on either *Avenue du President Wilson or Rue Cler*.

Each Christmas in Paris, I usually order a pheasant and tell my friendly butcher on *Rue Cler* to save some feathers for me for decoration. He loves Americans, regales me with stories of his last trip to Las Vegas or Florida, and always greets me with a loud "Hallo" that can be heard a block away.

One year, he got a bit carried away and I arrived home with my pheasant all wrapped up and prepared in a thin layer of lard for cooking, as promised, with lots of feathers and *two* heads. It made for a most original presentation.

CANARD AIGRE-DOUX
(SWEET AND SOUR DUCK BREASTS)

Ingredients:

1	duck breast, with skin
2 tbs	vegetable oil
	salt
	pepper
1/4 c	Dijon mustard
1/2 c	apricot jam
1 tbs	soy sauce
1 tbs	honey

Preparation:

Combine the Dijon mustard, the apricot jam, the soy sauce, and the honey in a sauce pan and heat over medium heat until bubbling, stirring constantly. Reduce to a simmer and keep warm. In a separate skillet, heat the 2 tablespoons of vegetable oil until a drop of water will bubble when dropped into the pan. Lightly sauté both sides of the duck breast, just a minute or two on each side. Important: Do not overcook the duck breasts. When cut, they should be bright red inside, which means that they have been quickly sautéed but not overcooked. Remove the duck breasts from the sauté pan, cut into thin slices, and place several sliced on each person's plate, overlapping the slices slightly. Place some Mustard-Apricot sauce on each plate, to the side of the duck breasts, and have some extra in a sauce serving dish in case people want more. (They will!)

Note:

This is the easiest sauce to make and is delicious as a glazing for ham, as well.

NUTTY CHICKEN

Stuffing:
- ¾ c   dry roasted, unsalted peanuts
- ¼ c   bread crumbs
- 2 tbs   unsalted butter, melted
- ¼ c   heavy cream
- ½ tsp   salt
- ⅛ tsp   pepper
- ⅛ tsp   cayenne pepper
- ⅛ tsp   nutmeg powder

Ingredients:
- 1   chicken breast, boned, per person
- 1   slice of smoked ham per serving
- 1   large onion, chopped
- 1   large carrot, chopped
- 2   tart apples, one chopped the other sliced thin (1/4 inch)
- 2 c   apple cider
- ½ c   unsalted butter (1 stick), melted

Preparation:
Preheat oven to 400°. Place nuts into bowl of a food processor. Process (on/off button) until smooth. Add the bread crumbs and process for a few seconds. Add 1/4 cup melted butter, salt, pepper, cayenne pepper, and nutmeg to the food processor, process again for a few seconds. Add the cream and process until smooth. Flatten each chicken breast and put a slice of ham on each one. Spread a heaping tablespoon of the stuffing made above on each slice of ham. Roll the chicken breasts, tuck ends in before last roll, fasten with skewer. In a large oven-proof casserole, place the onions, the carrots, and rolled-up breasts. Brush the breasts with some of the melted butter. Place the casserole in the preheated oven and bake for about 15 minutes. Turn breasts over, brush with the rest of the butter and bake 10 minutes more. When done, remove the chicken breasts from the casserole and keep warm. Place the casserole liquids into the food processor, add the apple cider, and process until smooth. Transfer the apple cider mixture into a saucepan and cook until reduced by half. Set aside

and keep warm. Coat both sides of the 1/4 inch thick apple slices with sugar. In a separate skillet, heat the remaining 1/4 cup butter. Brown the sugar-coated apple slices on both sides. They will be used as a garnish to the Nutty Chicken when served. Place one rolled-up chicken breast on each plate, drizzle with the apple-cider sauce, and serve with the browned apple slices to the side.

Chapter 23
Harvest

The season had been a good one. More than once, we were forced, with regret, to tell even some of our regulars that there was, indeed, no room at the inn, and that we couldn't welcome them.

Aux Trois Saisons was six years old. It had grown from an idea into a well-established inn. We were confident that we would have enough guests to fill the rooms the next year, and looked forward to seeing again those who had become "regulars." All of the hard work had paid off and we felt a sense of accomplishment. For two people with no prior experience at inn-keeping, we had, somehow, made all the right moves.

With the five rooms almost constantly filled, we considered adding five more. We talked it over with Bernard, our accountant, and came to the conclusion that it was a Catch-22 situation. If we added more rooms, we would have had to take out a loan and earn more to pay it back. We would also have had to find additional personnel, since it was all we both could do, working eighteen hours a day, to handle things as they were. We would have needed extra help with the cleaning, cooking, and serving that additional rooms would require, so we reluctantly decided to stay with the original five guest rooms. Besides, we were in good health, enjoyed what we were doing, and had created something we were very proud of.

In addition, a problem in France is that, since everything is pretty much covered by the State cradle-to-grave, if you hire a person, whatever that person's salary is, you must pay an almost equal amount to the government to pay for that person's Social Charges. In effect, you're paying two salaries instead of one. This may, in part, explain why nobody hires anybody and the unemployment rate is constantly hovering around the ten percent level, but I won't get into that now.

As each September arrived, we began looking forward to the harvest time because that meant the tourist season was almost over and we could begin to wind down. We knew it would take us at least a month after we left Burgundy to really relax, after the hectic seven-days-per-week schedule. The first few weeks resting in Paris would be just the remedy.

When our last guest left, the Burgundy air was still filled with the excitement that the harvest always brings. The vineyards were filled with people picking grapes, filling up the baskets they carried on their backs, and unloading the grapes into whatever vehicles could be commandeered to transport the precious cargo back to the processing buildings. We visited Jean-Claude more than once to taste the golden liquid of the first pressing before the fermentation process begins. It's a rich, sweet grape juice, yellow-white or pinkish-red, and it's delicious.

Closing up the house that was *Aux Trois Saisons* and preparing it for the winter ahead seemed to become an easier task and to go much quicker each year. Or perhaps we just became more anxious to get away.

We made the rounds of the post office, arranged with Monsieur and Madame LeFavre to have our mail forwarded to Paris, visited the *Mairie's* office to say goodbye to *Monsieur le Maire* and his secretary, dropped by Madame Turner's home to say our farewells, and then let our neighbors, the Neyrats, know that we were leaving and would see Monsieur Neyrat's sister, Florence, in Paris.

Florence lives on *rue Cherche Midi* in the same building where Andy Warhol had his Paris studio. It's also the street where *Poulaine*, acknowledged to bake one of the best breads in Paris, is located. Walk by it one day, even if only for the intoxicating aroma.

A telephone call from Sabine told us of a birthday surprise she was planning for Erik. She had arranged to rent a boat and cruise up the Seine while dinner was served and asked us to join them. It sounded like a wonderful way to begin the winter in Paris.

We loaded the car with cartons of wine to replenish the supply in Paris and installed *Mademoiselle* in the back seat, comfortably seated on a thick pillow. We locked the iron gates and left *Aux Trois Saisons* behind.

AUX TROIS SAISONS

Part IV
Le 4eme Saison

Chapter 24
All aboard

The guests Sabine had invited were sworn to secrecy. It was to be a complete surprise for Erik, his big 4-0! We assembled on board and began the party before they both arrived.

I misunderstood Sabine when she telephoned to invite us. The boat was not, as it turned out, one of the regular tourist *Bateau Mouches* that leave hourly from the *Pont d'Alma*. It was a special dinner boat that followed the same route on the Seine but catered to party groups such as ours.

A trip on a *Bateau Mouche*, by the way, offers one of the best ways of viewing Paris from another angle. The boat leaves the *Pont d'Alma* and glides along the river, passing some of the city's magnificent monuments. Then it turns around after it passes the *Ile de la Cité* and the *Ile Saint-Louis* and returns to its starting point. It's a two-hour trip through history. The recorded descriptions are very well done, and the trip is best enjoyed if you time it to begin the trip in daylight and finish it after sunset. It's then that the City of Lights lives up to its reputation.

For Erik's birthday celebration, the dinner, served by candlelight, of course, was specially selected by Sabine and was excellent, with a dessert

I later tried to duplicate and named "Lemon Cloud" because it was so light and airy. Most of the people were new to us, although we had met many at the gatherings that Sabine and Erik had hosted over the years. They were an interesting mix of Sabine's fellow artists, Erik's fellow architects, and civilians like us.

The architects were the most easily identified; they all were dressed in black from head to toe and wore their hair a bit longer than the rest of us. The artists seemed to prefer more colorful get-ups, still chic but a bit more inventive. It was easy to feel special surrounded by those people, gliding up the Seine, and sipping wine as Paris passed by the enormous windows.

Ever the perfect hostess, Sabine introduced us and gave everyone an abbreviated history of our adventures with *Aux Trois Saisons*. We soon became the center of much attention, the most often asked question being, "Why?"

Even with as cosmopolitan a group as the people on that boat, they asked "Why?" rather than the "Why not?" that would have been typical of a similar American group of people. The idea of changing professions mid-life would never occur to most Europeans, especially the French. They remain what they are until that day they all wait for..."*retrait,*" retirement. They wait for it, in fact, from the very first day they start working, which may explain, partly, the seeming disinterest most of them show for their actual work. It's just something to help kill the time.

On the boat that night, however, we all enjoyed dancing and lots of wine and champagne toasts to the birthday boy, who was beaming for the entire trip. Erik has been a good friend to us on many occasions, and he and Sabine can both be counted on to help us make sense of the nonsense sometimes encountered in French bureaucracy.

Sabine speaks several languages, including English, fluently. Her sculptures are free-form and modern, and she has been commissioned to create pieces in many parts of the world. The *Grand Palais* has an annual showing of modern art and several of Sabine's sculptures were on display one year, along with works by Picasso, Moore, and other artists.

A trip to their incredible home in *Chambourcy*, about twenty minutes outside of Paris, always meant a special preview of Sabine's latest sculptures in her studio, still in their formative stages. The house itself was Erik's baby and one of the most spectacularly beautiful modern buildings I've ever seen, with walls of glass meeting at angles, wrap-around terraces that brought the outside indoors, other walls made of hammered metal or leather, a huge salon with curved walls that met at fireplaces at either end, and a magnificent view over a golf course. The kitchen countertops were made of special two-inch thick glass, and the windows were huge, round panes of glass resembling portholes.

Their Paris apartment, before they bought the house in Chambourcy, was a penthouse in the 16th *arrondissement* that Erik completely redesigned. The upstairs bedroom, with glass walls overlooking the city, had a circular revolving bed which, at the push of a button, would turn to get the best view of Paris at any particular time of day. The bathroom had a shower room with fiber-optic lights set into the ceiling and floor. Their bathtub filled with a waterfall that could be started by remote control from the bedroom. The entire house had the feeling of a space ship.

We spent one memorable New Year's Eve with them in that apartment and, if I close my eyes, I can still see the *Tour Eiffel* from their dining room, glowing, as we toasted in the New Year with Champagne.

In a city that offers a million and one treasures to delight the eye and the soul, it's almost impossible to narrow the things to see to just a few. Visiting the major museums of Paris would take a year. New ones are constantly being added to the list. A museum dedicated to Maillol opened a few years ago, with the late artist's model and "muse," Dina Varney, acting as coordinator. I still haven't found time to go there and it's only a few blocks from where I live.

But if you have only a few hours stopover in Paris one day, I suggest that you spend them on a *Bateau Mouche*, sitting back and drinking in the glories of the most beautiful city in the world as it glides peacefully by.

LEMON CLOUD

Ingredients:
- 1/4 c   lemon juice
- 1/3 c   water
- 4   eggs, separated
- 1 tbs   grated lemon rind
- 1   envelope unflavored gelatin
- 1 c   heavy cream
- 1 c   sugar
-             fresh mint leaves for garnish

Preparation:
Mix water, lemon juice, lemon rind, 4 egg yolks and 1/4 cup sugar together. Sprinkle gelatin over mixture and cook gently until gelatin dissolves and the mixture will coat a spoon. Put mixture into a dish and place in the refrigerator for about 30 minutes. Beat the egg whites until they form peaks. Beat in 1/4 cup sugar until dissolved and peaks are firm. Whip heavy cream until stiff. Remove lemon mixture from refrigerator, fold whipped cream into the lemon mixture. Fold this into the beaten egg whites until well mixed. Wrap aluminum foil collars around individual small ramekins, secure with rubber bands and lightly grease the inside of the aluminum foil. Spoon the mixture into each ramekin until it extends well above the level of the ramekin. Refrigerate for several hours until set. Remove the aluminum foil wrappers and top with mint leaves for garnish and serve.

Note:
A really nice additional touch is fresh raspberries or raspberry coulis along with the fresh mint leaves. This dessert looks like a soufflé and is incredibly light, a true "lemon cloud."

Chapter 25
À La Table des Rois

One of the most exciting events of the Paris winter, several years ago, was an exposition in Versailles called *"À La Table des Rois."* It was an exhibit of table settings from the days of the king. Aside from being a glimpse into a long-gone lifestyle, it also turned out to be quite an educational experience.

The sumptuousness of the serving dishes and utensils, the manner in which they had been used, and the evolution of serving styles was brought to life on a series of tables set as they would have been for the king and his guests. We wandered between exhibits, discovering, along the way, the evolution of eating habits and the historical and economic events which they represented.

À La Table Des Rois traced the changing serving styles and tastes from earliest times. In the seventeenth century, there were only five types of bread available in Paris. Poor King Louis XIV had very bad teeth and could eat only the soft *"pain à la Reine"* named after Marie de Médicis, who popularized it. His doctor, Fagon, even eventually forbade Louis that small pleasure.

The most consumed meats in the seventeenth century were beef, veal, and mutton, since lamb was considered too insipid and tasteless. Pork was considered gross and coming from an "impure" animal and was used only in the second half of the seventeenth and eighteenth centuries as stuffing or chopped into small pieces. Ham was, however, quite popular.

Wine was the main beverage consumed, because water was of such poor quality that it was used only to cut the wine. Champagne began to be appreciated only toward the final years of the seventeenth century.

Liqueurs and alcoholic drinks made from pears and cherries were very popular at Court, particularly among the ladies. Fagon, the king's doctor, while forbidding bread, made sure that Louis drank his anisette daily.

Chocolate and tea appeared in the seventeenth century although the Princess Palatine declared that she did not believe in these "drugs" because they were "not healthy." Coffee became popular in 1669 as the result of a reception given at the Court in honor of the Turkish Sultan Mohamet IV. Coffee became so popular as a drink, in fact, that when the Duc de Luynes dined with Louis XV, he later reported that the king was absolutely hooked on coffee and wouldn't leave the table without it.

Cookbooks began appearing in 1651; between then and 1789 there were about 230 available. Monsieur de La Varenne, whose cookbook appeared in 1651, proposed "health, moderation, and refinement" in preparing meals.

A typical meal at Court, however, in the seventeenth and eighteenth centuries, consisted of five main parts: the *"potage,"* a sort of bouillon with cubes of bread cut into small slices; the *"entrees,"* consisting of several meat and fish dishes, sausages, *ragoûts*, and other warm dishes; the *"rôti,"* which were an assortment of meats cooked on skewers or on the spit; the *"entremets,"* which could include cold meats, artichokes, asparagus, ham, cold tarts, grilled meats, all sorts of mushrooms, pig's feet and ears; the *"hors d'oeuvre,"* which consisted of all the things that might have accompanied the other courses, or even salads; *"le fruit,"* which ended the meal and was, actually, "dessert." The nobility did not like this word because it was used by the *bourgeoise* class so they used "le fruit" instead, but no matter what it was called, this part of the meal consisted of various fruit tarts, platters of fresh and dried fruit, and *pâtisseries*.

The way in which the meal was served changed drastically over the centuries. The *"Service à la française"* was prevalent in the seventeenth century, and was the serving style in which a meal consisted of multiple courses, but all dishes were presented at the same time. With this manner of service, of course, the utensils were kept to a minimum and the guests even sometimes brought their own. Each guest also pretty much had his or her own personal waiter, so a variety of knives and forks were not set out, since each course was served by the waiter standing behind the chair. He delivered the utensils as they were needed, just as he poured the wine when the glasses were low.

The *"Service à la russe,"* which is the method used today, even in France, is the method in which the courses are served consecutively. Having one server per guest became impractical and difficult, except at Court, so individual waiters for each guest gave way to only several servers to provide for the needs of all the guests present. The tables began to have a few strategic utensils already set out when the guests arrived at table, depending on what was going to be served.

This *"Service à la russe"* has evolved into the elegant table settings we find in grand restaurants, with several various sized forks set to the left of the plate, and several spoons and knives set on the other side, and the dessert spoon and fork set above the plate. The utensils were arranged with the ones for the first course on the outside and the others placed further toward the center, so they could be used as the meal progressed. The sharp knife edges faced inward toward the plate and the forks were set with their tines down toward the table.

The most interesting feature of the entire exhibition, to me, was the display of *Menus* of dinners prepared for the king and his guests. There were as many as forty separate courses to each part of the five-course dinner, and the meal could take hours. The recipes were intricate and called for ingredients not always readily available today, but with the large kitchen staffs of those days, and the unlimited funds of the royal houses, anything was possible.

The menus themselves were works of art. Lavishly illustrated, meticulously printed, they speak of an age of luxury that was soon to end. If, for example, you had been invited to dine at the *Château de Choisy* on Thursday, April 19, 1751, the menu would have looked like the one you see on the next page.

One of the menus, which fascinated me, offered among its many choices "duck with oysters." I searched for something similar in a book of ancient recipes that I had discovered in a bookstall in Paris about twenty years ago. The recipe I found for *Canard Aux Huîtres,* obviously a favorite delicacy in those days, called for *"les canards sauvages,"* wild ducks, but since my butcher on *Rue Cler* in Paris was not about to go out and shoot one for me, I had to settle for the next best thing.

The recipe further instructed me to truss the wild duck very carefully, and "stuff it with truffles and fine herbs when it is almost done but still slightly red," and then turn it in the flame a bit more. The instructions were very specific and very involved, which, with a kitchen staff of fifty or so, would present no problem at all.

More in keeping with my own humble kitchen in Paris, I adapted the recipe slightly, and I'm delighted to present it to you so that you, too, may join me in dining at the "The King's Table."

CANARD AUX HUÎTRES
DUCK WITH OYSTERS

The original recipe calls for lots of truffles and some ingredients that were readily available in 1751 but somewhat scarce today. I've adapted the original recipe as follows:

Ingredients:

1	good-sized duck
16	fresh oysters
1 c	small mushrooms, sliced 1/8 inch thick
1 c	trumpet mushrooms, sliced 1/8 inch thick
1/2 c	smoked salt pork cut into 1/2 inch cubes
1	onion, sliced thinly
1	carrot, sliced thickly.
1	shallot, chopped fine
1 c	white wine
1/2	liter water
	Bouquet garni*
	Salt, pepper

Preparation:

Salt and pepper the duck inside and out and bake in a very hot 450° F. oven for 15 minutes. Reduce the oven temperature to moderate (350°) and continue to roast until it is tender but still dark pink on the inside. (Usually, you can allow about 15-20 minutes per pound.) Pour off the fat and baste often with some liquid from steps 2 and 3. While the duck is roasting, place duck gizzards, neck, and wings in a pot with the onion, carrot, and chopped shallot. Add the white wine, water, salt, pepper and the bouquet garni*. Cook gently for 30 minutes until the liquid is reduced to 1/2 liter. The mixture is then strained. Cook the salt pork pieces in a buttered sauce pan and add the two types of mushrooms which have been cut into slices. Add the liquid obtained in step 2 and simmer for about 20 minutes more. Remove the oysters from their shells and place into the simmering liquid, but only for a minute or so, until they swell slightly and the edges get all curled up. If you cook them too long they will lose their flavor and taste like rubber. When the duck is ready, cut it into 8 pieces and place the pieces on a serving dish. To serve, pour the sauce obtained from the simmering mixture over the duck pieces and cover with some of the mushrooms. Arrange the oysters on top of the mushrooms and serve hot.

Note:
(The original 1751 recipe further suggests that the pieces of duck may be surrounded on the serving plate by croutons cut into the shape of hearts and slightly browned in butter, and some chervil. Parsley will do just fine.)

*Bouquet garni:
A bouquet garni is very simple to make yourself and an absolute necessity for soups, sauces, stews and any dish that needs a little extra herbal flavor. You can easily make one by taking a 6-inch square piece of plain cheesecloth or muslin and placing an assortment of herbs in the center. You can use such basic herbs as a bay leaf, thyme, sage, rosemary, or whatever else you think will go well with what you're preparing. Tie the cheesecloth square into a bundle and then drop it in while the dish is cooking. When the cooking time is over, lift the bouquet garni bundle out and discard it. Voila!

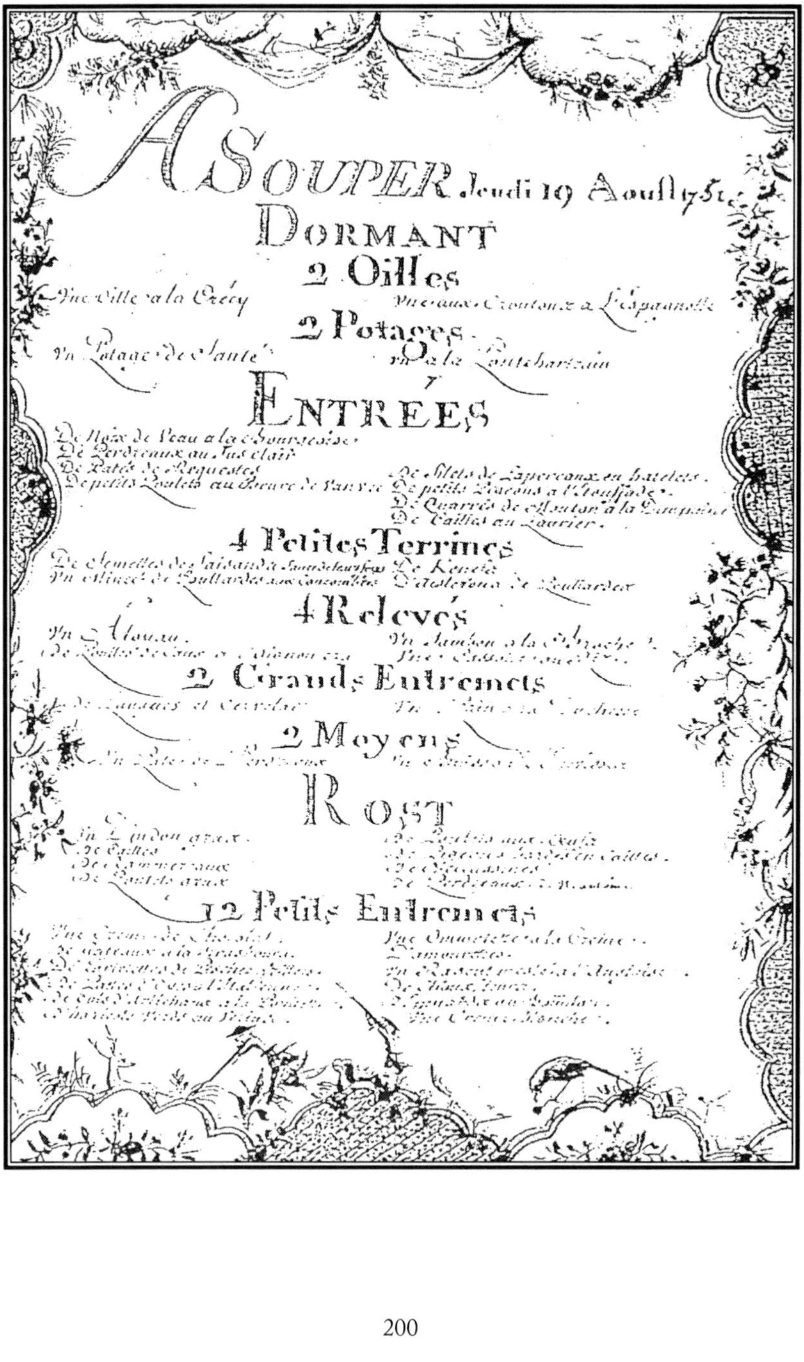
A SOUPER Jeudi 19 Aoust 1751

DORMANT

2 Oilles

Une Oille a la Crecy

Une aux Croutons a L'Espagnolle

2 Potages

Un Potage de Santé

ENTRÉES

4 Petites Terrines

4 Relevés

2 Grands Entremets

2 Moyens

ROST

12 Petits Entremets

Chapter 26
Politically Correct

It started innocently enough.

Frédérique and André are a young couple we first met in *Dracy Le Fort*. Frédérique's family owned a beautiful, rambling old stone house that had been in the family for centuries. She and André, her fiancé, lived in Paris all year long but came out to Burgundy on weekends during the summer. It was on one such weekend that we met them.

Frédérique speaks English perfectly and, at that time, worked for *Yves Saint Laurent*. She was paid to travel all over the world looking for counterfeit copies that illegally sported the *Saint Laurent* label. *Saint Laurent* is a multi-million dollar business and counterfeit items are a serious problem. Frédérique's disarming sense of humor must have come in very handy in some of the difficult situations that line of work can lead to.

André is a handsome young man, very athletic, with a fabulous smile that renders totally unimportant the fact that his English is somewhat limited. There's a great deal that can be accomplished with a warm smile and a twinkle of sky-blue eyes.

We were invited over for family feasts, always outdoors, where we met some of their Parisian friends, who often came with them for the weekend.

When Frédérique and André decided to get married, they asked if they could have the wedding reception and their *lune de miel,* honeymoon, at *L'Auberge Aux Trois Saisons.* The arrangements were made and they reserved the five rooms at *Aux Trois Saisons* for those guests who couldn't fit into the family house.

I will always remember one particular couple who stayed with us on that occasion. They were in their twenties, attractive, multi-lingual, and the gentleman was a count. They stayed in *Bellevue,* the room up the stairs from the kitchen and, unfortunately, as it turned out, directly over the private rooms in which Dierk and I slept.

All went well. The wedding banquet was a great success, and, eventually, all assembled went their separate ways. After *digestifs* in front of the fireplace, the count and countess adjourned to their room

When the kitchen was all cleaned up and the dishwasher loaded, we brought the bills up to date with that evening's dinners and wines added to them. Then we sent out the necessary FAXes confirming future reservations (this was before E-mail). Once all of the necessary details had been taken care of, Dierk and I flicked off all the lights, locked the house doors, locked the iron gates at the entrance of the property, and ended another day at the inn, exhausted but exhilarated.

That night, the flushing device in the count's bathroom decided to begin the steady drip-drip that indicated that the handle wasn't all the way down, or up, and water was gently seeping into the tank.

The delicate drops of water, as the house became quieter and quieter, began to sound like a waterfall. By 2:00 a.m., it was unbearable. By 3:00, with a 5:30 wake-up on the alarm clock, we realized that desperate measures would have to be taken.

We decided to shut off the house's main water supply valve, the famous *"robinet"* located next to our private quarters. It would mean that nobody in the house could flush more than one more time, but with the house filled with young people, all of whom probably still had strong bladders, we hoped for the best.

The silence was bliss. When the water was turned on a few hours later, we heard no sounds of major flushing. Our guests were none the wiser.

The next morning, as I was fixing breakfast, the count passed the kitchen dressed in his jogging shorts, ready for his morning run. To this day, I wonder what he thought as I politely sent him upstairs again with, "Please, go up and flush your toilet."

Frédérique, André, the count and his countess all laughed about it later on. We laughed with them, despite the sleepless night.

The other couple who enter into this story now are Serge and Dominique, whom you've already met. I'm the godfather of their second daughter, Alice, if you remember.

One Thanksgiving in Paris, years before Alice entered the picture, we thought it would be nice to invite both couples over for a typical American feast and to have them meet each other. After all, they were, all four of them, charming, intelligent, fun people, so the evening promised to be very special.

After introductions and *aperitifs*, dinner was served. The turkey, the candied yams—all the other trimmings, even the pumpkin and pecan pies—all met with approval. Dierk chose our best wines to go with each course, and everybody seemed content.

The after-dinner *digestif*, a fine old cognac, added to the good spirits. Then, since it was before the French Presidential election, I made what I intended as an innocuous attempt at conversation and asked who they thought would win. I learned a valuable lesson.

One couple was quite enamored of Monsieur Chirac, on the political

Right, and extolled his many virtues, including the fact that he had done a great job as the mayor of Paris. The other couple favored Monsieur Jospin, his challenger on the Left.

As preferences were expressed, the volume rose, eyebrows and shoulders busily entering the fray. I tried to change the subject but they were having none of it, so I quietly backed out of the room and withdrew to the kitchen.

The heated discussion went on as I put the dishes into the dishwasher. I ventured into the salon to ask if someone would like another *digestif* and was totally ignored.

Although the volume and gestures indicated otherwise, it was all sputter and no venom. They seemed, in fact, to be thoroughly enjoying themselves, so I just sat back and observed.

The French love to discuss things and they are passionate about the sounds of their language and their own cleverness in using it to best advantage. Politics, however, is a dangerous topic because they are so emphatically either Right or Left.

The Right, or the *Droite*, is the conservative element, whose members are always busy fighting among themselves, and the Left is represented by the Socialist/Communist coalition. The latter is so blurred that simply saying *Gauche*, or Left, may imply an infinite variety of combinations, ranging from liberal to downright anarchic. The unions, who comprise a relatively small percentage of the population, given their power, are all extremely Left, and capable of completely paralyzing the entire nation if they see fit to do so. Of course, since the government rarely comes through with what they promise in order to end the strikes, the following year there are usually the same strikes again.

Nobody in France has *no* opinion. And whatever that opinion may be, they're adamant about it. Combine this with a natural gift for expression and a language that is perfect for politics and diplomacy and it can lead to some very explosive social intercourse.

When they left, late that evening, I breathed an exhausted sigh of relief. All four of them are, however, still friends of ours. Dominique and Serge became almost family with the birth of Audrey and, later, my goddaughter, Alice. André and Frédérique have also since become parents of two beautiful children and have a lovely apartment near the Luxemburg Gardens.

Of course, they telephoned the next day to say what a wonderful time they had and to thank us. I think it would be nice to invite them all over for dinner again. In about twenty years.

Chapter 27
Les Ambassadeurs

When I close my eyes, I can see it very clearly. The magnificent room, the high, painted ceiling, the mirrors that reflect the glittering chandeliers, the impeccable service. When I'm having a particularly trying day, I close my eyes, take a deep breath, and I'm back at *Les Ambassadeurs,* my favorite restaurant in Paris.

I can't tell you how many times I had walked past the *Hôtel Crillon* on my way to the United States Embassy next door on *Avenue Gabriel.* Each time I passed, I peeked into the foyer beyond the revolving doors, saw a world of shining marble filled with beautiful people, and wondered what it was like inside.

For a very special occasion—I've forgotten exactly what it was—we decided to splurge and have dinner at the *Hôtel's* world renowned restaurant, *Les Ambassadeurs.* The first time must have been when we bought the house in Burgundy that became *Aux Trois Saisons,* or some such momentous event, and we figured that we needed a gift to ourselves to shore up our resolve.

When you enter the lobby, if you continue straight ahead and then walk up a few steps to the right, you'll be in the cocktail area of the *Ambassadeurs* restaurant. A chic young lady will take your coat, which will then reappear, as if by magic, when you leave.

Having a cocktail will give you time to drink in the grandeur of the rooms, the discreet, silent steps of the waiters along the marble floor as they unobtrusively go about their appointed tasks. More than anything else, it's an *aperitif* for the soul.

Then, a handsome young man—and I assure you, they're *all* handsome—will show you to your table. I hope that you've reserved Table Number 16, which is on the far left in front of the window looking out on the *Place de la Concorde*. You'll be able to see the lights come on and transform the largest, most magnificent open Place in the world into a wonderland. The two large fountains have been photographed thousands of times but look even more spectacular in person.

The waiter will hand you a large *Menu* which, at that time, perhaps still today, had on its cover a design by Sonia Rykiel, the famous designer. Each Menu is numbered and, over the years, I was able to collect a few, especially since they used to mail them to people who requested that they be informed of the various changes in the *Menus*. The chef's creations, you see, depend on the changing seasons.

Whenever I've treated myself to a celebratory dinner there, I always order the *Menu Dégustation,* which consists of about nine courses. They're all small helpings, but by the fourth one you'll begin to feel quite satisfied. By the seventh you'll begin to slow down considerably, and I once actually refused dessert because I simply couldn't fit it in.

I've got several *Menus* in front of me at the moment, and as I read them again I'm reliving those exquisite dinners. One *Menu Dégustation* offers *foie gras* with chestnuts to begin, then scallops in endives with an orange sauce, then duck breast in a black olive sauce, followed by various cheeses, dried fruits, and a dessert list which I cannot even begin to describe.

Another Menu offers sole with caviar, and red mullet with saffron-flavored vegetables. A third Menu begins with a lobster bisque, followed by salmon with truffles, and then lamb with tarragon cream. Their dessert *crêpes* are my personal favorite, especially when served with Grand Marnier and flamed at the table. Between courses, of course, there is an assortment of tidbits to "cleanse the palate" and stimulate it for the next assault. Usually, this is a sorbet of some sort.

There are also assorted goodies, tiny little taste sensations called *"amuse bouche,"* to tickle the taste buds before you even begin the dinner.

Each course is a work of art, beautifully prepared and superbly presented. I love it when the waiters all come out at once, each carrying a plate with a round silver cover. Then, in one synchronized movement, they remove the covers. It's a piece of choreography that somehow feels right in that setting. The French believe that when a dish is well prepared and then artfully presented, it should bring pleasure to the eye as well as the stomach. This, they say, is like "preaching to the converted."

The *Menu Dégustation* is, indeed, rather expensive, but well worth every centime. I would rather forego several dinners out at lesser restaurants and save up the money for one night in gastronomic heaven.

It's the little things that count. For example, in Europe, many men carry a small sac, a carry-bag, an elegant little leather affair in which the wallet, car keys, eyeglass cases, and other objects, can comfortably and conveniently find space. It makes so much more sense, I think, than trying to stuff these necessary accessories into pants pockets or jacket pockets, which cause them to poke out in less than flattering places. In America, if a man would carry this with him in public, he would most probably get stared at, but European men seem confident enough not to sacrifice their comfort.

The first time I went to *Les Ambassadeurs*, I was about to place my *sac* on the table when a little chair-height bench appeared out of nowhere right next to my chair. It was done so smoothly that I felt as if it was perfectly natural for it to be there.

The wine list is a thick, impressive volume and contains wines from every region. Dierk, whose wine expertise is greater than my own, chose a good wine that was fairly expensive. After all, the evening was designed to splurge.

The *sommelier* came to take our order for wine and, after complimenting Dierk on his choice, suggested that perhaps Monsieur would please allow him to suggest another wine which he, the *sommelier*, thought might go even better with the *Menu Dégustation*. The wine turned out to be, as he said it would, superb, and when we checked the wine list later on, we discovered that the wine he had suggested was, in fact, considerably less expensive than the wine we originally chose. It's this desire to please, to make the evening perfect for the client, not merely to inflate the bill, that turns a visit to *Les Ambassadeurs* into an unforgettable experience.

We remembered this when we welcomed guests to L'Auberge *Aux Trois Saisons*. The *aperitif* in front of the blazing fireplace or on the terrace at sunset, the five-course dinner presented by candlelight on a beautifully set table, the fresh flowers and the soft music, all were designed to please the senses.

Perhaps, today, some of our own guests at *Aux Trois Saisons* close their eyes and see it all clearly again.

SURPRISE DE TERRI (TERRI'S SURPRISE)

The crêpes in this dessert are as light and airy as the ones I remember from Les Ambassadeurs, but this dessert is named in honor of Terri, a guest at Aux Trois Saisons, and is made of all of her favorite things. The crêpes are so simple to make that I usually make many more than I need, freeze them, with a piece of waxed paper between each one, and use them, when needed, for lots of other dishes.

Ingredients:
4	large eggs, beaten
3/4 c	water
3/4 c	milk
1/4 tsp	salt
1 c	flour
3 tbs	oil (vegetable or peanut)

Preparation:
Combine all ingredients and whisk with a wire whisk until smooth. Refrigerate the batter for 2 hours. Heat a flat crêpe pan, paint the inside with melted butter, and heat until a drop of water flicked onto the pan sizzles. Wipe the excess butter from the pan with a paper towel. Put about 4 tablespoons of the crêpe batter, (poured from a ladle at one time), into the hot pan and rotate quickly to coat the entire bottom of the pan. Cook until the crêpe is slightly light brown and then turn with a spatula and brown the other side. Stack the crêpes with waxed paper between each one, refrigerate and/or freeze for future use.

MOUSSE AU CHOCOLAT

Ingredients:

8 oz	(250 grams) semi-sweet dark chocolate
3/4 c	sugar
1/4 c	water
3	eggs, separated
2 c	heavy cream
1 tbs	strong coffee
1 tbs	cognac

Preparation:

Melt the chocolate in the top of a double boiler. Combine the sugar and water and heat gently until sugar melts completely. Put the melted chocolate in a large, deep bowl, and, using an electric beater, add sugar syrup and 3 egg yolks (one at a time). Add the cognac and coffee and beat briefly again. Cool slightly. Beat the egg whites until stiff and combine this with the chocolate mixture. Whip the cream and fold the whipped cream and the chocolate mixture together until it is all one color and no streaks remain. Chill in the refrigerator for 4 to 5 hours. Serve as described for Surprise de Terri, or simply spoon into a lovely piece of stemware and serve. In either case, it's sinfully delicious. Enjoy!

RASPBERRY COULIS:

Ingredients:
4 c   fresh raspberries
1 1/2 c   sugar
2 tsp   lemon juice
1/2 c   water

Preparation:
Gently rinse the raspberries and place them into a sauce pan. Add the sugar, lemon juice and water, mash slightly and then cook, on medium heat, until it all becomes a thick sauce. Cook for another 10 minutes on very low heat, remove from the stove and strain through a wire strainer to remove the pips. Set aside until ready to decorate the Surprise de Terri. Prepare unsweetened whipped cream. For each serving of Surprise de Terri, place a rounded teaspoon of mousse au chocolat into the center of a crêpe, fold the two side edges over the mousse and then the other two sides to form an envelope. Invert the crêpe so that the folded ends are on the serving plate. To serve, cover each crêpe with enough whipped cream to hide it, put a few raspberries on top, and then drizzle raspberry sauce over it. Quel surprise!

Helpful Hint:
When the crêpe is done on one side, I tap the side of the pan against a hard surface and it loosens the crêpe enough to be easily slid around the pan. Then I turn it over with a knife or a spatula.

Chapter 28
Le Marais

One of the oldest parts of Paris was once a swamp. It has been totally gentrified in recent years, and is, presently, quite fashionable. Despite the up-scale boutiques and expensive apartments, it is still, however, called *le Marais,* the swamp. It's another French paradox, with a name that doesn't quite correlate with the place it describes, like the *Pont Neuf,* or "new bridge," being, naturally, the *oldest* bridge over the Seine.

The center of the *Marais* is one of the most beautiful enclosed squares in Europe, the *Place des Vosges,* originally called the Royal Square, which was built by Henry IV. Poor Henry II had been killed while jousting in the *Rue Saint Antoine* and Richelieu and Madame de Sevigny once lived there in the houses above the arcades.

Although Henry IV couldn't get his wife, Marie de Medici, to live there with him—probably because of his amorous pursuits of other ladies—it still became the center of fashionable life. Pageants, parades and duels took place there, and it is still one of the nicest places in Paris to spend an afternoon.

If you visit the *Museum Carnavalet*, you can see the old Paris of the *Marais* depicted in paintings. Many of the rooms, from houses in the area that were demolished, have been transferred intact to the museum and mirror the lives of the people who inhabited them. The history of Paris is arranged chronologically and you can, literally, walk through the centuries.

The *Marais* is also the old Jewish quarter of Paris and is still the place where one of the oldest synagogues in Paris and some good restaurants, such as "Joe Goldenberg," can be found.

Jasmine's apartment is one block off the *Place des Vosges*. It is a corner apartment with a huge fireplace; the ceilings are high and beamed so that the effect is one of enormous space. A dinner with Jasmine is especially nice because it's also an opportunity to walk through the *Place* to the other side and explore some of the shops along the way.

There's a pleasant restaurant with an outdoor terrace for a meal or a drink, and there's the Victor Hugo museum, which offers a glimpse into the home and life of this incredible man, an icon of French literature.

If you fancy a trip from the sublime to the ridiculous, you might go from the Place des Vosges to see an art exhibit at the *Centre Pompidou*, or the *Beaubourg*, which some of the French refer to as "the factory." Except for the fact that you can have a marvelous view of Paris from the top of it, I find the building to be thoroughly ugly, with its pipes on the outside and its rust spots there for all to see. As a showplace for modern art, which it was intended to be, however, it succeeds, because, as most of my French friends who love it insist, it offers unobstructed space. If nothing more, it's a great topic of conversation if things get quiet around the dinner table.

The same architectural firm has built a similar structure in London's financial district and, strangely enough, it's beautiful. At night, there is a blue light played on it and it looks ethereal. It houses an insurance company, so I think it's just fine. In London.

There's a marvelous junk shop at one corner of the arcade and browsing there can be great fun. It really is a junk shop, with some things like those you probably got rid of when you last cleaned out the attic, but there are also some interesting finds. You just have to spend some time looking around, and you can find few better occupations on a nice day in Paris than "just looking around."

Stores like this can be a treasure trove. I found an old, beaten-up frame in just such a store. The *antiquaire* assured me that it was "over one hundred years old, Monsieur, and truly a great bargain."

I assured her that I would treat it with the respect it was due, and I took it home, disassembled it and saved those parts of the original frame that I could. The original frame was about 18 by 24 inches. When I finished mitering the parts that remained, I was left with a beautiful little frame which is perfect for an ink sketch of Bacchus the god of wine that was given to us by a guest at the inn. It brings back many memories.

Chapter 29
Mademoiselle

Mademoiselle's favorite city in all the world was Paris. And, being the well traveled dog she was, her decision was not made lightly.

I can trace *Mademoiselle's* genealogy back to one evening in New York City. After working all day at the Children's Aid Society, I stopped to buy a newspaper at the kiosk that was then located at 86th street and 3rd avenue. Sitting on top of a stack of newspapers, I saw a black and white ball of dejected looking fur. It was love at first sight.

The lady selling the newspapers asked if I would like to adopt her. I answered that, if it was acceptable to the dachshund who already owned me, I would be quite willing to try. I returned home for the trial period with the ball of fur, who turned out to be a Cockapoo, and we were both greeted by Ludwig, who smelled Samantha in all the right places and, obviously, approved.

Ludwig was, actually, delighted because there were now *two* dishes of food placed on the floor, and he assumed both were his. Samantha took over the house, taught Ludwig about food-dish protocol, and they got along just fine after that.

When I stayed to teach at the university in Johannesburg, South Africa, Samantha joined me. Ludwig was well on in years and not quite up to the trip, so he moved in with my mother where, I suspect, he got at least two food dishes of his own. When I saw him on a trip home the next year, he ignored me completely and waddled after my mother wherever she went.

In Johannesburg, Samantha met Timothy Von Rensburg, a handsome white poodle, and he and Samantha hit if off quite well. Two months later, Samantha had me and Jill, a friend who was a registered nurse and who had flown up from Capetown for the event, in attendance when Corinne came into the world accompanied by two brothers and a sister.

She was a tiny ball of white fluff, part Cockapoo, part poodle, and all love, and, from the minute she emerged from a rather surprised Samantha, there was no question that she would be mine. Even if I had to arm-wrestle the five-year-old daughter of Timothy's parents for her!

Corinne, named after another friend, was a perfect lady from the time she was born and never gave Samantha a bit of trouble. I never quite understood whether they realized that they were, indeed, mother and daughter, but they were inseparable.

Samantha, ever the devoted mother, washed Corinne's face and ears, a chore which Corinne decided to perform on me after her mother passed on. Dierk, who had joined the family by this time, declined the honor, so Corinne devoted all of her attention to what she considered my personal needs.

Samantha and Corinne accompanied us to California after South Africa, and they took to the Beverly Hills lifestyle with ease. Then on to Puerto Rico for my attempt at retirement, which didn't last long. Next stop was Hoosick, New York, a village not far from Bennington, Vermont, where they lived in a lovely old house that had belonged to Grandma Moses' relatives, and then to Massachusetts, when I accepted a position at Harvard.

Samantha had passed on before we decided to move to France and begin the adventure that became *Aux Trois Saisons*, but Corinne was still a very important member of the family. Before leaving the United States, Corinne had to visit her doctor to have all sorts of forms filled out stating that she was in good health and had all of the required vaccinations. Most offensive to her, however, was that FDA form stipulating that she was, indeed, a dog and not a farm animal. She was not amused.

I've already told you the story of our crossing on the "Egon Oldendorff" with Corinne's beloved captain and the full suitcase of dog food which we carried *on* board and, later, *off*.

From the moment we stepped on European soil, Corinne felt right at home. The Customs inspectors admired her as she stepped brightly off the "Egon Oldendorf" to begin her new life.

We drove the rented car to Paris and installed ourselves in the tiny flat on *Rue de Lille*, really no more than a hotel room in size. I noticed a new spring to her walk as we investigated *Rue Allent*, a small street between *Rue de Lille* and *Rue de Verneuil*.

The first time we visited a restaurant and she was not only allowed to enter but was welcomed by people who truly appreciated her, "Corinne" became "*Mademoiselle* Corinne," later shortened simply to *"Mademoiselle."*

And the French certainly know how to treat a lady!

She was greeted royally in the best restaurants of Paris, waiters came running with bowls of water, one and all agreed how *"mignon"* she was. We went shopping together in department stores, where salesladies actually stopped chatting amongst themselves long enough to say how adorable she was, and I began getting better service.

Crossing borders was no problem at all, even without a passport, and *Mademoiselle* enjoyed her visits to Germany to visit Dierk's family, and to Switzerland and Belgium to visit friends she, and we, had made at the inn. Her life, when her duties at *Aux Trois Saisons* didn't monopolize her time was one long party.

Julia, our dearest friend in Paris, was not, before she met *Mademoiselle*, a dog lover, and animals played no part in her life. *Mademoiselle* changed all that.

Of course, *Mademoiselle* met Julia under the best circumstances. It was at a jazz concert arranged by the son of another friend, Marcelle, to which Julia and we had been invited. We had never met Julia before.

We took our seats around the tables of the small jazz club; *Mademoiselle* arranged herself under the table, and we were chatting with Marcelle when a lady arrived who is the living definition of the word "elegance." Julia doesn't walk, she glides. Her laugh is a gentle tinkle and her gracious warmth puts everyone at ease. She seated herself next to me. *Mademoiselle* looked up at Julia in welcome, promptly curled up at her feet, Julia pronounced her *"mignon,"* and they were friends from then on.

The next year, while we were in the midst of renovations at *Dracy Le Fort*, Julia invited us to *Mandelieu*, overlooking Cannes in the south of France, where she had a home. *Mademoiselle*, of course, was included in the invitation and accepted it as perfectly natural.

Her good manners were in evidence and in the years to come she was always part of the entourage. Every February, we drove down to *Mandelieu* for a week's visit with Julia and enjoyed the beauty of the hillsides covered with yellow Mimosa blossoms at their peak.

Mademoiselle never visited the inside of the casino in Cannes, but we did enjoy sitting in the café across the street and admiring the ladies and gentlemen who entered. It was one of the few places where she was not admitted, other than *Père Lachaise,* the cemetery in Paris, and she never seemed too upset about that.

Mademoiselle comfortably fit in wherever we took her, and her sunny dependability amid the turmoil of the early days of *Aux Trois Saisons'* creation made that difficult time more bearable. Nothing seemed so bad that a lick or a wag of the tail couldn't make better.

In Paris, as well as in her new role as the hostess at *Aux Trois Saisons*, she was a great success and much loved.

In her sixteenth year, in Paris, she became ill and passed away. In the years that followed, returning guests still spoke with affection of *Mademoiselle*.

We still haven't allowed another four-legged individual to adopt us, but it's time to start thinking about it.

Mademoiselle had us so well trained. The last year of our time with her, when she was almost completely blind and deaf, we were, of necessity, inseparable.

I still open doors cautiously, for fear that she might be behind them and caught unawares, and I listen for the soft snoring that told of her presence near me. It's quiet and I miss her.

I content myself with the knowledge that she lived 125 years in our time and was loved for every day of those years.

May we all be so fortunate.

Chapter 30
Candles and Torches

Some events or places are identified with candlelight. Two such special moments took place one year between seasons at *Aux Trois Saisons*.

The newspaper advertisement announced a candlelight concert at the *Orangerie* of the Bagatelle. The *Orangerie* is where the famous rose garden is located and there, to the left of it, is the small gazebo where the Empress Eugenie watched her son taking riding lessons. We often went there, sat in the gazebo, and imagined how the city outside would have looked in her time.

The Bagatelle itself is an elegant house surrounded by a magnificent garden in the *Bois de Boulogne*, a forest at the outskirts of Paris. The park is filled with Parisian families every weekend, and we once went rowing there on the large lake with Dominique and Serge on a lovely Sunday afternoon.

The house, called Bagatelle because it was originally built as a "folly," was a private home and has been lived in, over the years, by, among others, an English family who restored it to its original opulence. A small gem of a house, it has a particularly beautiful circular music room with high ceilings and large windowed doors looking out to the garden.

The Bagatelle often houses exhibits of one sort or another. One year, there was a collection of fabrics made by a Parisian manufacturer who has been supplying fabrics and wall coverings to chateaux for hundreds of years. And another year, we saw an art exhibit of the works of Lalanne, the artist who does those life-size sheep and other animals.

The concert of Chopin piano music was scheduled for an early fall evening and was to be held in the *Orangerie*, the large rectangular building which doubles as a greenhouse for plants that have to be taken indoors for the winter. Chairs were set up in the one-room building, and the gardens outside were filled with hundreds of little candles in tiny glass containers set along the paths. At intermission, we wandered the paths, and it seemed as if a million fireflies lit up the gardens for us.

The second, and even more memorable candlelit event, was the marriage held at the *Chateau de Condé*. The bride was the daughter of our friends Monsieur and Madame Khoury, a young lady who was one half of a set of twins. There are three girls in the family, each more radiant than the other.

Their parents became friends of ours when they came as guests to *Aux Trois Saisons* and have remained part of our lives ever since. Both the bride and her husband are architects and insisted on being married in a medieval church. After searching long and hard, they finally discovered the perfect church for their marriage, as well as a nearby chateau where their wedding reception could be held.

The *Chateau de Condé* is in a small village about sixty miles east of Paris. I discovered, with some disappointment, however, that this *Chateau de Condé* was not the one at which the Duke and Duchess of Windsor were married. That one is in Burgundy.

It was the middle of winter with snow on the ground, so, rather than brave slippery roads, we decided to make a leisurely weekend of it and reserved a room in a hotel near the *Chateau*. After the drive from Paris, we stopped at the one café in town to shake off the chill in the air with a warm drink.

The café owner and his wife were not used to visitors from outside and immediately began bustling around to properly welcome the newcomers. They were an elderly couple and very interested in the fact that we were *"étrangers"* who had decided to move to France from the United States. The owner made certain to put on a little jacket when he brought us the steaming hot cups of coffee and we saw his wife peeking out of the kitchen.

The wedding ceremony was held in the morning at the beautiful old church in the village. While the bride and groom had especially selected the church because of its authentic medieval architecture, the medieval architects, unfortunately, had made no provision for central heating. The damp cold seemed to penetrate and radiate from the stone walls. Prime seating was located as close as possible to the gas heaters placed strategically around the church. I sensibly positioned myself between a gas heater and a woman with a big fuzzy fur coat.

The wedding ceremony was lovely, and the church was, indeed, a superb setting for the nuptials. The young couple had chosen well. We went back to our hotel to thaw out, relax, and dress for the festivities later on.

That night, when we arrived at the *Chateau* for the wedding reception, the grounds were lit with torches set in the snow every six feet, and they had arranged for loudspeakers to play trumpet music as we walked up to the entrance. The effect was unforgettable.

The dinner was splendid, the chandeliers reflected the candles all around the main room of the Chateau, and the bride and groom glowed with happiness. They have since added to the family a beautiful little baby girl, Eva, and Madame Khoury, the proud grandmother, keeps us supplied with photos that make the miles between us fade away.

Myriam Khoury, herself, is a marvelously warm and gracious person and one of our dearest friends. She is of Egyptian descent and her husband, Michael, is of Lebanese descent. They live in the 16th *arrondissement* in a huge apartment, so large that you could easily put four apartments the size of ours into it and still have room to spare. Family apartments in the 16th are traditionally that large, at least the ones that haven't been divided up into smaller ones.

Myriam's kitchen in Paris is an enormous eat-in room, with granite countertops and modern appliances. Many wonderful evenings have been spent seated around her dining table, either the large formal one in the dining room, when the girls are there, or the round granite table in the kitchen, when it's just us.

The food is always the middle-eastern food that I love, with a mixture of spices, such as cumin, that make dishes from that part of the world so special. Myriam gave me a recipe for okra prepared as a dish that could accompany any main course, and she once served a delicious casserole containing okra that seemed to blend all of the special flavors she was born to. Okra is very popular in the southern part of the United States, as well, but it had always seemed to turn out unappetizingly slimy when I cooked it in New York. Myriam's recipe changed that.

Another evening, we were treated to Myriam's *Poulet Citron* and I watched her prepare it while we sat around the kitchen table. It seemed easy, but, of course, she had spent a good deal of time that afternoon cutting and preparing the ingredients. The result was delicious, and the sauce added a special piquancy to the potatoes served with it.

I tried to incorporate some interesting international dishes into our Menus at *Aux Trois Saisons*, and Poulet Citron became a favorite. When I prepared these dishes at the inn, the only thing missing was the warmth that we share with the Khourys when we gather around their table. It's the most important part of the feast, but I'm sure you can supply your own.

POULET CITRON

Ingredients:

6	chicken breasts, boned, skinned
4 tbs	flour
1/2 tsp	salt
1/8 tsp	pepper
2 tbs	vegetable oil
2 tbs	butter
3	medium onions, chopped
3	cloves garlic, chopped fine
1/2 tsp	paprika
1 tsp	ground cumin
1/8 tsp	cayenne pepper
	pinch of thyme
1 c	chicken broth
	juice of 1 lemon
1/2 c	green olives, sliced thinly
1	lemon, sliced thin

Preparation:

Coat chicken breasts in flour to which salt and pepper have been added. Heat the oil and butter in a large skillet, and sauté the chicken breasts on both sides until they are lightly browned. Remove the chicken breasts from the skillet, sauté the chopped onions and garlic until the onions are transparent. Add the paprika, cumin, pepper and thyme and cook for 1 minute longer. Add the chicken broth and the juice of 1 lemon to the pan. Bring the mixture to the boil and then reduce to a simmer. Return the chicken breasts to the pan, along with the thin lemon slices. Cover and simmer for about 35 minutes, then sprinkle with the olives and cook, uncovered, for another 10 minutes. Serve hot with some of the cooked olives, a little of the cooking juices, and a slice of cooked lemon over each piece of chicken..

MYRIAM'S OKRA RECIPE

Ingredients:
1 1/2 lb fresh okra
3 tsp ground coriander (add more to taste)
1 tsp turmeric
2 pinches cayenne pepper
1 1/2 tsp salt
5 tbs vegetable oil
2 tsp cumin seeds (add more to taste)
1 tsp mustard seeds
1 c grated coconut
1 1/2 tsp sugar
1 c water or more depending on the okra
   juice of two lemons

Preparation:
Cut off the two ends of the okra. Put okra in a mixing bowl and sprinkle with the ground coriander, turmeric, cayenne pepper and salt. Toss. Heat the oil, drop in the cumin and mustard seeds. Cover the pan for a moment to prevent the mustard seeds from popping out. Fry the mustard seeds for a few seconds. Add the okra, mix, and cook for a few minutes. Add the coconut, sugar and water. Cook at low heat until okra pods are tender, about 20 minutes. Sprinkle with the lemon juice and serve hot or at room temperature.

MYRIAM'S EGYPTIAN CASSEROLE

Ingredients:
1 1/2 lb beef (cut into one inch cubes)
1/2 c   pearl onions
1/2 lb   okra
1   large eggplant (cubed)
1 c   chick peas
1 c   string beans
1 c   cubed potatoes (1/2 inch cubes)
3 tbs   olive oil
1/2 tsp   salt
1/4 tsp   freshly ground pepper
1/8 tsp   cayenne pepper
1 tsp   ground mint leaves

Prepartation:
Put the olive oil into a large casserole, heat until a drop of water will sizzle when dropped in. Cut beef into 1 inch cubes, brown on all sides in the hot oil, remove and set aside. Clean okra, cube eggplant, and place them into the casserole, together with the pearl onions, cubed potatoes, and string beans. Sauté vegetable mixture . Add browned meat, mint, salt and pepper. Cover with water, bring to a boil, cover casserole, and simmer for 30 minutes.

Chapter 31
Beaujolais Nouveau

When I telephoned the *Rivaldière* to make reservations for dinner, Frederic informed me that, in honor of the annual *Beaujolais Nouveau* celebration, dinner that night would be a special *Menu Fixe*. It would, he said, consist of typical regional fare with one full bottle of *Beaujolais Nouveau* per person.

Frederic, who had been the waiter at the restaurant since we began going there many years before, also served as the *maître d'* and knew my tastes well enough to suggest, "Perhaps, Monsieur might not like all of the specialties."

He proceeded to list a number of courses, one of which was blood sausage, which, along with tripe, have never gotten past my lips a second time. The French and the Germans salivate with the mention of these delicacies. When I think of them I shudder.

I thanked him and hung up the phone, ready to call *Le Fregate,* another of our favorite restaurants, then thought about it and decided that, with all of the other items on the Menu, I would certainly not starve. Besides, Dierk absolutely loves blood sausage. So I called Frederic back and made a reservation for two.

We arrived at the restaurant that evening, and Frederic asked if we would rather sit at one of the back tables since the restaurant had been completely booked by a group that might be a bit noisy. The usual table near the window was ours if we wished, however, so we chose to sit there, curious to see what the party would be like.

A few people had gathered there already, who stood around the tiny restaurant chatting while they waited for the others to arrive. And arrive they did, in two's and four's until the restaurant was full to capacity. They seemed pleasant enough and acknowledged us with the usual courteous French nod of the head and *"Bon Jour"* as they entered.

Two bottles of *Beaujolais Nouveau* and a basket of sliced baguette appeared on our table and the first course was brought out. Frederic told us that the meal was á *volunté*, which meant that, if a particular course met with our approval, he would be happy to bring out seconds, thirds, as much as we wished.

The infamous blood sausage came wrapped in a *crêpe*. Even though the filling was hidden, I, knowing what was inside, could barely look at the *crêpe*. Surrounding the *crêpe* was a pool of lentils, one of my favorite things. Especially when accompanied by the *Beaujolais Nouveau* which was beginning to disappear. I asked for more lentils, which Frederic brought out in a small tureen.

The next course was *rillette,* a mashed meat preparation that is delicious when spread on fresh baguette. The *rillette* was served in a bowl and was deceptively filling, which did not deter me from asking Frederic for seconds. I have subsequently learned to control myself when this dish is served because it is one of my favorite French specialties.

The group surrounding us consisted of about forty people, all French *functionnaires*, government employees, and one of them was a former minister who was now affiliated with the police department. He and his wife were quite friendly and Madame was fascinated by the two *americaines* sitting in their midst. She was a typical middle-aged Frenchwoman, blond hair tightly pulled back, impeccably dressed, with a million-dollar smile that was both shy and inviting at the same time.

The self-appointed master of ceremonies stood to say a few words of welcome. He was a huge bear of a man, and his audience, many of whom had already gone through most of the first bottle of *Beaujolais Nouveau*, were decidedly in a party mood. He soon began leading them in a sing-along. The songs, obviously quite naughty and complete with hand signals, were received with loud laughter, but it was all in fun and tastefully done.

One of the songs required putting both hands up with tips of fingers touching, simulating a mountain, then outlining circles, simulating a curvaceous lady, then undulating them in a hula movement, signifying the sea, then a motion which I'm not too sure of as I write this, but which certainly was a crowd-pleaser.

Dierk and I, not wanting to set ourselves apart, joined in the hand maneuvers, and, when they hit a tune we knew, chimed in. The ex-minister's wife kept pointing to us and giving us the thumbs-up sign, and one of the other women in the group produced a little book with lyrics of songs from many different countries.

Perhaps it was the *Beaujolais*, perhaps just the setting, and perhaps it was just being with nice people wanting to have a good time, but the next thing I knew, the lady with the book of lyrics was sitting beside me, flipping through the pages to find *"chansons americaines."*

Unfortunately, the "American songs" in the book were either old Simon and Garfunkle or Beatles songs and they just didn't lend themselves to a French Beaujolais party.

And then we found "The Red River Valley" with some five or six verses, and I was asked to sing in *americaine*. I feigned embarrassment, the applause grew, they insisted, and, to be honest, the Leo in me was delighted.

I have a fairly acceptable tenor voice, which, although perhaps lacking in professional versatility, makes up for it in volume. It was greeted by momentary silence, then approving nods, and then they all joined in. We were, and I say this in all modesty, superb.

Many, many verses of "Red River Valley" later, and just about the time that fresh bottles of *Beaujolais Nouveau* were brought out, the lady with the lyric book got Dierk up to dance and they did a waltz between tables. Her hands, in typical Java style, were planted on his rear end. The applause was deafening and an encore was in order.

The evening progressed until the time came to leave our new-found friends. We said our *adieus* all around, and, accompanied by the French lyrics to "Auld Lang Syne," backed out the door with them all waving glasses of *Beaujolais Nouveau* in a toast to the Americans who had joined in the festivities.

A few steps later, we discovered that we had left our umbrellas behind. Dierk returned to the restaurant while I waited on the pavement outside. It seemed to take him a rather long time and, when he finally came out, he was grinning from ear to ear.

The group had decided that he couldn't leave without another toast, which they proceeded to do, and then they started singing a song about the joys of wine and friends and he had to join them in still another toast. As he tried to leave, someone put a bottle of *Beaujolas Nouveau* in his coat pocket, and another chorus of "Auld Lang Syne" rang out loud and clear on rue *Saint Simon*.

We returned to the *Rivaldière* several nights later, and the owner and his wife came running over to kiss us and to say that we were the hit of the party and that we simply had to return the next year.

Sitting at one of the tables having dinner was the fellow who had acted as master of ceremonies the night of the *Beaujolais Nouveau fête*, and he jumped up, gripped us both in a bear hug as if we were long-lost brothers, and thanked us for taking part. The party had continued until 3:00 in the morning and, the year before, there had been an accordion player who led the group in a conga line along *Boulevard Saint Germain*. Who knows what would happen next year?

We have reserved the same table for the *Beaujolais Nouveau* fête for next November and I'm busily trying to find other songs in addition to my theme song, "Red River Valley," that might be suitable for my Paris audience.

Just in case they ask for an encore.

BAGUETTE

Ingredients:
2 c   warm water
1 1/2 tbs salt
1 tbs   sugar
6 1/2 c unbleached flour
1 1/2 tbs active dry yeast
       white of one egg, beaten

Preparation:
Preheat oven to 450°. Place large rectangular pan on bottom of oven, fill pan halfway with hot water and allow water to boil. Mix flour with salt, sugar, and dry yeast in a large mixing bowl. Add water slowly, forming a wet dough. Allow to rise for 1 hour in a warm place, then turn out onto a floured surface and knead for 10 minutes Put dough into a bowl in a warm place and allow to rise for another hour. Separate dough into two balls, and form each one into a long loaf. Make several slashes on each loaf with a razor blade or very sharp knife. Brush each loaf with beaten egg-white Place loaves on perforated baguette-baking forms that can be found in any good kitchen store. Bake for 30-35 minutes, depending on how brown you like the baguette. The finished baguette should have a hollow sound when tapped, with a firm outside and a soft interior.

Note:
The key to a successful baguette is baking it in an oven in which there is steam, so be certain to keep adding water to the pan on the bottom of the oven, as the water evaporates.

RILLETTE

Ingredients:
- 1 lb roast pork, chopped into pieces
- 1 small onion, chopped (about 1/2 cup)
- 1 1/2 tbs chopped parsley
- 1/2 tsp grated nutmeg
- 1/2 c stock (either pork or chicken)
- 1/2 tsp powdered mace
- 1 1/2 tbs cognac
- salt to taste
- pepper to taste
- 1/4 lb softened butter

Preparation:
Put all of the ingredients except the butter into a large pot and cook for about 20 minutes. Cool and place contents of pot into a food processor. Using stop/start action, process the mixture until it is the consistency of ground meat. (Be careful not to purée too finely. You do not want a smooth mix.) Stir in 1/2 of the softened butter, reserving the rest for later. Add salt, pepper, and cognac. Put the mixture into either a large serving bowl or, if you prefer, individual ramekins and put into the refrigerator until completely cool. Melt the other 1/2 of the butter and paint a thin layer of the melted butter on the rillette mixture. Serve at room temperature with slices of baguette.

Note:
Makes a delightful first course or, accompanied by wedges of toast, as an accompaniment to the aperitif before the meal.

Chapter 32
Marie

When I met her, Marie was eighty-seven years old. The word that I chose then, to describe her, is the only one I can use now, so many years later, to do her justice. Marie was, quite simply, beautiful. Truly beautiful, as only someone whose face contains a lifetime of experiences can be.

It was the first time Julia had invited us to spend a week with her in her "country place" in *Mandelieu-Capetou*, a town on a hillside overlooking Cannes. I wasn't quite sure what to expect, but, knowing Julia, I knew that our time there would be nice. It turned out to be far more than that, and the annual visits each February that followed, would be anticipated all year long.

Originally owned by the Belgian Ambassador to France, from whom Julia had bought it forty years before, the villa sat in the midst of acres of Mimosa trees that covered the hillside, turning it into a blaze of yellow each year when the flowers bloomed. The view from the villa and the terrace surrounding the swimming pool took in all of Cannes and the sea beyond.

In February, there were no tourists, and it was delightful. We relished that week and savored every moment of it, because it represented almost our last week of freedom before we would have to return to Burgundy in March to prepare for the new season.

Marie had worked for the ambassador and stayed on when Julia bought the house, so she had, in effect, come with the house. She lived in her own quarters in the spacious guest house, which was anchored on the hillside. It was to one side of the entrance gates, and, in addition to Marie's private wing of the guest house, there were five superbly decorated bedrooms for visitors. There was also a lovely little kitchen, tiled in the vibrant colors of *Provence*. But all of the cooking, except for the times that Julia and I prepared a special dish together, was done in the huge kitchen at the main house that lay at the end of the long, curving driveway. That kitchen, unlike the smaller one in the guest house, had four ovens, two refrigerators, and would have been the pride of any restaurant in the world.

In addition to Marie, her daughter and daughter-in-law came to help out when Julia was there with her invited friends. The daughter, although middle aged and well married to a judge, still considered it her duty to come for part of each day to help Marie with the extra housework, and the daughter-in-law, a great cook herself, assisted in the kitchen and served at table. Marie, however, was totally and unquestionably, in charge. The house, in many ways, belonged more to her than to her successive employers.

Marie, after forty years, knew Julia's likes and dislikes perfectly. She and the two other ladies were equally attentive to the guests Julia invited each year to share the time she spent there. We were among the lucky few, along with *Mademoiselle*, who was the only four-legged person ever in evidence.

Mademoiselle and Julia, as you remember, had become acquainted at the jazz concert at the *Café de la Danse*, where *Mademoiselle*, whose hearing was almost gone, had curled up at Julia's feet and happily snoozed away, unaware and undisturbed by any musical sounds other than the occasional vibration of the drum. They had became fast friends, *Mademoiselle* taking Julia's often repeated *"Mignon"* and *"Adorable"* as her due, and nonchalantly adding her new friend to a long list of conquests.

It was actually *Mademoiselle* who was responsible for the special friendship that was forged between Marie and me. The first day there, *Mademoiselle*, still possessed of a fully functioning nose despite her advanced age, had simply strolled into the kitchen and introduced herself. Marie was there in her domain, of course, as she had been for fifty-odd years, hands flying as she chopped away and prepared the meal for whatever guests *Madame Julia* had invited.

Marie and *Mademoiselle* had also taken an instant liking to each other. Perhaps they both, being rather on in years, had certain things in common that escaped the rest of us. Whatever the reason, when I finally found *Mademoiselle*, after frantically looking all over the property and fearing the worst, she was contentedly sitting at Marie's feet being fed yesterday's leftovers in a dinner plate Marie had set out on the floor.

I began to apologize for *Mademoiselle's* intrusion, and Marie, without skipping a beat, looked up at me and offered a smiling, *"Bonjour Monsieur."* She had blue eyes that radiated warmth, with clear, alabaster skin, wrinkled into a permanent smile that spoke of a lifetime of memories. Some, as I found out later, were not particularly happy, but all had done their part in contributing to that unforgettable face.

Marie's son had passed away the year before. But even the loss of a child, the worst thing imaginable for a parent, had not dampened her joy in living. She had mourned him, pulled herself together, and continued doing what she had always done, cared for others.

Marie was tiny and thin and reminded me of a hummingbird. Always in motion, only alighting for a moment and then hurrying on. I saw her every morning, out and about long before anyone else, bending over to remove some offending weeds, or cutting the Mimosa blossoms. She could arrange ordinary flowers into stunning arrangements, and each room was filled with fresh arrangements every single day. She never seemed at rest, unwilling to waste one moment of life's offerings, both the good and the bad.

I wanted to spend time with Marie, but it was the wrong moment to intrude on her work. Offering to help would have been considered an insult, so completely in charge was she. I backed out of the kitchen, on my way out, picking up an unwilling, and rather annoyed, *Mademoiselle*. To *Mademoiselle*, I was the intruder.

Luncheon was served, as were all formal meals, in the dining room of the main house. The room was filled with Spanish antiques. Julia had bought a truckload of them on a trip to Spain long ago, and they filled the entire guest house as well.

The lunch was served by Marie's daughter-in-law, Ginette, and each course was brought around on large platters so we could help ourselves to as much or as little as we wished. Marie herself came out to serve a platter of *crudités* to begin the meal. It was her specialty and she was very proud of it. A work of art, the vegetables bought at the market that morning had been chosen and arranged to create a master's palette of colors. The platter was about three feet long and a foot wide and was clearly a labor of love that had taken hours to prepare.

There were six of us that first year, and in subsequent years the number would sometimes swell to as many as nine or ten. There were years when Dierk and *Mademoiselle* and I stayed in the guest quarters in the main house. It was a separate little apartment that took up almost the entire basement and opened onto a private terrace. There was a comfortable sitting room with an upright piano, and an armoire and a huge carved wooden desk taking up one corner of the bedroom. I imagined some bearded Spanish *señor* seated at the desk, centuries ago, signing a document that might decide someone's fate. And there sat I, making my diary entries seated behind the same desk. I wonder what he would have thought.

There were also some years when Dierk, *Mademoiselle* and I were the *only* guests. Those were the visits I enjoyed most, especially since they gave me a chance to get to know Marie better. *Mademoiselle* was my excuse, at first; but then, over the years, I simply went in to chat with Marie when I knew she wasn't too busy.

We passed many hours together. She spoke of all the years she had been at the house, of how beautiful the garden had been when there was a full staff of gardeners all year round. Now a gardener came by only to do the planting and the heavy yard work. The rest of the time it was Marie who tended it as best as she could, with some help from her "daughters."

She told me of the famous people who had been at the house, from Elizabeth Taylor when she was a guest at the Cannes Film Festival, to *Monsieur Citröen,* who had stayed in the quarters we occupied in the main house. Marie spoke of the parties the house had seen and the people it had been her responsibility to take care of. And she spoke of it all with dancing eyes, a song in her voice, and affection from her soul. They were good days and she would create more of them for as long as the Lord spared her. All who came to the house became *hers*.

We talked of food, the dishes she had grown up with and that she now prepared for *Madame Julia's* guests, the flavors of the *Côte d'Azur,* the spices that made the food from that part of France so special. Although she was not formally schooled as a chef, every meal she prepared was delicious. There were none of the rich cream sauces of the Normandy cuisine, but the variety of foods that Marie could produce was incredible.

One of Marie's specialties was *Soupe de Pesto*. Again, no one else was allowed to serve this, only Marie. It was made of white beans, stewed in a broth that tasted of pesto and *herbs de Provence*. Marie brought it to the table with pride and was delighted when I more than willingly accepted her offer of a second helping. Before we left that year, she shared the recipe with me. Unlike Marie, I make the pesto in the food processor, but I remember Marie grinding it all in the wooden mortar and pestle that had served her so well for many years.

When Marie and her helpers had the day off, Julia and I would prepare a simple meal in the little kitchen in the guest house. I would roll thin slices of cooked chicken breast around chunks of provolone cheese, sprinkle on some *herbs de Provence*, pop them into the oven until the cheese melted, and then serve them on a bed of salad with a drizzle of olive oil. Another time, when I saw them in all their fresh glory in the local market, I bought asparagus, cooked them slightly and then stuffed them in along with the cheese, and it was delicious. Or I would prepare some *tapenade* with the luscious black olives so readily available in the market, and serve it with a salad of assorted greens.

The wine was usually a chilled local *rosé*, which I rarely drink except on those occasions when red wine is not available. In that setting and for that climate, they were refreshing, satisfying, easy meals and great fun to prepare.

Dessert, however, was always Julia's contribution. She has a very active sweet tooth and loves baking, so, in honor of Dierk's birthday, one year, she decided to make something special. It turned into *Délice de Julia*, which later became a favorite at *Aux Trois Saisons*. At that time, though, chocolate gave him terrible migraine headaches, the most awful allergy I, as a chocoholic, can imagine. It fortunately disappeared after two years, and he can now enjoy those incredible Belgian *Neuhaus* chocolates which, I'm firmly convinced, can cure anything.

AUX TROIS SAISONS

Faced with the birthday cake dilemma, Julia solved the problem quite artistically. She simply coated one half of the cake with chocolate icing and made a coffee-butter icing with chopped hazelnuts for the other half so he could enjoy the cake too. It was a splendid success.

In Marie's ninety-fifth year, she passed away, still active to the end. We were tearfully informed of this by Julia, shortly after Ginette called her in Paris to tell her the sad news.

We mourned Marie and the world she had created that was gone with her. It was filled with purpose, love, caring, and pride, and I treasure the times we shared. They live in my memory, and my heart. As will the face I saw for the first time those many years ago in the kitchen in *Mandelieu....*

PESTO

Ingredients:
4 c	fresh basil
½ c	pine cone nuts
2	cloves garlic
½ tsp	salt
½ c	parmesan cheese
⅔ c	olive oil

Preparation:
Wash and drain the basil leaves, remove stems, and allow leaves to air-dry for several hours. Grate the cheese. Put all ingredients in the food processor and blend (stop-start motion) until smooth. The pesto may be refrigerated or frozen in small plastic containers until ready to use.

Note:
If you put the pesto in a transparent freezer bag and flatten it out, you can then easily break off as much of the frozen pesto as you need for any future recipe.

MARIE'S SOUPE DE PESTO

Ingredients:

1 lb	dried white beans
1 lb	lima beans
4	large potatoes, cubed
4	large onions, cubed
4	large carrots, (1/4 inch slices)
2	leeks, (1/2 inch slices)
3	stalks celery, (1/4 inch slices)
3	medium zucchini, (diced)
2 tbs	olive oil
1 c	string beans (1/2 inch slices)
1 c	chopped cabbage
1 c	diced salt pork
2	bay leaves
1 tsp	salt
1/4 tsp	pepper
1/4 tsp	sage
1/2 c	pesto, prepared as above

Preparation:

Soak white beans overnight. Combine white beans with lima beans. Prepare the other vegetables, as above. Put the olive oil into a large pan, heat until a drop of water will sizzle when dropped into the oil, then add the salt pork and the onions and sauté until transparent. Add the other vegetables and sauté for several minutes. Transfer vegetables into a large pot and cover with water, bring to a boil, and add bay leaves, sage, salt, and pepper. Cook over low heat for one hour. Just before serving, add the pesto, stir well, and serve with grated parmesan cheese on the side.

Note:

The above proportions and ingredients are really a matter of preference. Check the seasonings and add more or less to your own taste. The same holds true for the amount of pesto, although I can never seem to add too much.

TAPENADE
ALSO KNOWN AS "POOR MAN'S CAVIAR"
"CAVIAR DES PAUVRES"

Ingredients:
- 1 c — black olives, pitted
- 3/4 c — anchovy fillets
- 1/4 c — capers
- 1 tsp — Dijon mustard
- 2 tbs — lemon juice
- a dash of pepper
- 1/2 c — olive oil

Preparation:
Place the olives, anchovies, capers, mustard, lemon juice and pepper in a food processor bowl. Using the stop-start motion, carefully purée the ingredients. Add the olive oil in a stop-start fashion until a thick paste is formed, being careful not to over-purée. You want to end up with a coarse paste not a fine one.

Helpful Hint:
At Aux Trois Saisons, I served the tapenade as part of a salad course. I mixed two different varieties of fresh lettuce, one of which was a frizzy kind. Then I filled one half of an egg shell, which I had previously cleaned and dried, with the tapenade. (A tiny quail egg makes for an even prettier presentation.) To serve, I set the filled egg shell in the center of the bed of lettuce, drizzled the lettuce sparingly with olive oil, and served the salad with thick slices of bread to be spread with the tapenade. This presentation looks like a bird's nest and tastes delicious.

DÉLICE DE JULIA

Ingredients:

1	layer yellow cake
12 tbs	Cointreau
6	eggs, separated
8 tbs	powdered sugar
1 1/2 c	crushed hazelnuts

Preparation:

Cut the layer of yellow cake into 1/2" thick slices and arrange them to cover the bottom of a baking pan. Sprinkle with the Cointreau. (You can use your own favorite yellow cake recipe or a bought cake. It will be happily doused in Cointreau either way.) Beat 4 egg yolks and 6 large tablespoons powdered sugar until the mixture turns slightly white. Add 1 1/2 cups crushed hazelnuts to the beaten mixture. Spread this mixture evenly over the yellow cake in the pan. Beat 6 egg whites with 2 tablespoons of powdered sugar (plus a bit of regular sugar for firmness) until firm. Pile this meringue over the other ingredients already in the baking pan. Place the pan into a hot oven for 5 or 10 minutes, just to brown the meringue peaks. If desired, (and Julia most certainly does!) pour melted chocolate sauce over the cake at serving time.

CHOCOLATE SAUCE:

Ingredients:

2	slabs of unsweetened cooking chocolate
1/2 c	heavy cream
1	egg yolk

Preparation:

Break chocolate into pieces and melt chocolate in the top of a double boiler. Add cream, egg yolk, and, if desired, a little more milk to thin, plus sugar to sweeten to your taste. (I don't like too-sweet chocolate, so I add very little.) While hot, drizzle the chocolate sauce over the cake, and please leave some in a separate bowl for Chocoholics like me.

MORT SOBEL

Part V
No Room At The Inn

Chapter 33
Les Guides

When we returned to *Aux Trois Saisons* from Paris each year, we had about half of the rooms reserved for the season. By the sixth year, we had a sixty percent return rate of people for whom we were an annual stopping off place every year on their way north or south.

The Belgian guests brought us those marvelous "Neuhaus" chocolates and some very special parsley seeds. When you're dining out in Belgium next time, ask the waiter if the restaurant serves fried parsley. It's a specialty that requires a very particular frizzy type of parsley and very careful frying of the parsley. Otherwise it can burn to a crisp very quickly, but, if prepared properly, it has a unique taste and is a delicious and unusual accompaniment to the meal.

Our Dutch friends brought us the *"hageslakke"* chocolate bits that I sprinkled over desserts, at least those that survived my midnight raids on the refrigerator where they were kept. It's a breakfast favorite in Holland but delicious any time of the day, or night, even dry right out of the box.

All of our guests, with the very few exceptions I've already told you about, the "horrors," became our best advertisements. It was the old *"de bouche à l'Oreille,"* the word of mouth, that makes any venture a true success. The other forty percent came to *Aux Trois Saisons* either because they had heard about us from their friends or had read about us in one of the tourist guides.

One of these guides was the Hilary Rubinstein "Good Hotel Guide." This is a guide printed in the United Kingdom and a pretty good one. Unlike the "Guide Rivage," which really was the turning point for us, this one did not have any photos and the write-up was very short.

One of our guests had obviously written to them about us, so they put us in the guide sight unseen. We would have preferred it if they had seen us personally, but we still appreciated the mention. The guide is very popular in England and brought us some nice guests, including the young man who sat cross-legged in the garden and presented us with a sketch of the tower when he and his family left.

Another guide book, which probably had more effect on our success than we ever really knew, was the one printed in France and named, with typical French understatement, *"La Bible des Week Ends, Seminaires, et Receptions."* We were included in that one somewhat by chance.

One of the finest restaurants in Burgundy is the *"Moulin de Martorey,"* located in Saint-Rémy and housed in an old mill. The superbly prepared meals are the creation of one of the younger chefs of Burgundy, Jean-Pierre Gillot. He is a true artist and a visit to his restaurant is an experience. We dined there several times and were very impressed with the food and his friendliness.

Monsieur Gillot's restaurant was already included in the guide. When they asked him for the name of a place in the vicinity where his dining guests could stay overnight, he had recommended "la maison des américains" because a lot of his clients had spoken to him favorably about us. He said that it was a place that seemed to pay as much attention to the guests' comforts as he did in his restaurant. High praise, indeed.

The next year, we were surprised to receive a beautiful hard-cover volume with *Aux Trois Saisons*'s picture inside. The description said that *Aux Trois Saisons* was "neither a hotel nor a restaurant, but better than that: a place where life is warm and happy," with *"confort adorable,"* and where there is a "relaxed welcome unique in Burgundy."

Without our knowledge, they had probably paid an unheralded visit to *Aux Trois Saisons*, because the description went on to say that they didn't want to say too much because the proprietors wished to remain "discreet" and the guests wished to guard their *"privilèges."* Then they listed such amenities as the luxurious bathrobes and numerous towels in the bathroom, the chocolates Dierk placed on each pillow at night, my "gâteaux maison" for breakfast, the unusual and delicious dinner *Menu Fixe*, the promenade along the river, and the *apéritif* on the terrace.

Those three were the only official tourist guides that we were in. But they, together with the articles that appeared in various newsletters and magazines, and the reputation that the inn had created by word-of-mouth, seemed to indicate that we had, indeed, arrived.

Arrived, in fact, at the point where, halfway through the season we were usually exhausted. After the initial mistakes and the growing pains, the operation worked smoothly, and we managed to get through the eighteen-hour days.

The first two years were slow ones. There were some days when only two or three rooms were occupied, so we had more time to spend enjoying our guests. By the third year, we were almost fully booked, and, by the fourth year, we began to actually welcome the occasional cancellation.

As the inn became more successful, it became an all-consuming, seven-month long, eighteen-hour-per-day, seven-days-per-week enterprise that left no time for recuperation. Five months off, between "seasons," sounds wonderful, doesn't it, but when we closed the gates for the last time each

October, we were so wound up that we needed a few weeks to unwind. Then, of course, when we returned to Burgundy from Paris each year in March, repairs had to be done, and the garden cleaned and planted before the official opening on Easter weekend.

Eventually, by the end of the fourth year of *Aux Trois Saisons'* existence, we decided that we had to just block out a long weekend, several times during each season, tell people who called that we were all booked up, and then lock the big iron gates, get into the car, drive up to Paris and hide for a few days. We began doing this the fifth year. We felt sorry, especially when calls came from people we knew and would have loved to welcome again, but it became a matter of survival.

And the people truly were the fun of it, so we felt a strange mixture of feelings…fortunate, grateful, and terribly guilty.

GÂTEAU MAISON

This breakfast specialty is what the Guide called our "Gâteau Maison"

Ingredients:

2	good sized onions, sliced very thin
12	slices of bacon
12	slices of dry day-old baguette (or other thickly sliced bread)
4 c	milk
8	eggs
1 tsp	salt
1/4 tsp	pepper
1 lb	grated Swiss cheese

Preparation:

Fry bacon until crisp, remove bacon from pan, leaving bacon fat in pan. Dry fried bacon on paper towels and crumble into small pieces. Fry sliced onions in bacon fat until transparent (do not brown). Generously grease a large casserole dish with butter. Spread half of the bread slices to cover bottom of casserole. Sprinkle half of the dried bacon pieces, half of the fried onions, and half of the grated cheese over the bread. Put a second layer of bread over this, and spread the other half of the bacon pieces, fried onions, and cheese over the first layer. Gently beat together the eggs and the milk, salt, and pepper. Pour the milk mixture over the bread layers in the casserole. Bake in a preheated 350° oven for about 45 minutes until it puffs up. Serve while still hot.

BABOTIE

This is a recipe I learned while I lived in South Africa and which our guests loved. It became a favorite at Aux Trois Saisons.

Ingredients:

½ kg	(1.25 pounds) ground beef
½ kg	(1.25 pounds) ground lamb
	large onions, finely chopped
	slices bread (may be stale)
1½ c	milk
2 tbs	vinegar
2 tsp	salt
½ tsp	pepper
2 tbs	sugar
1 tbs	curry powder
2 tbs	oil
2	eggs
2 oz	each: raisins, dried apricots, dried apples.
3	bay leaves

Preparation:

Preheat oven to 300°. Soak raisins, dried apricots, and dried apple slices overnight in water. Soak bread in milk until soft, squeeze off excess milk, retaining it for later use. Fry onions in oil until brown, then add spices and bread. Add ground meat and mix well. Add drained raisins, apricots, and apple slices. Transfer meat mixture to a large greased baking dish. Beat eggs and add the milk from step 2. Pour beaten egg mixture over meat mixture, and top with 3 bay leaves. Place baking dish in preheated oven for approximately 35 minutes, or until golden brown. Serve with rice and sliced bananas or stewed apples.

Chapter 34
Place de la Corinne

When a lawn extends over two acres, and all of your time is spent running an inn, it's almost impossible to do either one justice if you try to do both. Each year, the basic and necessary tasks of just planting flower seeds and cleaning up the leaves left over from the last autumn took several weeks.

We needed the flowers, during the season, because there were a total of thirty-five vases in the guest rooms and the salon and dining room areas that had to be filled with fresh flowers regularly.

I left the planting to Dierk, who, unlike myself, knew what he was doing. I must admit, though, I rather enjoyed the mindless task of raking and burning the leaves on those brisk March days before the inn opened officially. We raked for hours each day, piled the leaves in pyramids, set the fallen apples to one side, set the fallen chestnuts to the other side, and then began the burning, which was perfectly legal in Burgundy.

The chestnuts posed special problems. The three enormous trees outside the dining room windows produced "horse chestnuts," the inedible kind. When they bloomed, they were lovely, but their beauty somewhat dimmed for me by the fact that I was terribly allergic to the delicate pinkish-white blossoms and spent two weeks sneezing incessantly.

With the hard spikes that surrounded each chestnut, if we inadvertently left one of them in the leaf pile, it would explode and emerge from the flames like a cannonball. We dodged a great many and over the years became very wary.

Anything more than cleaning the park was a Herculean effort. The lawn, when the grass started growing, required about five hours of work, even with a self-propelled lawn mower.

We made a valiant attempt the first year, but when the inn began to be busy, we realized that we needed help. Finding people to work, in France, is not easy. There are not enough people who actually want to work since the State will supply everything anyway. And this in a country that has had over a ten percent unemployment rate for over a decade. But more of that later.

We put the word out to all of our friends and the people from whom we bought the wine, croissants, indeed, everything we used at *Aux Trois Saisons*, that we needed someone to come in and help us.

The lawn posed no urgent problem for me but, when it grew a few millimeters above what he considered acceptable, Dierk, with his Germanic need to do things absolutely right, insisted that it was time to find someone, even if only for mowing the grass once a week. We contacted a garden service. Their representative came out to see the property, shook hands with us, made voluminous notes in his dossier, shook hands with us again and departed.

Two weeks later, we received his devis, the estimate of what his company would charge us for just a weekly lawn-mowing. The figure was double what our total profits had been for the previous season. We respectfully declined.

There followed a succession of local people who helped us out, the first of whom was David. He was a student in nearby Chalon-Sur-Saône and arrived regularly on his little moped that invariably wouldn't start up again when it was time to leave.

David worked for us for a few years and then went off to school in another city. He was a really nice young man, very polite, and I've often wondered what the future held for him. I hope he has done well.

Wherever you are, David, thank you for helping us out when we needed it so much.

David was followed by Arnaud, a lanky, good-looking young man with beautiful blue eyes and a pleasant personality. He was the strong, silent type and began each sentence with a prolonged "Baaaaaaaa" before anything was actually said.

The "Baaaaaaaa" in France is very common. It's comparable to the "Ummmmmm" in the U.S., which can be disconcerting when it delays the answer you're anxiously waiting for.

When I first arrived in France, I actually thought that "Baaaaaaa" was a word. Each time I heard "Baaaaaaaaaa, oui," I took it to mean more than just a simple "oui," which, of course, it doesn't. I've even used it myself, on occasion, to buy some extra time when I didn't have an answer to a question. It's very handy.

When Arnaud, too, left us to go on to higher education, his father, who had been laid off work and was looking for odd jobs, filled in for him. It was Arnaud's father, bless him, who did, indeed, come through for us when we needed extra help after Dierk's injury years later.

My major contribution to the garden, the only one except for leaf burning, in fact, had been to create and plant the *Place de la Corinne* the first season. This was a large circular area in the back garden which I claimed, in *Mademoiselle's* name, the first month we were in the house. I laid out the *Place* in pie-shaped wedges and designed the plantings so that each wedge was a different color and there was always something in bloom.

I cleared the area of rocks, put in some top soil, planted dahlias—in both seeds and little flats—pansies, and sunflowers. I meticulously planted the pansies in color-coordinated rows so that they could be interpreted as either the American red-white-blue or the French blue-white-red, in honor of my two beloved countries. The order of the colors also depended on whether you were coming or going. It was most effective.

My patriotic efforts failed, however, because some of the snails, the ones who survived *Monsieur Lagrange*, decided to eat all of the blue flowers and we were left with only the red and white ones. Our Swiss guests must have felt right at home.

My sunflowers became the talk of *Aux Trois Saisons*. Not knowing any better, instead of buying sunflower seeds in commercial seed packets, I bought a big sack of bird seed and scattered it in rows, and dumped loads of fertilizer over them.

The sunflowers that came, and eventually took over that part of the *Place de la Corinne*, grew to over two meters high, which is about seven feet, and were magnificent. In the years to come, my only contribution to the garden at *Aux Trois Saisons* was to plant the sunflowers, since I was obviously doing something right.

When the first planting of *Place de la Corinne* was finished, we asked *Mademoiselle* to sit in the center of it, opened a bottle of champagne for ourselves, toasted her health, and fed her some of the *foie gras* she loved so much as a special treat. We continued the tradition each year, even after she left us.

After all, it isn't every dog that had her own Place named after her in France.

Chapter 35
Two Weddings and a Birthday

Aux Trois Saisons was the perfect place for celebrations and we had many of them. Once they had visited for the first time, guests seemed to begin planning their return and who to bring with them to show off their "find."

Two young people from Germany, Stephan and Kristina, arrived the first year and fell in love with the inn. They decided that, for their marriage, they wanted to have their family and friends join them at the "most romantic" place in the world for the happy event. They asked us to check the required formalities and let them know what had to be done to arrange the wedding for the following year.

I went off to the local *Mairie* to ask *Monsieur le Maire* what the procedure would be. A visit to the Mairie was, invariably, a social occasion, with handshaking all around, inquiries as to how the inn was faring, comments on any new local beautification plans, mutual health, vacation plans, or, more often than not, how to respond to the latest instrument of legislative torture we received in the post that morning.

This time, Madame, the mayor's secretary, made some telephone calls and we were informed that, in order to be married in France, at least one of the prospective partners had to reside in the community for at least thirty days, something neither Stephan or Kristina could do.

We turned to Jean-Claude Brelière for help. He took us to meet the priest at the little church in *Rully* across from his vineyard. The elderly priest was most cooperative and said that, although an actual marriage was not legally possible under French law, he was certainly not averse to a religious "celebration" of their union, a wonderfully French way of getting around the problem.

Stephan and Kristina had their legal civil marriage in Germany on Friday morning, then drove, with their closest family and friends, and their priest, to *Dracy le Fort*. I prepared dinner for them on Friday night, and on Saturday morning we all were there as they stood up in the ancient church in *Rully* and vowed their love before God.

Jean-Claude and Anna and their two young boys were waiting to throw rice at them as they came out of the church and Jean-Claude prepared a special *dégustation* for all the guests in their honor. Fully fortified, everyone returned to the inn, where they had reserved all five rooms for the weekend, and I prepared a special Wedding Banquet. My *Mousse au Saumon avec Sauce Aneth*, (the Salmon Mousse with Dill Sauce that M.F.K. Fisher had asked about in her letter) was the hit of the dinner.

Kristina and Stephan are still good friends. They've visited us in Normandy, where I baby-sat outside with Indy, their enormous black *Bouvier de Flandres* dog while they and Dierk toured the inside of the cathedral at *Honfleur*. And they spent a few days with us in Paris shortly before they welcomed baby Lars to their growing family.

The other wedding that stands out in my memory started innocently enough when Madame W., who lived in *Dracy le Fort*, drove into the courtyard one day to speak with us. She is a tiny lady with a perpetual smile and a charming personality. Would we, she asked, be willing to allow her daughter and son-in-law to be photographed on their wedding day in the park of *Aux Trois Saisons?*

We agreed with pleasure, and a few weeks later the entire wedding party arrived led by the bride and groom, who looked like they had stepped off the top of a wedding cake. They were an adorable couple, she blond and petite, he dark and handsome, and both looking as nervous as one might expect.

The photographer posed them all over the park, in front of the flowers in the garden, along the path of the trout stream, and then with the house as a backdrop. Somewhere along the way, someone took out a bottle of champagne and we started toasting the young couple. Then we toasted the mothers and fathers. Then, of course, we couldn't leave out the members of the wedding party, or, *bien sûr,* the kind hosts who had allowed them to be photographed in their park.

We followed them along and this went on for about an hour. We all got so carried away that Dierk and I insisted they come inside and be photographed in the salon and the library, as well. The photograph of them looking adoringly into each other's eyes was on our mantelpiece soon afterwards, a gift from Madame W.

One very positive result of this particular wedding for us was that we and Madame W. took an immediate liking to each other and Madame agreed to come in to help us with the rooms, something she had done for Madame Fournier, the previous owner of the house that became *Aux Trois Saisons.*

She showed up every day after that, beautifully groomed and smiling, and stayed for two hours each morning, even on her birthday. She and Dierk became a great team and I could leave for my shopping expedition each day a little less exhausted.

One year, the daughter of Madame Fournier, the previous owner, contacted us by letter from Lyon, where she lived. The letter, a long and typically flowery French one, said that she had heard from ex-neighbors and townspeople that we had done lovely things to her former childhood home and also that we had shown ourselves to be welcome additions to the community, even taking part in the *Fête Patronale*.

The letter, as letters do in France, took a while and lots of meaningless flattery to get to its main point, which was that the daughter and her husband wanted to arrange a surprise eighty-sixth birthday party for Madame Fournier and they felt it would be perfect to hold it at the inn. It was, after all, where they had spent so much of their lives.

Would we, it inquired, be "so kind as to have the graciousness to let them know if we could grant them this special request" and reserve all five rooms for the evening and would I give them the pleasure of preparing a *Menu Gastronomique* for the occasion?

Out came the dictionary and three or four hours later a letter in my own unique variation of the French language was sent off. Several weeks later, I met with Madame's daughter at a café in *Chalon sur Saône*, and together we planned the whole surprise from beginning to end. All of the townspeople who had worked for Madame Fournier over the years would be invited to the *aperitif*, and we talked over the Menu and wines for the ten overnight guests who would be there for the sit-down dinner.

As the day approached, I became a little anxious because I still heard Madame Fournier's final words in the notaire's office. How would she react to all the changes we had made to the house where her children were reared, a house she had shared for most of those years with Monsieur Fournier?

On the appointed day, with the guests all settled in their rooms, her daughter escorted Madame Fournier into the entrance foyer before the party was to begin. Her smile began at the entrance when she saw the cheerful Monet-yellow of the walls. We had hand-mixed the paint ourselves to arrive at a color that would complement the cobalt blue of the old floor tiles. The smile grew wider in the salon, where the *boiseries* had been painstakingly brought back to their original nineteenth century splendor, and it grew wider still in the present library with its comfortable sitting area and the wall of bookcases we built, stained and varnished ourselves. Her face lit up in the new dining room, where we had created one large room out of two smaller ones and spent days removing the plaster hiding the foot-thick beams and hand-scrubbed and waxed them to gleaming perfection.

Madame was delighted with the house, telling everybody in sight, almost with pride, how beautiful she found it.

The townspeople arrived for the *apéritif*, all dressed up in their Sunday best and unable to hide their curiosity about what we had done to the inside of the house. Madame Fournier sat in a high-backed chair in the salon and welcomed them regally.

The birthday party itself was great fun. We set all the tables in a row down the center of the dining room, and the family was together again just as they had been for all those years. My Menu and the wines chosen to accompany each course were a great success. The dinner was followed by a fifty-year-old *Marc de Bourgogne* that was uncorked and handled as gingerly as a newborn baby.

This was the strongest alcoholic beverage I have ever tasted. The precious liquid had been saved for so many years and it was such a momentous event to all assembled that I didn't have the heart to tell them I found it undrinkable. The French love their Marc, but give me a good cognac any day.

When Madame was being escorted to the door, at the end of the evening, she turned, took my hand and Dierk's in hers and said, "I'm happy you have the house. You have made it beautiful. No French person would have done so well."

MOUSSE AU SAUMON AVEC SAUCE ANETH (SALMON MOUSSE WITH DILL SAUCE)

Ingredients:

Mousse:

1	envelope unflavored gelatin
3 tbs	lemon juice
1 tbs	finely chopped onion
½ c	water
1 c	mayonnaise
¼ tsp	paprika
1	crême fraiche (or sour cream)
1 lb	canned or fresh salmon (skinned, boned, and drained)

Preparation;

Lightly oil individual ramekins or molds of your choice. Put the lemon juice and finely chopped onion into the food processor bowl. Slowly dissolve the gelatin in the water and gently bring it to a boil. Once the gelatin is completely dissolved, add this mixture to the lemon juice and onion and process until smooth and frothy and no onion bits are left. Turn off the processor and add the mayonnaise, paprika, and drained salmon. Process again until smooth. Stop the machine and add the crême fraiche 1/3 cup at a time, processing after each addition. Pour into very lightly oiled individual molds. Prepare one day ahead and chill. Unmold before serving, surround with sauce, and decorate.

Dill Sauce:

½ c	mayonnaise
½ c	crême fraiche (or sour cream)
2	sweet cornichons (gherkins), finely chopped
1 tbs	juice from cornichons
1 tbs	dried chopped dill

Preparation:

Blend all of the ingredients in the food processor until smooth. Chill until ready to serve.

Helpful Hint:
It's easier to unmold the mousse if you fill the mold slightly above the top. This means that, when inverted, it will stick to the plate and help release the suction inside the mold. When ready to unmold, simply run a warm, sharp knife along the edges to break the seal, dip the outside of the mold quickly into hot water for several seconds, dry the outside of the mold and invert the mold in the exact position you want it on the serving plate. The mousse will adhere to the plate and the mold will just slide up like magic! Then pour some of the dill sauce around the salmon mousse and decorate with sprigs of dill and some sprigs of chives

Chapter 36
The Annual 30- Year Flood

Our neighbors in the adjoining field, at *Dracy le Fort*, were successive herds of Charollais cows. This breed is particular to Burgundy and is white with curly heads, giving them the general appearance of a bovine Harpo Marx. They prospered, while we lived there, thanks to Dierk's visiting them daily with barrels of fallen apples, which he deposited over the barbed-wire fence separating them from *Aux Trois Saisons*. The apples would otherwise have simply been thrown away, so Dierk considered it an act of kindness with a practical side.

This went on for several months and, eventually, the cows saw him coming from the other end of the field, came running, and lined up for their daily treat. They were the happiest and friendliest cows I've ever met.

When we or our guests took off on hot-air-ballooning trips, it was usually from our front lawn, unless the wind dictated otherwise. The cows would line up along the fence, totally unafraid of the activity, and act as a sort of farewell committee as the *montgolfier* wafted up, up, and away.

The first year, when the warmer days had melted the snow in the higher lands and the water flowed into the rivers, the trout stream that marked the border of our property started rising. It stopped short of our back lawn. Our house sat quite a bit higher than the stream, so we had no damage at all, but the adjoining field ended up under several inches of water.

Our curly-headed friends stood there looking very perplexed and uncomfortable as the water rose to what, I guess, were their ankles.

When I went to buy the croissants and baguettes, I asked the lady at the *patisserie* if this flooding happened often. *"Mais, non,"* she replied. "There is, perhaps, flooding like this every thirty years or so."

I returned home, reassured, by her words, that we were safe for at least another twenty-nine years, and got on with the day's chores.

The next year, of course, it happened again. I felt even safer since this meant that for the next fifty-eight years we didn't have to worry. After that, I would take my chances.

As you might guess, the flooding occurred every single year at precisely the same time, which led to our greeting it each year as "the annual thirty-year flood".

The flooding, one year, was worse than usual in Burgundy and I saw on the television screen homes only a short distance from *Aux Trois Saisons* that were under three feet of water. The misery was etched on the faces of the people who lived in them. Many of the farmers had made spaces in the attics of their barns for the livestock, and they were forced to arrive by rowboat to feed them.

These events seem so far removed when we see them on television. We've become immune to them, possibly because they *have* become so familiar. Modern television-addicted viewers dine with disasters somewhere in the world every evening, and announcers recite statistics that can't be very good for the digestive processes. But the reality of it, in terms of human and animal suffering, is impossible to imagine.

The aged man and his wife who were interviewed by the *Canal 5* reporter had been drained of sadness. They just shook their heads in quiet disbelief that a whole lifetime of memories lay under a meter of water.

Those people were our neighbors, perhaps not personal acquaintances, but, for a while, we shared the same destiny with an unspoken but mutually understood dependence on an often capricious nature.

Each year, after the annual thirty-year flood came and then subsided, our four-legged neighbors could again graze and await Dierk's daily largesse. The beautiful summer days arrived. The inn became busy, so that I saw the cows only when I gave arriving guests a tour of the property. They seemed content.

One day, when the summer was almost over, the inevitable happened and they were led onto a flat-bed truck and driven away.

We missed them, and Dierk vowed to feed next year's herd fewer apples so that they would appear a bit thinner. Then we might have them around longer.

Chapter 37
Assignations

L'Auberge Aux Trois Saisons, over the years, came to be a place where people could feel safe, discreetly hidden from prying eyes, yet still surrounded by the comforts of civilization.

Perhaps because it was a small, romantic spot a bit out of the way, or perhaps because we did not welcome very young children and it was, therefore, peaceful; or perhaps because the word got around that the inn was elegantly appointed; or perhaps simply because it was in France…at any rate, the inn served as a place to which people came to spend time with their own special people.

Part of the early success of *Aux Trois Saisons*, in fact, was due to one assignation in particular.

Michelle was a lady of advanced age with a heart of gold. She'd been divorced many years ago from her first husband, with whom she had three children. We met Michelle in Paris at a mutual friend's house. I still see her entering the room, dressed in Chanel from head to toe, announcing that her recent hip replacement surgery was a complete success, and proceeding to do a high-kick to prove it.

Michelle was a product of "old money" whose family had once owned an entire house on *Avenue d'Iena*, complete with a full staff of servants. As a young girl, she spent weekends with the Rothschilds on hunts, and indulged in other pastimes I couldn't even begin to imagine. Her present home was an enormous apartment in a high rise, just outside the *peripherique*. It was on the twenty-fifth floor, and the apartment had a magnificent view of all of Paris from every room. If I had been blessed with an unobstructed view of the Eiffel Tower from my kitchen window, as she was, I would never have gotten any cooking done.

When her first husband was dying of cancer many years after their legal parting, it was Michelle who took care of him in his last days. She was, and is, to this day, always there for friends in their time of need.

Michelle had been, in recent years, the companion of an English gentleman named Ian, also in his seventies. She refused his offer of marriage, and he had responded that he did not want to continue in a relationship that offered no "security," since he, unlike Michelle, was not wealthy.

They parted and, in anger, Ian had vacationed in Florida, married a wealthy, attractive, and much younger American widow, and made no bones about letting Michelle know. She was there to comfort and forgive him when the marriage failed and Ian returned to Europe.

When Michelle called *Aux Trois Saisons* to make a reservation, she volunteered that she would bring Ian with her and that she, therefore, wanted the prettiest room in the house. It was to be a last attempt at a reconciliation.

We filled *Bellevue* with flowers, served a complimentary drink on the terrace when they arrived, and, except for the bow and arrow, we did quite a good job of impersonating Cupid for the two lovers.

The dinner music was soft and romantic, the wines Dierk helped them choose were perfect for the meal, and there was a fine old cognac served in front of the blazing fireplace before they went up to bed. In short, nothing was left to chance.

They asked for breakfast in their room, a service which we gently discouraged after the first few years, and came down the next morning holding hands and looking very happy.

Aux Trois Saisons worked its magic and they've been together ever since, still not married but that's a technicality that must have been worked out somewhere along the line. At some point, I also adopted Michelle's recipe for Avocado Soup and named it after her when I served it at *Aux Trois Saisons*.

This assignation did, as I mentioned above, have a lot to do with the early success of the inn. Michelle's brother-in-law, the brother of her late ex-husband, lived in the south of France and had many friends who made the north-south trip each year as part of their vacation. Shortly after Michelle's successful reconciliation with Ian, we started receiving calls from people saying that a Monsieur X had recommended our inn very highly and they wanted to make reservations.

The name wasn't familiar to us, but the mysterious Monsieur X, it turned out, was Michelle's brother-in-law, who we never actually met in all the years we had *Aux Trois Saisons*. He was responsible, however, for recommending it to some of the most memorable guests who ever came to the inn. They were people who, once they discovered the inn, returned there at least twice each season and made reservations, when they left, for the next year.

By the sixth year of *Aux Trois Saisons*' existence, they had all returned so often that they became almost family to us, and we met many in Paris during the winters. They filled us in, each successive year, on their children's lives, their children's children's lives, and we, I think, in showing genuine interest, became part of their own lives.

They almost all belonged to the large non-French community who own homes in the south of France, although they maintain their residences in various parts of Belgium or Holland. As a group, they were charming, interesting, well-traveled, usually at least tri-lingual, of a certain age, very appreciative of our efforts, and a joy to welcome back each year.

Somewhat more in the category of "assignation," suspected but unproven, was an episode involving a businessman from Paris who, when he made the reservation, instructed us to, please, not communicate with him in any way. He sent a blank check with his reservation, asked that we not cash it until his arrival, and we were dying of curiosity by the time he arrived a few weeks later.

He was middle aged, distinguished looking, if rather furtive, and the lady with him was quite pleasant. A good deal younger than Monsieur, true, but friendly and attractive. Although he wore a marriage ring, she did not, so we discreetly avoided any small talk about family and delighted in his choice of two bottles of the most expensive champagne on the Wine List.

When we were safely in the kitchen, we decided that he was creepy and, regardless of the perks, she deserved better. We wondered what his wife would have thought if she'd been there.

A third assignation that remains vivid in my memory involved an extraordinary threesome from Belgium. One part of this strange triangle was an elderly physician. The second part was his equally aged wife. The third was their female "companion," "nurse," "caregiver," or whatever else one might wish to call the formidable woman who accompanied them and who completely ran the show.

They requested the two tower rooms, *Tour Nord* and *Tour Sud*, which were the only rooms in that wing and, therefore, totally private. Dinner was accompanied by several bottles of wine, after which the doctor's wife retired to bed and the other two stayed behind drinking more wine, and cognac after cognac, in the salon.

Eventually, the companion would tap on the kitchen door, where we were busily cleaning up and adding up the bills, and announce that they were going up to bed and would see us in the morning. They took another bottle of wine and one large bottle of water up with them as they lurched their way upstairs.

We never did figure out the sleeping arrangements, but they were obviously satisfied because they returned at least twice each season for all the years we were there. The companion brought with her, after that first year, some rather macabre books about the supernatural, which she proudly presented to me.

Perhaps categorizing their visits as "assignations" is a stretch of the imagination, but the whole thing certainly seemed a bit unusual. Three pickled octogenarians, pleasant as they might be, especially if one of them arrives bearing books on the supernatural, can lead to some very interesting speculation, indeed.

POTAGE MICHELLE

Ingredients:
- 3 ripe avocados (average 1/2 avocado per serving)
- 1 lime
- 1 c chicken bouillon
- 1/4 tsp salt
- 1/8 tsp pepper
- dash of curry powder
- 1 c crème fraîche (if not available, use sour cream, although the taste is not as good, I think)

Preparation:
Cut the avocados in half, remove pips, scoop out avocado flesh and put into the bowl of a food processor. Add the lime juice, chicken bouillon, salt, pepper, and a dash of curry (more or less to your taste). Process until very smooth. Add the crème fraîche 1/2 cup at a time to the food processor container, with an on/off motion. Add more water or crème fraîche until a smooth, creamy consistency is obtained. Chill for several hours in the refrigerator and serve very cold with a dollop of crème fraîche with parsley in the center or a very thin slice of lime floating on the top.

Note:
When you put this into the refrigerator, be certain to cover it with clear plastic wrap so that the wrap touches the surface of the avocado mixture and no air can get to it. If air gets to it, it will turn dark and not too pretty. If this happens, you can just skim off the dark part and the rest underneath will still be perfect.

Chapter 38
The Countess, Jus d'Orange, and I

When the countess arrived, around the middle of *Aux Trois Saisons'* third year, we were, by then, far more relaxed about welcoming visitors. We showed her to her room, explaining along the way the house's history, or, rather, what we knew of it. She was perfectly coiffed, impeccably dressed, and arrived with a small dog in tow.

With one fast sweep of her eyes, she took in the room and smiled approvingly. She was staying in *Suite de Jardin,* which opened onto the courtyard in front and the garden in back. The garden met with her obvious delight.

The little dog, whose name I don't remember, sniffed the flowers and regarded *Mademoiselle* with disinterest, which was reciprocated. *Mademoiselle* never had any patience with pretentiousness and titles did not impress her.

Actually, *Mademoiselle* got along with just about everybody, with only one major exception. The exception was a hyperactive wire-haired terrier named "Octabelle" who lived with Françoise, a friend in Paris. For some reason, which we never understood, *Mademoiselle* and Octabelle, when in the same room, immediately withdrew to opposite ends. They simply could not stand each other.

The countess, unlike her dog, was charming, not effusive but agreeably pleasant. She participated in the small talk of the *apéritif* hour, dined alone that evening, at a table near the window, and seemed quite pleased with us and with *Aux Trois Saisons*.

As I always did, I made the rounds of the tables after dinner, inquiring if everything was satisfactory, and asking what each guest wanted for breakfast. The countess opted for regular coffee, not the decaffeinated variety, the usual croissant and baguette, and a bowl of corn flakes.

The next morning, I prepared the breakfast plates for each table. There were separate little platters of cold cuts and cheeses, and three different types of jam and jelly on each table. There were individual pots of coffee, tea, or hot chocolate, depending on what each person had requested. It was really quite a nice spread and much more than the usual continental breakfast fare of most French hotels. The most time-consuming breakfast chore was squeezing the oranges for the fresh orange juice I prided myself on serving. No canned or prepared juice for our guests!

The countess and her little friend arrived at their table and I smilingly approached with the pitcher of orange juice to greet them. I'm a little unclear as to what happened immediately after that, but I do remember pouring the orange juice into the glass and then, somehow, lurching over the table and, as if in slow motion, pouring the contents of the glass over the countess.

Fortunately, most of the juice landed on the table and only a few drops landed in the countess' lap, which was protected by the over-sized cloth napkins we used. The table was soaked and I tried my best to sop it up, put another table cloth over the wettest parts, with the countess' gently reassuring, *"Pas de problème, Monsieur"* making me feel even more stupid.

She didn't miss a beat, said that everything was fine and I shouldn't worry about the mishap, laughed, and went about eating her corn flakes.

I returned to the kitchen and asked Dierk to please go out there with a glass of orange juice for the countess. I was genuinely convinced that I would douse her again if I approached the table.

I don't know what it is about me and orange juice. A similar catastrophe happened on a return flight to Paris from a vacation in Florida. We scheduled a stop-over in London that left us just enough time to get to the Ritz, have high tea, and get back to the airport for the flight to Paris.

We try, each time we visit London, to schedule a high tea at a different restaurant. So far, we've sampled high tea at the Ritz, the Langham-Hilton, Fortnum & Mason, and several other lesser-known establishments. A personal favorite for the food is the high tea offered at Fortnum & Mason, although, in my humble opinion, the Ritz is the most elegant one.

Despite the Florida heat, we dressed up in shirt and tie, jackets and trousers elegant enough for high tea at one of the top hotels in the world.

When we were comfortably settled into our airplane seats, the stewardess came around with a glass of orange juice for each passenger. I accepted it and was about to bring it to my lips when, again, it somehow got away from me and landed on Dierk's trousers, on my left, and just missed the left cuff of the shirt on the man sitting to my right.

I apologized profusely. The stranger with the lucky shirt-cuff made appropriate noises of disgust, moved as far away from me as a seat in coach could permit, and said not one more word to me for the remaining five hours. The most painful comment of all, however, came from Dierk. He merely sighed softly, looked away, and said nothing.

As they dried, his trousers developed a tie-died motif and became rather stiff. In case you care, the Ritz Hotel in London, one of the world's top establishments, has absolutely no facilities for instant dry-cleaning of tie-died trousers.

The countess, for the rest of her stay at *Aux Trois Saisons*, also seemed to back almost imperceptibly out of my range whenever I approached her table. She was as charming as before, and did, in fact, return to *Aux Trois Saisons* the next year, but I never again served her orange juice. That became Dierk's job.

Chapter 39
After the Fall

It happened on August 9th. We were well into our seventh season, all rooms almost completely reserved for the two months that remained, except for the weekends we had blocked out for survival. Dierk was in the garden, trimming back the tall Wisteria bushes so that we would get another bloom out of them. I was in the kitchen preparing something or other for that night's dinner, chopping away. The phone rang.

It was Dierk on the other end of the telephone and he sounded strange. Could I, please, come downstairs? I knew him well enough to feel that there was something wrong. I wasn't prepared for the shock when I opened the door. He was lying in bed, a bloodied towel around his head, and his face was ashen.

He had stepped from the six-foot ladder on which he was standing, misjudged the position of the ivy-covered stone wall below, and missed it, stepping out into thin air. He hit the wall, the trunk of the huge walnut tree alongside it, and then, when he landed, the gravel of the courtyard. I helped him clean off the wounds, a nasty cut on the forehead, scraped arms, bruised wrist, and bloodied toes.

Dierk does not complain, never has, but I knew that he was in terrible pain without his saying so. The hospital was nearby, but he insisted that he felt all right, that it looked worse than it was, and that, besides, we couldn't just leave. All the rooms were reserved and the ten people were gone for the day, off to see nearby chateaux or tasting wine. What would they think if they returned to an empty house? We both still had a full day's work ahead of us and there was no time to go to the doctor.

His toes were so swollen that evening that getting into shoes was impossible. He wore two pairs of black socks and hobbled along, still not complaining, praying that nobody would touch him or notice that he wasn't wearing shoes.

It was August, one of our busiest months, and, with only the two of us, we couldn't just close up. Dierk valiantly carried on, but by the second week, when his swollen wrist started turning all colors of the rainbow, I just locked the front gates, put a sign on them saying we would be back by 3:00 p.m. and dragged him, literally, to the hospital.

The verdict: a broken right wrist, two broken toes, and a head-wound that, thank God, did, indeed, look worse than it was. The doctor put a cast on the wrist, Dierk protesting all the while that the cast, if it had to be placed, must leave him with full mobility of his fingers.

Don't you love it when doctors tell you to just go home and rest?

With still so many weeks to go until the end of the season, Dierk tried his best, but such simple things as ironing, cleaning, making beds, cutting cheese, or opening wine bottles were impossible. Madame W., bless her heart, stayed an extra hour a day to make all of the beds, a chore she had shared with Dierk. Somehow all of the work, amazingly, got done, but after a month of double duty, I was a wreck.

I put through a frantic telephone call to Jean-Claude Brelière in Rully, asking if he knew of anyone who could help us out while Dierk recuperated. He called back a few days later to say that the first person who had grudgingly answered his appeal announced that she wouldn't, *bien sûr*, work weekends, our busiest times. The second one, before even finding out what the work entailed, asked how much vacation time there would be. Jean-Claude was sorry that he couldn't be of help and, I suspect, a bit embarrassed. We got the impression that they were not exactly applicants whose work-ethics inspired confidence.

We realized that the accident could just as easily have happened to either one of us, and if *I* had happened to be the one put out of action, we would not have been able to offer dinner, since I was the chef. The dinner and the wine that went with it were the most profitable things about the inn; the five rooms would have just allowed us to break even.

It made us realize that things worked fine when we were both at levels of optimum performance, but the balance was destroyed when a major problem hit one of the team's only two members. Hiring a third person, in France, as we'd already considered, was not in the cards.

We knew that if we changed the inn's operations, either with additional personnel or by adding more rooms, we risked losing the intimacy, character and friendliness of a small country inn. After all, that had been one reason for starting the whole project in the first place, and a major reason for its success.

We were managing to survive this particular catastrophe, but there were sure to be others, the probability only increasing with time. If this had happened at the beginning of the season instead of towards the end, it would have been impossible to continue, and the financial consequences could have been disastrous. It was simply too risky to continue.

We talked it over very carefully, decided to face reality, turn the page and move on. That seventh year of *Aux Trois Saisons*' existence was a turning point, one which we had never even contemplated when the dream was taking form eight years before.

Dierk continued hobbling around in two pairs of black socks, calling me out of the kitchen to open the wine bottles and cut the hard cheese. He insisted that we continue the cleaning and ironing chores together, but I could see that every movement he made came with difficulty. We continued to go over each room after Madame W. departed for the day, and the faucets and sinks sparkled as before. Our people had entrusted us with their precious time and they deserved our best efforts.

We vowed to finish the season, somehow, and, once back in Paris, we would make decisions about the future. But the decision had already been made for us, really, the accident only hastening it. The house would have to be put on the market as soon as we returned to Burgundy for the next season. Things move slowly in France and we anticipated at least a year or two of uncertainty ahead of us.

The gray, damp winter is no time to sell a property in Burgundy, and, besides, all of the nicest things either went into storage each winter or traveled with us back and forth to Paris. The house didn't look happy without them. We determined to start the selling process as soon as we returned in the spring, cleaned up the park, and opened up the house again.

We would leave ourselves plenty of time, because I can't think of another group of people in France who are, in general, as consistently and shockingly inept as French real estate agents, charming though some of them may be. Since they have not yet cottoned on to something called "Multiple Listing," each agent handles his or her own listings and might very well show you an unsuitable property, which he has on his own list, even though he knows that a property across the street is perfect for you and is also for sale, but is listed by another agent. Or, he may not even be aware that the other property is for sale, since there's no professional communication. I think that French real estate agents will do anything to avoid having to split a commission, even if it means not making a sale.

All agents jealously guard whatever listings they can sign up. They then sit back and patiently wait for the hordes of potential buyers to storm their offices demanding to have their money taken. Waiting patiently is something which, along with street demonstrations and anything having to do with food, the French, however, seem to do exceedingly well.

Chapter 40
La fin

We called Catherine, but she had by then, eight years after our first meeting, given up real estate and devoted herself to a full-time job promoting and managing the ladies' basketball team.

We returned to the house in early March. In between raking and burning leaves, repainting and retouching the ravages with which winter can punish a 350+year-old tower, and taking care of the dozens of little details of re-opening the house, we sought out real estate agents in *Chalon-sur-Saône* and in *Beaune*. Because it was so heavily frequented, we thought Beaune a particularly good idea.

The real estate agent from Beaune came out to the house the week before our season officially began, we signed the listing agreement, and he took photos of the house, promising not to show them to *anyone* except serious prospective clients.

We felt as if we were betraying the guests who began arriving the following week, some for the sixth time in as many years. Greeting them, we almost forgot that we were trying to sell "their" inn out from under them. But the eighteen-hour days soon kept us occupied, Dierk's injury was long forgotten, and *Aux Trois Saisons* continued.

Then one day, two guests returned from their visit to the *Hospice* in *Beaune*, and strode into the kitchen with a surprised, "You're selling the inn?"

So much for the assurances of the real estate agent. There in the window of the largest real estate agent in Beaune, right in the center of town, was a lovely photo of *Aux Trois Saisons* in all its glory!

I got into the car, drove to Beaune, angrily confronted the real estate agent and the photo was removed from the window, but the damage had been done. If news of a possible sale got around, the word-of-mouth and good-will that had made the inn a success would certainly come to a halt. There was no telling how long we might have to wait for the right buyer to burst into the real estate agent's office brandishing Franc notes.

We swore to secrecy the couple who had seen the photo, explained our reasons, and, they became, in a fashion, our accomplices, albeit sadly. They were two lovely people from California, Irma and Sam. Irma and I had, early on, established a correspondence and exchanged recipes and news between their visits to *Aux Trois Saisons*. Sam, her husband, was the Los Angeles "Donut King," a friendly fellow we took to immediately. We liked them both so much that we even forgave them for "Minsk and the Monster," who were one of the couples that came with Irma's brother and his wife.

Selling a house without its occupants knowing is no easy task. Whenever an agent called to say that a potential buyer wanted to see the house, we arranged it for a time of day when we knew that all of the guests would be out sight-seeing. The "official" word was that the potential buyer was simply a person who wanted to see the rooms with the intention of renting them for a large party. It wasn't exactly the truth, but it worked.

Since French real estate agents have no concept of customer service, and since they invented the seventeen and a half-hour work-week long before the French government came up with the thirty-five hour work-week, dealing with them is an experience. There were a few people who, we felt, we had to tell ourselves. Stephan and Kristina from Germany, who had been married at *Aux Trois Saisons*, had made us promise to give them first option on the inn if we ever decided to sell, so we called them and told them the news.

They were ecstatic and started making plans immediately. They would have been perfect. They were young, energetic, and had a large immediate family they could summon to help out in busy times. They are delightful, friendly people, and Kristina loved to cook.

When it came down to actual decision-making time, there were just too many things standing in the way. They had no children at that time, but what would happen if a baby entered the picture? They both had flourishing careers. Was it the right time to give them up and start on a new project?

A few years after all of this happened, when they visited us in Paris, we spoke about what, at the time, was a great disappointment for us all. They had, by then, welcomed Indy, an enormous furry black *Bouvier de Flandres* to their family, and Indy and I took long walks together in Paris and, still later, when they all visited us in Normandy. The next year, Lars, an adorable baby arrived and *Aux Trois Saisons* had faded into the distant past.

When the possible sale to Kristina and Stephan didn't work out, we went about our chores, hoping that one of the agents would come through. There were several "lookers" among the few people they brought to see the house, but no "takers."

One potential buyer who stands out in my memory was a lady from *Chalon-Sur-Saône*. She walked through the house, ooh-ed and aah-ed appropriately, began making plans where to place her furniture, and asked if she could return. We were pleased. The second time, she returned with a gentleman she introduced as her brother-in-law, who was, also, a lawyer. We were even more pleased. The third time, she returned with two other ladies from her tennis team, and they all ooh-ed and aah-ed appropriately. We were still pleased and waited for an offer to buy. Any offer.

The fourth time, it was with her sister. Still no offer. We were not pleased.

Another call came from the agent in *Chalon*, who wanted to show the house to buyers from Lausanne, Switzerland. This agent had been the only one to have the business acumen to do a little advertising in other than local newspapers, especially in Switzerland. House prices there are astronomically higher than in France, so, for the Swiss, our house was a give-away.

The Swiss people arrived, a father and son. Charming people, the son with a video camera slung across his shoulder, the father looking into every nook and cranny and inspecting beams and walls. They walked all through the house, videotaping every room, every staircase, every corner, every alcove. The lady of the family could not accompany them because she had to work in her boutique, but they would tell her everything when they returned to Lausanne and if she liked what she saw, they would return. All of this transpired in a very pleasant, professional, and businesslike manner.

The father was an architect and the son, a young man in his twenties, was a student. He was, at that time, considering dentistry, among other professions, as a career. Forget the house sale, we hit it off on sight. They left and we waved them off in the courtyard.

No nibbles, no offers, no action, so we bid the last guest of the season farewell, closed up the house, locked the iron gates again, and returned to Paris. It was the beginning of October. The closing date at *Aux Trois*

Saisons had been advancing each year and had gone from end-November, the first year, to early October by year seven. Had the inn continued, we would probably have had to change the name to *L'Auberge "Aux Deux Saisons."*

We fully expected to have to contend with this state of limbo for the next few years, despite the one or two calls from real estate agents during the winter months, summoning us back for a showing.

Of course, the lady from *Chalon-Sur-Saône* wanted to see the house yet again and called us directly in Paris to arrange a meeting. We drove down to Burgundy in the dead of winter, opened the house especially for her and another of her sisters, and remained in the kitchen, trying to warm up near the electric heating unit while she showed her sister around "her" house.

When she came into the kitchen, exclaiming how beautiful the house was, and was evidently about to leave, I finally lost patience and, with a smile pasted on my face, said, "Madame, you've seen the house six times already. Do you like the house enough to make an offer? Because, if you've got a large family, this could take years."

She never returned.

We drove to Hamburg for Christmas and went from there to a beautiful island called Amrum in the North Sea. Amrum is very much like Cape Cod, except that it has thatched-roof houses and delicious German food. We bundled up and walked for hours on the paths along the beach, with only wild rabbits as our companions. We totally relaxed. *Sehr gemütlich.*

The message was on our answering machine in Paris when we returned. The Swiss people wanted to see the house again, this time with the mother.

We arranged a meeting time, drove down to Burgundy from Paris, met them at *Aux Trois Saisons*, and Madame fell in love with the house in person, just as she had loved it in the video her son took on the first visit. From the very first moment, she felt absolutely at ease in the house.

They made what we considered a fair offer, we accepted, and the sales agreement was signed that afternoon in the agent's office.

We silently drove back to Paris with very mixed emotions.

Chapter 41
Au revoir...

So much to do, so many little details. We drove back and forth from Paris much more frequently once *la promesse de vente* had been signed. Between that day in January and the date in mid-March set for the *signature*, when the home would legally belong to the people from Lausanne, there were a million and one things that had to be taken care of.

We filled the car with things to take back to the Paris apartment each time we returned. But all of the contents of a huge, six-bedroom house couldn't possibly fit into the small one-bedroom flat in Paris. Deciding what to keep, what to put into storage, and what to give away took several weeks of time.

Madame W., the little lady from the village who had helped us with the cleaning, had two other married daughters, in addition to the one who took her wedding photos at *Aux Trois Saisons*. We visited her at her immaculate house in town and told her the news.

We had a glass of wine with her, and, when we had all dried our eyes, we asked Madame to offer the newlyweds and her other children the pick of all of the contents of the house that we couldn't keep. They all arrived the next weekend and left with enough towels, beds, bed linens, dishes, stemware, and assorted housewares to begin their own inns. They were grateful and we were happy for them.

Madame's birthday is on August 5th and we still call her each year to wish her well.

We visited our neighbors across the way and told them of our decision. One of the umbrellas they gave us is still in service in Paris.

I stopped by the post-office and arranged with *Monsieur* and *Madame Lefavre* to have our mail forwarded. Their daughter had grown into a lovely young lady with other interests than playing the organ. She and her brother shyly shook my hand, and the family promised to let us know when they were ever in Paris. It hasn't happened yet.

Madame Turner, when she learned of the sale, invited us to a farewell tea. We promised to see this lovely lady in Paris. The baron wasn't there this time. He was at another of his properties in the Beaujolais area that day.

The storage people were called in and things that would not fit into our Paris flat were packed up. One day soon they would help furnish the weekend place in Normandy that we had decided to buy.

As the movers were leaving, a car drove into the courtyard. It was a couple who had seen the inn in the *Guide Rivage* and wanted to know if, by any chance, we had a room available for that night.

"Sorry. No room at the inn. In fact, no inn."

The house was emptied and would be delivered clean to the new people. We touched up the paint where it was scratched by the movers and polished the floors. Two bedrooms were left intact and fully furnished so that the new people could move right in that night if they wanted to. One room for the parents and one for the son. And, of course, a bottle of champagne in the fridge.

We returned to Paris and filled the days with trips to Normandy to find the right small weekend home. On one of these outings, we discovered a beautiful little village called *Beaumont-en-Auge*, where we saw a real fixer-upper that we bought for very little down.

Erik and Sabine came out to see it and Erik predicted how much it would actually cost to renovate the house. It was a lot more than we had imagined. Unfortunately, he ultimately turned out to be right on target, but we went ahead with the purchase anyway because the location was perfect. Only two hours from Paris on the A-13 autoroute, fifteen minutes from the beach at Deauville, and small enough to manage easily, it was just right.

The house, about 300 years old, had thick, square-tile floors which, it turned out, had been set directly into the soil centuries ago. It also had an outdoor toilet tacked onto the side of the house, but no running water connected to it. No bathroom inside the house, just one lone sink in what was used as a kitchen, and an overgrown garden that cried out for help. The lady who lived there had been moved to a retirement home by her daughter. She had lived that way for forty-seven years. But all of that is part of another story.

We waited for the day in March when the sales papers for the house in Burgundy would be finalized. The time went by quickly, and on the appointed day, we drove down to *Chalon-sur-Saône*, met the agent and the buyers in the lawyer's office, and signed what seemed like several hundred papers.

It didn't take very long. We drove back to the house with the new owners and they opened the bottle of champagne we had left chilled for them. They spent their first night comfortably installed in the house, unlike us, eight years before. They would, of course, create their own memories, but we had ours.

The house that was *l'Auberge Aux Trois Saisons* legally became the private residence of a very nice family from Lausanne. We were happy that they loved the house as we had and, in subsequent visits, were pleased to see that they kept it beautiful.

Mademoiselle wasn't at the notaire's office for the *signature* this time, but her spirit was there, curled up and happily snoozing away.

Part VI
Menus "Aux Trois Saisons"...and why...

Chapter 42
Menus "Aux Trois Saisons"...and why...

Were the casual observer to take inventory, my bookcase contains books in primarily three categories. The first category, "Biographies," mirrors my fascination with the famous and infamous people who have, for better or worse, influenced human events. The second and third categories, although diametrically opposed, have to do with food. I am the proud possessor of a great many books on "Dieting" and "Cooking" that vie for space as my interests, and waistline, permit.

I began cooking as a matter of necessity, while living at home. In the ensuing years, my experiments in the kitchen slowly began to be associated with where life has led me. Food is inexorably bound up with social situations. Each meal is a cultural as well as a gastronomical event. When people sit down to dine with other people, they are really saying, "I trust you, so let's share this experience together."

The handshake began, in ancient times, as a way to prove that the person facing you was not bearing a weapon and, therefore, not potentially dangerous. Similarly, sharing a meal, the act of physically "breaking bread" with another person, says something about your relationship with that person. Unlike the business "power lunch," where people may dine together because they're seeking something in return, the only ulterior motive in most situations involving food is to *give* something to the other person.

That something may be the sharing of a new and exotic taste experience, a memorable evening of discussion, or simply sharing in the celebration of a happy event.

During the two years I spent in Turkey, when I was in the U.S. Air Force, I discovered new spices and the marvelous things they could do to an ordinary dish. Cumin is used a great deal in the Middle East. It is really a versatile spice and combines beautifully with other spices, but I had never used it very much before then.

For example, I tried mixing a teaspoon of ground cumin, a teaspoon of ground cinnamon, and 1/4 teaspoon of ground nutmeg together and adding the mixture to a puree of carrots and potatoes. The result was delicious, somewhat like sweet potato but more interesting. It was a great hit and went well with my Pork Paprika at *Aux Trois Saisons*.

In Paris, at the university, one of the doctors I had the pleasure of working with is a woman from Algeria. Her own flat was a bit small, so she offered to prepare a *couscous* dinner for Dierk and me in our flat. I watched her as she went through the elaborate preparations. The *couscous* grains were cooked and fluffed three times in a special pot called a *couscousiere*. It was perfect when served, not soggy or pasty. The meal was a delight. Perhaps because it was prepared with joy for friends who would receive it with pleasure, it created a special evening for us all.

The recipe I had put to paper while watching Mama prepare her own special stuffed cabbage was a part of my own life as well as of her European heritage. I prepared it at *Aux Trois Saisons* and loved watching the reaction from our guests.

You can't imagine how flattering it is to have a Parisian lady, who is herself a gourmet cook, a graduate of the famed *Courdon Bleu* cooking course, ask about my recipe for *Mousse au Saumon avec Sauce Aneth,* as did M.F.K. Fisher in the letter from her that began the book you're reading.

I've had the kitchen filled with French people who came for my cooking course and shared with them the secrets of Shoo-fly Pie, Pecan Pie, Chili, and other dishes from our American tables. Believe it or not, the French are as fascinated by our food as we are with theirs. It was also great fun teaching some of our American guests the tricks to a great *Boeuf Bourgignon* or a heavenly, light *Sauce Moutarde de Dijon,* which is incredibly simple to prepare.

The years at *"Aux Trois Saisons"* were good ones. The best part of it all was the sharing of ideas and of cultures. Each evening, over pre-dinner *aperitif* and post-dinner coffee and *digestifs* we chatted about every possible subject, in any number of languages. The exchange was never dull and I took pleasure in blending my unmistakably American ideas and approach with the, sometimes, less flexible traditions of Europe.

The letters and telephone calls we received in Paris, when we announced the inn's closing, were proof that the inn was a dream come true for a lot of people, as it was for us.

There had been so many adjustments, so many new people and patterns to assimilate. I noted them all while they were still fresh. The interminable delays, the mountains of French bureaucratic paperwork plowed through, the kind, funny, exasperating, endearing people who loomed so large in my life over those years, the self-doubts, the challenge itself and then being able to catch my breath for those few exhilarating moments of success between hurdles.

I wrote about each new situation, each unexpected crisis, in my daily diary and in letters to friends. This continued from the day the freighter pulled out of Baltimore with *Mademoiselle* and us aboard. It still continues.

I suspect that writing about them put the "crises" in perspective. Laughing at them, and myself, made it all less traumatic than it might otherwise have been.

Aux Trois Saisons taught me another good lesson. It taught me that there's much truth to the old joke about attempting the impossible: "Nobody told me it couldn't be done…so I *did* it."

I've told you about the choice of wines for the *Carte de Vin* and the fun we had finding them. But the most fun of all was creating the dinner Menus, which were my responsibility, since I was the chef. This was a distinction that, I suspect, few other American dentists can claim.

Along with the suitcase of dog food for *Mademoiselle*, I carted a suitcase full of my favorite recipes onto the "Egon Oldendorf" when we set sail for the "Old World." They were all neatly catalogued and in folders. As I had so carefully collected them over the years I wasn't about to trust them to any old moving company. If the ship went down, the recipes would go down with me.

Cooking at *Aux Trois Saisons*, however, was a new experience for me, because it was the first time that I would actually be paid for doing what I'd done for years purely for pleasure. It added a slightly different element of pressure to the meal. After all, with people paying for it, there was little room for forgiveness as there might be with a friendly dinner party at home.

I tried not to dwell on this or I would have been too worried and self-conscious to do anything. I decided to treat each evening as if I had invited a group of friends over for dinner, with the sole purpose of providing a setting for them to enjoy themselves. I was determined to avoid the frazzled condition some hosts and hostesses arrive at by trying to be absolutely perfect. They are so intent on getting the details right that they sometimes forget the reason for getting together is to enjoy the people as well as the food.

I enjoy cooking. Nothing tedious can really be enjoyable. I also enjoy being with guests, one of our main reasons for creating *Aux Trois Saisons*, or, for that matter, for entertaining in your own home. I came to the conclusion that the food we served had to taste terrific but not take five hours to prepare. I simply didn't have the time. And, I suspect, neither do you.

I wanted to spend as much time with guests as possible, to be *part of the party*. My very American no-nonsense attitude toward food preparation and organization and Menu planning resulted in fourteen Menus which I rotated, so that guests didn't have the same thing for dinner twice during their visit.

If you remember the logistics, each evening the *apéritif* was served at 7:30 in either the salon or on the terrace. It was complimentary, which meant that everyone showed up on time. After serving the drinks, usually a Kir, I chatted with guests and Dierk disappeared to turn down the beds, put a chocolate on each pillow, and either turn off the lights in each bedroom or close the windows. This was a necessity since, in most parts of Europe, there are no screens on the windows and bugs of all varieties are attracted to lights. It was harder for American guests to get used to this, but Europeans have grown up with it so it comes naturally to them. You either read with the lights on and the window closed or you risk being eaten alive, and you open the window when the lights are out and you're ready to go to sleep.

Then, when Dierk finished his rounds, at about 7:45, he returned to chat with the guests and I disappeared into the kitchen to put the finishing touches on the first two courses. They had been prepared earlier and just had to be arranged on the serving plates. The Menus at the inn were specifically designed for this approach, but the same approach could just as easily be used for making home entertaining easier.

At 8:00 sharp, dinner was announced and the guests were ushered into the dining room, each couple to the table that was theirs for their visit.

When they were seated, Dierk inquired as to wine choices, went down to the cave to get the wine, and I put the first course on the serving plates. I served the first course while Dierk uncorked the wine. After this course, he did most of the serving, since the other courses required a bit more arrangement in the kitchen.

I helped gather the dishes, put them into the dishwasher while he was serving the cheese course, and, after the dishwasher was going, I could put the dessert onto the serving dishes to be ready when the guests had finished the cheese course.

If this all sounds rather like a military operation, it was! None of this necessary precision, however, was noticed by the guests. Everything flowed smoothly, the courses appeared effortlessly on the table, the soft music played in the background. It was like a well choreographed performance, just as you, and I, want every celebration to be.

You've probably noticed that all of the desserts are named after ladies. These were the first fourteen ladies who came to *Aux Trois Saisons* as guests. I asked them each what their favorite dessert elements were and then fashioned a new dessert dedicated to each lady.

Terri, of *Surprise de Terri*, was a delightful lady from New York who came to us from Paris, where she had been taking a *Cordon Bleu* course specializing in desserts. She and her husband, an airline pilot, had decided to open a restaurant in the south of France, and Terri came to *Aux Trois Saisons* after hearing about us in Paris. We visited them at the house they bought in the south of France a year later, and got caught up in the excitement they were feeling about their own dream.

Terri's two favorite dessert tastes were chocolate mousse and fresh raspberries. The *Surprise de Terri* was born. It's a traditional crêpe filled with chocolate mousse with raspberry *coulis* drizzled over it.

Julia, who remains our dearest friend in Paris, has a particular love for hazelnuts and chocolate. *Délice de Julia,* which featured both, was the dessert she made for us when we visited her in *Mandelieu* that first winter while the renovations were in full swing.

They, and the other twelve ladies, had their very own desserts served at dinner each time they visited *Aux Trois Saisons*. It was my way of saying "Thank You" to some very special people.

The following Menus are just two out of the fourteen Menus I served at *Aux Trois Saisons*. I've already given you most of the recipes that went into their creation, and I hope that they bring the taste of a very special inn in Burgundy into your own home.

Thank you for reliving with me the adventure that was *Aux Trois Saisons*.

Au revoir…

AUX TROIS SAISONS

Menu One

❧

Mousse au Saumon—Sauce Aneth

Salade Tapenade

Roulade de Veau—Timbale d'Epinard

Fromage

Dessert—Surprise de Terri

Thé—Café

Menu Two

❧

Potage Michelle

Salade Printemps

(Finely chopped red, green and yellow peppers, celery, ham, and hard-boiled eggs, arranged by color.)

Boeuf Bourguignon

Fromage

Délice de Julia

Thé—Café

Epilogue

The French don't color their lives or their calories with regret. They don't feel guilty about taking time to savor a meal, a situation, or another person. Even those whose lives are hard and lacking in the comforts I took so much for granted in America still find time to chat with the postman or the baker and take delight in what they do have.

To the French, the banquet is life and they're not afraid or embarrassed to enjoy it to the fullest.

A bientôt…

Acknowledgements

When I try to reconstruct the path that led from this book languishing in my cupboard, as it had been for so long, to arriving in your hands, the trail begins with Holly Brassard, who read the pages of my manuscript and went a step further to get me in touch with a local Florida publisher. That publisher, Jeff Schlesinger, of Barringer Publishing, read the manuscript and believed in it enough to go ahead with the many stages of getting it into print, aided by Carole Greene, the superb editor who patiently put up with my mad habit of inserting commas wherever there was an empty space. Their confidence in the book and expertise in getting it into print have earned my everlasting gratitude.

My sincere thanks to LeRoy Neimann and his gracious wife Janet, who came to *Aux Trois Saisons* as guests and left as friends. I saw them walking in the garden one afternoon, LeRoy with his ever-present sketchbook in hand, and when they left he presented us with the special gift that ultimately became the cover of this book, in his own words, "Sketched well rested on a full stomach."

To all of the people who filled the house with love and appreciation over the years of its existence, thank you for sharing our dream.

To tell the truth, though, the journey would never even have started without Dierk Volckers, my long-suffering partner of many years who has always encouraged and supported my dreams and made them his own. Nobody really deserves to be that fortunate!

Testimonials

"At Aux Trois Saisons heaven is close. Merci to the two hosts for having been the creators of this magic place."

~**Jean Charles de Castelbajac,** Paris, Fashion Designer

"An Enchanted Garden. Lovely walks along the river, superb food, a delight in every way."

~***24 Heures,*** a leading Swiss newspaper

"A place of warmth and hospitality, never to be forgotten."

~**Nicolas Bouvier,** noted Swiss artist and prize-winning author

"A special moment in time spent in beautiful surroundings with most agreeable hosts."

~**André Festjens,** Belgian historian and author

"We thank you for creating this place of enchantment."

~**Janet and LeRoy Neimann**

"Neither only a hotel or a restaurant, but much more than that, a place of happiness with very comfortable rooms and a welcome that is unique in Burgundy."

~**Roland Escaig,** *The Bible of Weekends in France*

"Supremely picturesque, an old ivy-covered manor with a tower dating from 1622, now the home of two Americans who have converted it into a very personal five-room hotel. It is welcoming and charming, the dinner is excellent and is preceded by drinks on the terrace where guests can meet each other. A delightful haven amid a pretty garden and orchard with a marvelous welcome."

        ~**Hilary Rubinstein,** The Good Hotel Guide: France

"Deep in Burgundy we have discovered an 'art de vivre à la française' created by two Americans."

        ~**Isabelle and Jean-Claude de la Clergerie,** Paris, France